Master Yourself

CHERYL AND
EDWARD AND
FAMILY
I FEEL SO GRATEFUL
FOR HAVING YOU AS MY
FRIENDS. I HOPE THAT THIS
BOOK MAY BRING YOU PEACE
AND LOVE.
YOUR FRIENDS EVER.

05/05/2007

Master Yourself
Ten Steps To Loving Yourself, Having Good Relationships, And Being Successful

Claudio Vargas Silva

2007

Master Yourself

Table of Contents

Endorsements

"Your book is A plus and proves my beliefs in the human being as the key to transforming pain into glory. It all depends on the ingredients and determination for it. Thank you for publishing such a rich piece loaded with life experience in a real and instructional way." Sandra Silva, Psychologist.

"Master Yourself enables us to move from letting circumstances determine our joy to letting our groundedness in God determine our joy and that makes all the difference in the world!" Rev Dan Hoffman, United Presbyterian Church of Watsonville.

"Claudio Vargas Silva' unique and uplifting testimonial is a life guide to being the best you can be. By paying attention to your inner drive and motivation, Claudio says "you can do it" by arranging your life like a beautiful piece of music." Dave Garcia, Assistant Project Manager with Ross Construction

"This book is an inspired work by a man blessed by God with many talents, his music and preaching and desire to help people rule his life. I know you would find this book informative and helpful." Lance Almond, Realtor on Ridgefield, WA.

"I would never imagine how many improvements in my daily life these book's ideas would bring. You have an opportunity in your hands...Enjoy your life." Cleber Dutra, MBA, System Engineer

"His is a compelling story and the change wrought in his life is nothing short of a miracle!" Sharon Thiel, Nurse.

"The best word to describe Master Yourself is 'bright.' Each page turns on lights that powerfully show the practical and winning aspects of being on a positive journey in life!" Pr. Robson Oliveira. SDA San Ramon Church

Acknowledgments

To my parents, Elias Henriques Silva and Leni Vargas Silva, for giving me the self-discipline and dedication that helped me write this book.

To my daughter, Carolina Vargas Silva, for helping me to revise this book. In one of our readings at night, I asked her help and she proudly accepted the idea. We worked on it for six months, and she has corrected almost every sentence (including this one). I feel proud when I see her ability to take an awkward sentence and turn it in a beautiful piece of literary work.

To Judith Jacob, Sharon Thiel and Pr. Robson Oliveira for helping me revise Master Yourself. It wouldn't be the same without your input.

Introduction

When I was eighteen years old, I read a self-help book written by Norman Vincent Peale entitled *The Power of Positive Thinking*, which was very helpful to me. Then I bought Peale's book, *You Can if You Believe You Can*, but I never read it. I wanted to dedicate all my time to studying, and felt like it was a waste of time. Six years later, I read three self-help books and stopped again. Two years ago, I started reading again, and I realized that I should have kept on reading when I was eighteen.

If you really want to grow and overcome your emotional problems, you'll have to pay the price. I can tell you from my own experience that there's no quick fix. You need to commit yourself to work until you get the results you expect. You'll need to spend a fair amount of time reading and meditating.

Unfortunately, most people don't have that commitment. The majority of people give up when they're a hair's breadth away from the solution. Although there's abundant literature, there are millions of people who either choose to live in ignorance or think that self-help books are glorified scams. As a result, there are all kinds of problems in our society. Shootings in schools, abductions, rapes, and child abuse don't shock us as they once did.

When I was fourteen years old, I asked myself some fundamental questions: "What is the purpose of my life? Why do I exist? Who Am I?"

At this time of my life, I was very depressed and I stayed depressed for more than ten years until, through hard work, reading, meditating, and counseling, I found the solution to my problems.

Although my childhood was problematic, my father helped me in ways he wasn't aware of. He taught me that through hard work, I could get anything I wanted in life.

He told me several times, "You need to be a man of honor, a superior man."

I heard those words so many times that they were recorded in my subconscious mind and gave me the motivation to seek excellence and success. Although I had to face almost insurmountable problems, I kept pressing forward in an unrelenting effort to overcome my depression and to achieve my dreams.

My father also encouraged me to read books that taught me about the importance of living by principles. I can't remember how many books I've read since I was six years old. I confess that I found them boring at that time, but when I look at my life and try to understand what gave me strength to conquer my hardships and be successful, I'm now thankful for those books.

My father embodied responsibility and commitment. He did everything he could to make me a winner. He saw my struggles and my suffering, and he was very patient. He stayed by my side until he was sure I no longer needed his help. He set an example of commitment and the courage to face hardships that was the best gift he ever could have given me.

Maybe you didn't have an example of commitment and hard work such as I had. However, something that you'll see throughout this entire book is that you can change whenever you wish. If you haven't done your best, you can change it right now by committing yourself to excellence. Don't conform to mediocrity. You don't need to stay put in your self-defeated image. You can rise above your problems and be a happy person. You can overcome virtually all of your emotional problems if you work hard. Your happiness is at stake. Why be a failure when you can be a winner?

You need to be aware of some roadblocks that may prevent you from growing. One of them is the very problem you're trying to overcome. You may avoid looking inside of yourself because it makes you suffer. That's why many people don't want to go to a counselor or read self-help books. They don't want to feel as if they have a problem. They prefer to live in denial rather than facing their issues.

If you don't want to read and seek counseling because you fear that people will see you as a problematic person, that's reason enough to do it. If you learn to value yourself, you'll never worry about other people's opinions. What makes you feel inferior isn't going to a counselor or reading a book, but the fact that you don't value yourself.

Emotional growth is a process. There are no shortcuts or quick-fix solutions. Many people give up on themselves when they realize that they can't overcome their problems in a week. They stop their process of growth, like I did after reading *The Power of Positive Thinking*.

Emotional growth is similar to physical growth. When I was a child, my teacher asked the class to do an experiment with beans. She asked us to pour water on a plate, put cotton in it, and then put a bean on the cotton.

When I got home, I did everything the teacher had told me to do, then proceeded to stare at the plate. After a few minutes, I got impatient and asked my mom why nothing had happened. She patiently explained that I'd have to wait.

When you look at a tree sprout today and it looks the same as it did yesterday, you'll be tempted to think it hasn't grow at all, but when a month passes, you'll notice that it did grow. It's the same with emotional growth. If you look at yourself today and compare yourself with yesterday, you'll think you've made no progress. You'll be like me, waiting impatiently for my bean to sprout.

Since emotional growth is invisible, you may think that you aren't growing. The reason is because the emotional growth happens inside. You can't enter your heart and watch the changes. However, I can tell you right now that you aren't the same person you were when you started reading this book. Something has already happened that has changed your life. You can say goodbye to the old you.

Emotional growth is ruled by laws that weren't invented by us. Although you may accelerate your emotional growth by the amount of time you dedicate to reading, counseling, and meditating, you can't overcome your problems all at once.

The rush to be mature is in itself immaturity. You want to overcome all of your emotional problems overnight because you think you're inferior in your current state. You may think that you have a terrible problem and that if it isn't healed immediately, you'll suffer permanent damage. However, as you grow, you'll realize that there's nothing seriously wrong with you, and you aren't inferior, either. You *can* do your work and enjoy the growing process.

Although we have a tendency to celebrate our victories only when we reach the final stage, we need to learn to value the small victories that combined make the final victory possible. For example, to get a Ph.D., you need to study for many years. You go to school, study long hours, and take many tests. When you finally get the diploma, you celebrate. However, you need to learn to celebrate every small step you took to get to the point of graduating. A great victory is composed of many small victories on a daily basis. The mere fact that you're going to school and studying is reason to celebrate.

Therefore, why not celebrate finishing the first chapter of this book? You started the process of emotional growth, and you're already a different person. Without a series of small victories, you'll never reach the final stage of emotional growth. You deserve to be proud of yourself, because you're better than you were yesterday.

Emotional growth is a miracle. When you look around at plants and animals, you're amazed to see the miracle of growth. When you look to a pregnant woman or when you see a child being born and growing, you can't help but thank God for the miracle of life. Likewise, your emotional growth is miraculous. Although you'll still make mistakes, remember that you're part of a miracle. Therefore, instead of beating yourself up every time you fail and chiding yourself, be thankful for the fact that although you're still not perfect, you're in the process of growth. The beauty of emotional growth isn't solely reserved for the end, but for the means, as well.

Step One
Valuing Yourself

1.
Unconditional Value

A lack of self-esteem is the root of all emotional problems. When you don't value yourself, you feel guilty, you have a victim mentality, you don't believe in yourself, you're angry, you fear, you can't say no, and as a result, you're unhappy.

To value yourself is to have a positive image of yourself—seeing yourself as important and special. Appreciate and respect yourself. Think well of yourself and be happy and satisfied with the person you are. Your flaws don't matter. You can still have a sense of dignity.

Cause of an inferiority complex

Self-esteem is developed during childhood, through your relationship with your parents. Children see themselves as their parents see them. Like radio waves in the air, parents communicate to their children what they think of them. Through their words, tone of voice, and body language, they convey either a positive or a negative message.

Children are extremely vulnerable to their parents' opinions. They know instinctively if their parents value them or not, and they believe everything. That's why they take everything personally.

Most parents are unaware of their influence. They don't realize how much power they have over their children's self-esteem. That's why, when things go wrong, they tend to act like victims. They desperately want to change their kids. They don't realize that by changing themselves, they'll change their children.

If you're a parent, be aware of the influence you exert on your children. Be sensitive to the words you use, the way you talk, and the expressions in your eyes. Develop your parental skills so that you impact your children positively. You're either teaching your children to love or to hate themselves, to believe or to disbelieve in themselves, to fear or to be courageous.

You're your child's role model. What you are has a powerful effect on what they'll be. They're being shaped by your example. Think about what kind of role model you are. What you think of yourself affects what they think of themselves. If you think you aren't fit for anything, they'll think the same of themselves. They're living with you and looking at you everyday. They perceive your lack of self-esteem and they copy you. If you degrade yourself, you're teaching them to degrade themselves, as well.

If you want your children to be winners, you need to be a winner. Be what you want your children to be, set the example, love yourself, believe in yourself, think big, and reach for your dreams. Instead of being perceived as a victim, let them see you as a victor. Make them proud of you, and then you'll be proud of them, too.

I've talked to my daughter about the effort I've made to rise above the abuse I suffered in my past and all the scars it left. Despite everything I went through, I still became a conqueror. I told her that I'm the transition person in our family tree. I didn't accept my fate. I wanted to be better. I've conveyed to her by words and example that she can be everything she wants to be. I'm proud when I see her grades. She has the absolutely certainty that she's a genius.

I've told her thousands of times, "You're intelligent, you're capable, and you can do anything."

Treat your children the way you want them to be. If you want them to be intelligent, talk to them as if they're intelligent. Imagine that someone introduced you to a genius. How would you talk to that person? Like an idiot? How can your child be smart if you treat them like an idiot? How can they be good if you treat them as if they're evil? Whatever you want them to be, treat them as if they already *were* that. Believe in them. See them in a positive way.

When you value, you value everybody

You can't value one person and degrade another. It's impossible. It's the law of love that when you love someone, you love everyone. Your respect spreads out in every direction. You consider all humankind to be important and worthy.

On one occasion, there was a man who parked his car in front of a bar. The bartender was closing the door when the man asked him for a drink. The bartender didn't want to sell it to him because the cash register was already closed, and the man got furious. He started screaming and cursing at the bartender.

The man drove a little bit further and found an open bar. He entered the bar, and even before asking for a drink, he noticed a beautiful woman. He almost melted in appreciation and reverence. He couldn't help but be kind and respectful to the lady. It was a prime example of hypocrisy. How could someone go from one extreme of ignorance to another of kindness in less than five minutes? You can be certain that if, from that fleeting encounter, a relationship had been born, that man would someday treat that woman the same way or even worse than he had treated the bartender. He wouldn't be able to hide his disrespect for long. He'd eventually show his contempt for the woman at some point.

When I talk about family in my seminars, I emphasize that the way people treat their parents is the way they'll treat their spouses and children. If they're rebellious, if they hold a grudge, they'll end up hating their family in the same way.

Manoel told me that he wanted to marry Fiona because she wanted desperately to leave her parents' home and didn't have anywhere to go.

I told him, "Don't marry her, because in just a few days, she'll try to escape from you to go back to her parents' home."

He didn't believe me, but exactly one month after they were married, she visited her parents and didn't want to go back. One day, she attacked Manoel with a knife and he jumped from a two-story apartment to save his life. She hated Manoel the same way she had hated her parents.

The first people you need to forgive, if you want to love, are your parents. If you're at peace with them, you're at peace with everybody. You'll know you've forgiven your parents if you've forgiven yourself. If you degrade yourself, it's because your past still affects you. You have emotional hang-ups with your parents that make you not accept yourself. Your parents' opinion still influences you. You believe them, so you can't accept yourself. When you're completely independent of your parents, when you have your own self-image that isn't distorted or affected by past wrongs, you've conquered yourself.

When you feel good about yourself, you can look at people and see their beauty. You believe in them as much as you believe in yourself. You're able to value all humankind—without exceptions. You won't favor some while despising others. Everyone will be special to you.

Your value is unconditional

Your worth isn't a consequence of money, culture, social status, or beauty. If you're rich or poor, pretty or ugly, famous or unknown, it doesn't matter—you're important, anyway.

The only thing you need to merit value is *life*. If your heart beats, if you breathe, if blood runs through your veins, you're worthy. You aren't important because of what you have, but because of who you *are*.

You can dream about having money, knowledge, or status, thinking that those things will make you important and special. However, those things can't change your worth, because what's valuable isn't the money, knowledge, or status—it's *you*. It's not what you have that makes you important—it's *you*! To value what you have instead of valuing yourself is to materialize yourself, taking away your life and making you an object.

Imagine that you have a wealthy family member who dies, leaving an inheritance of $100 million, and you're the only relative who's alive, but you never knew him. The money stays in the bank, waiting for somebody to inherit it, but you aren't aware that it's yours. That $100 million dollars doesn't have any value, because there's no one to use it. However, if you discover that the money is yours, it suddenly has value, because there's someone who can own and use it.

Material things have value only when they're the property of somebody who can take advantage of it. A house has value only when it belongs to someone. A car can be beautiful, but if nobody owns it, it has no value.

On the other hand, a human being has value *without* material things. You're important without a car, without a house, and without $100 million! Although it would be marvelous to have $100 million, you wouldn't be any more special for having it.

Valuing things is a consequence of valuing people

There's a difference between achieving a goal as a *result* of valuing yourself and achieving a goal in *order* to value yourself. When you want to reach a goal in order to value yourself, you don't value yourself in the present. You place your value in the future, so you reach for the goal to feel important.

However, if you don't value yourself in the present, you don't have the power to reach your goals. Power comes from *love*. You need to love yourself to have power. The more you love yourself, the more interested you are in your own happiness and development. Therefore, if you want to be rich, you need to first accept being poor. Loving yourself when you're poor will give you the power to be rich. If you want to get a Ph.D., you need to accept yourself, even if you can't read. If you really accept yourself in your illiteracy, you'll empower yourself to eventually obtain a Ph.D.

Love is so important that your primary goal needs to be *loving yourself*. Instead of thinking about being rich to value yourself, think about valuing yourself to be rich. Love is the most powerful thing in the universe. That's why the bible says that "God is love." You can also reverse the words and say that love is God. If you love yourself, you have God's power, and with that power, you can achieve any goal you want.

Don't degrade yourself for any reason. Don't put yourself down because you're fat, ugly, or not famous. If you put yourself down, you'll get stuck. Hatred has no power; hatred is all weakness. If you don't accept yourself, you don't have any motivation or energy to get anywhere. You'll just be fat, poor, sick, and unhappy, like you've always been. Therefore, get leverage—love yourself.

Look in the mirror and say, "I love myself."

Get a minimum-wage job, and then tell yourself, "I'm important."

Then say, "I deserve to be fit and rich. I'll get everything I want because I love myself, and I'll love myself every step of the way until I get there."

When you value yourself conditionally, you push yourself too hard. You demand that you get things you think you need to be valuable. You don't accept your limits. You don't sleep well, don't eat healthy food, don't relax, and don't take time for your family. You don't have balance.

When you push yourself too hard, you value things more than you value yourself. Things are so important to you that you're willing to harm yourself to get them. You treat things as if they were people, and yourself as if you were an object. That's the essence of materialism—to love things more than you love yourself.

You need to put things in the proper perspective. You weren't created for the objects, they were created for you. Your money, your house, your car, your education—all those things exist *for* you, not the other way around. They were created to serve you. You're above them.

What's the point of getting everything and losing your soul? There's no meaning in becoming rich, famous, and educated at the cost of your health or happiness. You need to put yourself first. Let things serve *you*, don't serve them. Maintain balance! Allow yourself time to recharge, relax, and enjoy the company of those you love.

You can't lose your value

When you value yourself conditionally, you're afraid of losing things, because you've placed your importance in them. You're afraid of losing your money, your spouse, your reputation, your job, or your health. You can't even enjoy what you have, because you're afraid of losing it. You're a hostage of what might happen in the future.

To overcome that fear, you need to realize that losing things isn't the same as losing your value. Your importance is your greatest treasure, and nothing can take it from you. Life has its moments of glory and its moments of despair. Sometimes you're on top of the world and other times you're staring at the edge of the abyss. Sometimes you're healthy and sometimes you're sick. Sometimes you're loved and sometimes you're hated. It doesn't matter if you're weak or strong, rich or poor, loved or hated—in any situation, your value remains unchangeable until the end of your existence. Your value can't be acquired through money, the conquest of an ideal, or by becoming famous, because you're above those things.

You're 100% important

We tend to measure our value. We think that the more money we have, the more important we are. Therefore, if we have $10 million, we're two times more important than if we had $5 million dollars. If we have a master's degree, we think about getting a doctorate degree to become more important.

We also measure people's value. We look up to those who have more than we have and look down on those who have less. If we're with someone famous, we feel embarrassed, but if we're with a "low grade" person, we feel comfortable.

Value can't be measured. You can't be 50%, 70%, or 90% valuable. You can only be 100% important. You can't compare yourself to other people. If you're richer than someone, you aren't superior to that person, and if you're poorer, you aren't inferior, either. Although people differ in aspects such as beauty, education, health, and assets, in their value, they're all equal. Isn't that wonderful and liberating? There isn't anyone in this world who's superior to you. You don't need to feel embarrassed in anyone's presence. You can feel absolutely comfortable with any person, because you're just as important and special as any other human being.

Sometimes, you can be amazed by the genius of some people to the point that you think they're somehow superhuman. You think they aren't normal, or maybe they're on a superior level. However, *everybody* is equal. Although someone might be a famous singer or actor, they aren't superior to you. Being famous doesn't put a person above any other human being. Many beggars could become celebrities if they believed in themselves.

There are professions, like singing or acting, that give people status and make them famous. Other careers, like cleaning houses, working in the fields, or collecting garbage, will never make a person a star. But a house cleaner can be just as good at their profession as a singer in their performance, and a worker in the fields may be as skilled in their job as an actor on the stage.

Your value isn't in your hands

You can't make yourself inferior. You don't have power over your value. There isn't anything you can do to be important, and there isn't anything you can do to be worthless. You can make any mistake imaginable, and you'll still be special. All you can do is believe in your value, but even that won't make you special. You're always *important*—believe it or not.

Peter decided to have therapy because he suffered from depression. After three years of treatment, he learned to accept himself. However, the three years of therapy didn't change what he was. He was as important before the therapy as he was afterward. The only change was the image he had of himself. He saw himself in a different way.

To be important without realizing it is like being a millionaire without knowing it. There's a story about a father who died and left a big inheritance to his son who didn't know it. The money was hidden in the pages of a book the father wanted his son to read, but it took several years until the son opened that book and found the money.

The same will happen to you if you aren't aware of your own importance. You have a great treasure, but you don't enjoy it. You're a millionaire, but you live like a beggar. You're sad, when you could be happy.

Your value isn't in other people's hands

People don't have power over your value. They can't do anything to put you down. You're important, no matter what they do to you. You feel inferior because you don't value yourself. Your lack of self-esteem makes you think they're humiliating you, but you're the one who's putting yourself down. If you value yourself, no matter what they do, you'll never feel humiliated.

Your self-esteem is like a shield that protects you from people's disrespect. When you value yourself, you don't take anything personally. When they try to hurt you, you know the problem isn't with you, but with them. They try to humiliate you because they don't value themselves.

When you don't value yourself, you're overly sensitive. Anything people say or do makes you sad. Your inferiority complex makes you vulnerable. You let people control your emotions.

When you value yourself, you're strong. You have a sense of honor that no one can destroy. People feel hopeless when they try to put you down. They feel your self-esteem and they shrink back. They know they can't influence you negatively.

It isn't what people do to you that makes you suffer, but what you do to yourself. It isn't the contempt that comes from them, but the contempt that comes from you. To feel embarrassed is to suffer twice—first because of the humiliation coming from people, and second because of your own humiliation.

Knowing that isn't enough. For a long time, I felt humiliated by people, though I knew a lot about myself. I knew that people didn't have the power to put me down, but I felt embarrassed every time they mistreated me. I knew intellectually, but not in my heart.

What really helped me overcome that sensitivity was to understand that I could control my emotions. I could feel up or down, if I wanted to. Whenever people tried to humiliate me, I could choose to feel inferior or to value myself. Once I understood that, I decided to feel valuable in any situation, but I had to be vigilant, because the old me was always prone to believing whatever people said about me. However, my new self disagrees. I remind myself that it's up to me to feel valuable or inferior. People can't put me down unless I allow them to.

Becoming independent of people's opinions is a constant battle. You always need to be on guard, not against their attempts to hurt you, but against your tendency to believe they can. Every time you overcome the battle, you become stronger. Every time they try to put you down and you don't believe them, you're less vulnerable.

Therefore, don't worry about other people's opinions. What matters isn't what they think of you, but what you think of yourself. Happiness comes from the inside. When you become independent of people's opinions, you discover that no one can make you sad. Your self-esteem is like a rock that sustains you amid the storms of life. You find security in your own love. People can take everything but your self-respect.

Love is inside

When you don't value yourself, you seek people's approval. You try to fill your emptiness with their love. You think that the solution is outside of yourself. You think you feel inferior because people put you down, so you want to convince people that you're important. You believe that when you convince them you're important, you'll *feel* important.

You can't overcome your own inferiority complex through other people's love. They can't fill your emptiness. No one can make you feel important if you feel worthless inside. You're your own guru, and the antidote to your inferiority complex is inside you. You have all the love you need. You must change the direction of your search. Instead of looking for respect *outside* of yourself, look for it *inside* of yourself. Instead of asking people to value you, you need to value yourself.

On the other hand, to demand respect from people when you don't respect yourself is contradictory. How can you ask them for something that even you aren't willing to give yourself? You should be the first person in the world to respect yourself.

When you don't value yourself, you don't value other people, either. Then you want them to value you, when you don't value them. When you value people, you don't demand that they value you. You aren't worried about what they do to you, but about what you do to them. Instead of focusing on yourself, you focus on them. When you're with people, you aren't paying attention to the way they treat you or the words they say. You focus on your attitude and behavior toward them. You're aware of your actions and you're attentive to the way you treat them. You want them to feel great about themselves because you know you can make a difference in their lives.

That's the secret of happiness. You find happiness when you *forget about yourself*. Looking for other people's approval is selfish. When you act in a self-centered way, you become unhappy. You can't find contentment unless you live a life of service.

I radically changed my state of mind when I found the purpose of my life. I became passionate about life when I decided to *live to give*. All of my goals are addressed toward people. If you want to live with passion, stop being selfish. Don't look for their approval. Just approve of them, value them, and love them. Give people what you want to get from them.

Making the purpose of my life serving others was also an enormous source of power and strength. I only felt motivated to reach my goals when they were addressed toward people. I found energy and power in my commitment to help people master their emotions.

When you don't value yourself, you think that other people also don't value you. Although they like you and they do everything to show you how important you are, you still think they don't like you. It's hard to feel respected by people when you don't respect yourself.

We tend to think that people see us as we see ourselves. Sharon worked in an industry where she felt rejected by other employees. She thought that people were saying bad things about her. Yet, on her birthday, her colleagues surprised her with a party and gave her lots of gifts. She realized that she had been wrong in thinking they didn't appreciate her.

To feel valued by people, you need to value yourself first. When you value yourself, you're able to feel how much people value you.

JoAnne was a scientist who worked in the laboratory of a respected university. She had a doctor's degree in chemistry and was very competent. Her colleagues had great admiration for her and the university was proud to have her as a member of their staff. However, she was very shy and withdrawn. She was always insecure about showing the results of her research, and she felt that no one would value what she'd done. Although she was very competent, she didn't believe she was. As a result, she thought other people didn't respect her.

You may think that if you were perfect, you'd get everybody's appreciation, but being perfect doesn't guarantee that people will respect you. There will always be people who reject you and won't recognize your qualities. It's impossible to gain everybody's respect.

People who don't value themselves can't value you, either. They look down on themselves, so they're unable to recognize your importance. What they see in you is a reflection of what they see in themselves. There's nothing you can do about that. You can't make people respect you, because you can't make them respect themselves, either.

Shame is caused by an inferiority complex

One thing that made me suffer a lot was my shyness. I often felt humiliated whenever I was with a group of people. I avoided being with people so I wouldn't suffer. When I had to be with a group, I told jokes and tried to be cool so people would look at me in a positive way.

When I started preaching, I was so shy that I wanted to crawl under the pulpit or flee from my audience. One year before I graduated from the theology seminar, I decided to do an evangelism series, and I was very successful. A church that had been empty on Sundays and Wednesdays nights was full every night during that evangelism period. All the evidence showed that I was a great preacher. However, I still doubted myself and was embarrassed when I preached. If someone left the sanctuary while I was preaching, I took it personally and believed it was an indication that they didn't like my performance.

My shyness wasn't exclusive to when I was with a group of people. I also felt very shy when I was with someone in particular. Asking a woman out was a very difficult thing for me. I acted as if it was a privilege to be with a woman and had to grovel. It didn't matter who I was talking to. I always felt uncomfortable, because I thought the other person saw how inferior I really was.

You feel shy when you think you're inferior. Shame is a product of a feeling of inadequacy. When you think other people are superior, you feel uncomfortable in their presence. You think you don't deserve their companionship because you're ordinary.

There isn't any reason for you to feel ashamed, because everyone is the same. Shame is a product of your fantasy. When you feel ashamed, you elevate people and degrade yourself. Even if people are famous, pretty, or wealthy, you don't need to feel embarrassed. Their external qualities don't interfere with their value. They don't become more important because of their status, beauty, or wealth.

Shame makes you think you don't deserve other people's companionship and that you aren't worthy of love and affection. You think there's something weird or ugly about you that needs to be hidden so people won't be disgusted. You become introverted and withdrawn because you're afraid people will see your flaws. When you accept yourself, you aren't afraid to be who you are. You don't fear rejection.

You don't need to be perfect to be valuable

When you don't accept yourself, you try to be different so you can be accepted by other people. You try to be special so people will accept you. You think that if you were more attractive, funny, or sexy, you'd be admired. Nevertheless, by trying to be someone else, you end up not being yourself. Instead of being yourself, you become a lie.

You're good, just the way you are. Your goodness resides in being yourself. When you give up being what you are in order to be what you aren't, you're not good anymore. What is good is what God did, just the way he did it. What is forced, faked, or manipulated isn't good. To be good, you must be yourself. Be natural, be spontaneous—don't be a lie. You must let your own nature flow, without being afraid something evil will appear. The effort to be causes you not to be.

An inferiority complex makes you think that other people are better than you. It seems that other people are perfect, but you're a disaster. Even your virtues become flaws. Don't be blind to your good qualities. Sometimes, what you despise about yourself is exactly what other people love.

People try to find your mistakes when they're trying to make up for their own inferiority complexes. They want to find your imperfections because they think you're better than they are. As a result, you don't need to worry about other people judging you. If they're judging you, it's because *they're* insecure.

Humility vs. inferiority complex

There's a difference between humility and putting yourself down. Sometimes, to avoid appearing proud, you fall into the trap of degrading yourself. Although you shouldn't act arrogantly, you mustn't go to the extreme of degrading yourself. The kind of humility in which you put yourself down is anything but humility. It's artificial, forced, and doesn't come from the heart.

Although you need to be humble, you can't do that at the expense of your dignity. In every encounter you have with people, you must exhibit self-confidence and respect. Believe in your goodness and talents. Be sure of who you are and what you're able to do. You're someone unique and special. Therefore, don't settle for less than you are. Don't let people have a poor impression of you because you're afraid of appearing to be arrogant and conceited.

There are many different ways you exhibit self-confidence, such as your posture, your voice, and the clothes you wear. When you value yourself, you're not hunched over or careless. When you value yourself, you're poised, whether you're standing or sitting.

When you value yourself, you look people in the eye when you talk to them. You speak with respect, and the tone of your voice inspires confidence. You must also be careful about the clothes you wear. I remember one day, I visited a member of my church in the hospital. Although I didn't have a lot of money to buy expensive clothes, I used the best clothes I had.

When I said to the nurse that I was a pastor and that I'd come to visit a member of my church, she told me, "I knew you were a pastor because of the nice way you dressed."

In every situation, you're selling your image. To be successful in your relationships and career, you need the respect and confidence of people. That's why it's so vital that you know how to sell your image. Although you mustn't make false pretenses, you can't make people think you're inferior.

2.
Symptoms of Conditional Value

When you value yourself conditionally, you define yourself through external things. You think they'll give you importance. Below are some standards you may impose in order to value yourself. Analyze yourself while you read them to see if you've been placing your value on external things other than yourself.

Financial

Sometimes we think that if we have more money, we'll be more valuable. We may strive to be richer so we can be appreciated by people. We exhibit our possessions as a way to attract attention. We buy things we aren't really interested in because we think they're going to impress people.

There's a drawback. Because we're trying to define ourselves through material things, we fear losing them and not being valuable anymore. Our sense of worth will be as fickle as the things we place our value in. If we lose our possessions, we'll feel desperate.

It's a delusion to place our value in material things. Deep inside, we don't feel important at all. We value the money we have or our material possessions, but we don't value the person who owns it—us.

When we define ourselves through our possessions, we compare ourselves to other people. When we find someone who possesses more than us, we feel inferior and idolize that person. If we meet someone who has less, we degrade them and show off our possessions. We feel superior or inferior, depending on who we're comparing ourselves to. When we value ourselves unconditionally, however, we never feel superior or inferior, because we know that material possessions don't change the inner value of people.

Knowledge

Another way we define ourselves is through knowledge. We think that to be important, we need to have knowledge and to have as many titles or diplomas as possible. There's no doubt that knowledge is useful and necessary, but when we place our worth in the knowledge we have, it becomes a problem.

Some people become so focused on acquiring knowledge that they forget other aspects of their lives. They want others to work for them so they can dedicate all of their time to studying. They ignore people and they never get to a point where they're satisfied.

They like to use their knowledge to make a good impression. I remember listening to preachers who talked to simple people, using complex words that made it impossible for them to understand the message. Those speakers were so desperate for attention that they ignored their audience's need to understand.

Beauty

Many people place their value on their exterior. They spend a lot of money and time trying to be attractive. They use beauty as a way to feel important. Entire industries have created billions in profit by taking advantage of that need.

Undoubtedly, beauty is an asset. The only problem is when people become obsessed with it and make it the center of their lives. People who place their value in their beauty show off their body to attract attention. How often have you seen a bodybuilder in a tank top?

The problem with placing value in your beauty is that you become as superficial as your prettiness. Instead of focusing your attention on your character, you focus on your exterior. In addition, you're never satisfied with your exterior. You'll always be worried about whether people think you're pretty or not.

Placing value in your beauty can cause you to reject yourself. If you're fat, old, have some physical disability, or just don't have the perfect body shape, you'll hate yourself and feel embarrassed when you're in other people's presence.

You can't be defined by your beauty. You're just as valuable as any movie star. Although it's good to take care of your body (as long as it doesn't become an obsession), it won't change your value. Although you can become prettier, you can't become more valuable than you already are.

Status

People also use status as a way of feeling valuable. Some people want to climb the social ladder only because it brings them fame. They want to feel as if they're the center of attention because they think they'll be superior.

When the desire for power comes from a necessity to define oneself, it corrupts a person. The problem with looking for status to feel valuable is that a person isn't interested in other people's welfare, but in their own. They don't hesitate to step all over other people who get in their way and will resort to gossiping, bribing, and sometimes even killing. (Take dictators, who kill thousands of people who disagree with them or who want to dispose of them.)

Consider what happens among politicians in their search for power. Members of a party avidly try to find fault in the other party to get attention. They accept an idea or reject it not because they really believe it's for the good of citizens, but because it will either bring popularity to their party or to themselves. However, the worst thing is to see one politician trying to destroy another's reputation. If there was no greed for power, there would be a completely different spirit among those authorities. They'd respect each other and they'd be united in seeking the good of the nation. They wouldn't take advantage of each other's weaknesses to gain popularity.

It's also possible to see that attitude in many companies. To keep their position of authority, some executives step all over other people, just to guarantee their own status.

Once there was a meeting to discuss a problem with an executive who was doing something the president and a few others disagreed with. Most of the committee members present thought the executive was right. However, they were afraid to show their opinion and to lose their positions in the organization. After the meeting, one of the committee members came to the executive, saying that he supported his position. The employee then asked why he hadn't spoken out during the meeting.

There are many politicians or executives who apparently defend an irrational position of a government or a company with beautiful speeches when they actually disagree with it. Their addiction to being important makes them sacrifice their deepest values. They even defend their positions through rationalization in an attempt to smother their own consciences. But the truth remains, eating away at their hearts and integrity. Eventually, they won't be able to value themselves anymore, because they'll feel ashamed for what they've done.

You can't forego your integrity in order to feel valuable. How many of Hitler's assistants, generals, and soldiers disagreed with him? You'd be amazed to find out how many of them abhorred Hitler's ideas—and themselves for what they were doing. They ignored their integrity because they didn't want to lose their status or worse—their lives.

Being loved

Being loved is probably the strongest desire we have when we don't value ourselves. We want to make up for our low self-esteem by being accepted by other people. Being loved by people doesn't change our value. We aren't important because they think we are. Our importance is beyond their opinion of us. If we place our importance on their opinion, our value will go up and down depending on how they see us at any particular time.

Health

When we think our value is conditional, we tend to think that if we're sick, we're inferior. That causes many people to be neurotic about health, making it the center of their lives. I've seen people get sick because they tried so hard not to. There was a couple who were so careful about not eating unhealthy food that they became weak and sick. Their weakness intensified their worries, making them even more neurotic about their food intake.

When you place your value on your health, you become afraid of dying. Any symptom or health problem makes you think that you have a serious health issue that will disable or kill you. Behind that fear is the thought that disease takes away your value. You think that people will despise you because of your health condition.

Some people become desperate when they learn that they're sick. Others even think about killing themselves. When I worked as a chaplain, I saw how people became deeply disappointed when they knew they had a disease. I remember a man who totally lost his interest in life after learning he had AIDS. It took him only one month to die. Some thought they were monsters after they knew they had AIDS. When they needed to love themselves the most, they reject themselves instead.

Perfection

People sometimes think their value depends on being perfect. It's a common problem among religious people. They become strict and worried about the rules and laws they must follow in order to be valuable. They don't follow those rules because of a desire to be a better person, but to be important and to receive other people's recognition.

A true relationship with God is fundamental to reaching a sense of purpose in life and serving others. When it becomes a mere attempt to overcome an inner sense of inferiority, in addition to losing their real purpose, a person can commit serious mistakes that will hurt themselves and others. Many wars, crimes, injustices, and abuse have been committed in the name of God. The reason is that people put religion, rules, and laws above human life instead of doing the opposite.

Evil

Although it may seem like a contradiction, there are people who place their value on being evil. They go to the extreme in their search for strength and power. In some gangs, for example, a member is praised and rewarded according to the intensity of his evil deeds. The greater the atrocity, the greater the reward. The maximum reward would be for murder.

Many people, especially the young, are attracted to gangs because they feel inadequate. They feel abandoned, rejected, and disrespected by their parents, so they think that by joining gangs they'll become strong, powerful, and valuable.

The problem with that belief is that inside every human being is a sense of justice that can't be violated without making a person lose their integrity. That means that even when gang members are praised by their colleagues, they don't feel good about themselves because of their own inner sense of justice. In addition, their value is in the hands of their colleagues. If they're approved of, they approve of themselves, but if they aren't approved of, they reject themselves. In other words, they still get their self-image from other people, just as they got their self-image from their parents. They simply changed the source of their search for approval.

On the other hand, when those kinds of people encounter someone who hurts them, they feel inferior. They think that being evil makes a person superior, so they believe that someone who hurts them is above them. When they're the ones who do wicked things, they feel valuable, but when they're the ones who suffer from wickedness, they feel inferior.

Step Two
Overcoming Pride

1.
The Difference Between Pride and Valuing Yourself

There's a difference between pride and self-esteem. Pride is an attempt to overcome an inferiority complex by putting yourself above others. It's a natural defense mechanism. If you feel inferior, you automatically try to show off and to get applause from other people. It's natural, so you don't even realize it.

Pride isn't the solution for the feeling of inadequacy, because it doesn't cure the soul. It's a defense mechanism, so you continue feeling inferior. While you try to prove that you're special, you feel substandard. The more proud you are, the more inferior you feel.

Valuing yourself is the opposite of pride. Valuing yourself isn't a defense mechanism, but the real solution for an inferiority complex. When you respect yourself, you don't feel the urge to put yourself above others or to get applause and praise. You don't need to impress people, because you already value yourself. You know you're important, and even if people don't recognize your importance, it doesn't make you feel inferior. You aren't sensitive to people's negative opinions and you don't feel down when they try to humiliate you.

When you value yourself, you also value other people. You have a sense of reverence for the greatness of people. You treat every person with distinction and honor.

Pride doesn't cure a feeling of inferiority, because you can't value yourself while putting other people down. If you degrade people, you'll end up degrading yourself. When you're proud, you don't have respect for other people, and if you don't have respect for other people, you don't have respect for yourself. Therefore, it's important to recognize the difference between valuing yourself and being proud. When you start a process of self-knowledge and growth, you'll sometimes confuse the two emotions. I remember that sometimes when I thought I was defending my rights, I was actually being arrogant. While attempting to show my importance, I put other people down. It took time to learn how to assert my value without humiliating other people.

Pride and childhood

Pride comes from your childhood, through your relationship with your parents. Parents who don't value themselves think their children don't value them, either. When their kids do something they don't like, they think they're doing it to humiliate them and try to reverse the situation by humiliating their kids. However, everything originates from the parents' mind.

A defensive attitude from parents provokes a defensive attitude in kids. Kids who are humiliated try to humiliate their parents. A competition is born that will endure for the rest of their lives. When those children become adults, they'll feel as if other people are trying to humiliate them, too, and they'll defend themselves by humiliating others. Their relationships will become an unceasing competition.

When those children become parents, they'll humiliate their children the same way they were humiliated by their parents. A chain reaction is established, in which pride passes from parents to children, from generation to generation.

Pride is a person longing for love

Pride is an attempt to get people's attention in order to feel loved. If you don't love yourself, you show off to attract other people's love. However, despite other people's attention and praise, you continue to feel unloved. You don't feel loved, because you don't love yourself. Even if people praise you, you don't feel they appreciate you, because you don't appreciate yourself. To feel appreciated by others, you need to appreciate yourself.

The solution for your longing isn't other people's praise, but loving yourself. When you love yourself, you don't need to attract the attention of others. When you love yourself, you're satisfied with your own love, so you don't need to show off anymore.

Pride is a fantasy

It's impossible for you to be inferior, so it's also impossible for you to be superior. If you have a real mental image of yourself, you'll feel neither inferior nor superior. When you try to overcome your sense of inferiority by putting yourself above others, you're just wasting your time. You aren't inferior, so there's nothing you can do to be superior. Therefore, competition is also a waste of time.

Nobody can humiliate you unless you agree with them. When you feel humiliated by what people do to you, it isn't because of what they did, but because of your own inability to value yourself. When you don't value yourself, you believe whatever people say about you. However, when you value yourself, you don't feel humiliated, because your self-esteem is like a shield that protects you.

If you meet a person on the street and that person says you're stupid, you may accept their comment or reject it. If you accept the criticism, it's not because of what the person said, but because of your own feelings of inferiority. Before they called you stupid, you felt that way already, so you suffer the accusation because you have a poor self-image.

When people try to humiliate you, it isn't because you're inferior. It's because *they* feel inferior. People who feel inferior attempt to humiliate you because they project their feelings of inadequacy on you. They feel inferior, so they think you are, too. They humiliate you because they humiliate themselves. What they do to you is a reflection of what they do to themselves.

People look at you as if you're a mirror. What they see in you is what they see in themselves. They project their opinions of themselves onto you and believe you're like them. If they value themselves, they value you, but if they degrade themselves, they degrade you, too. Therefore, when people try to humiliate you, you don't need to take it personally.

Pride causes materialism

When you're proud, you worry too much about exterior things. You think that to be important, you need to be beautiful, rich, or famous. You focus too much on material things and don't pay attention to your inner self. You don't consider that your character or virtues are the most important factor in getting people's appreciation. Kindness, honesty, and humility are more admirable than assets, beauty, and status.

On the other hand, there are people who are attracted to material things. They look for someone who is rich, famous, or beautiful. However, they don't want someone because they love them, but because they're interested in what that person can give them. That's why wealthy and famous people are so targeted by others. Everyone wants to be their friend or fiancée. As a result, they have to have bodyguards, and avoid public places. It's hard for them to know who really loves them and who just wants to take advantage of them.

When you try to obtain material things to attract people, you end up having people who want to be with you for status. They love your fortune, fame, or beauty, but not you. You shouldn't worry about exterior things.

Every once in a while, we hear about someone wealthy getting a divorce and losing a large portion of their assets. Unfortunately, famous and prosperous people are greatly targeted because of their wealth.

There are selfish people who prey on other people because of their wealth or status, with the purpose of getting their money and attracting attention from the media. Those unscrupulous people mistreat their prosperous spouses, don't support them in anything, and sometimes harm their career and damage their prestige. Finally, they divorce them and get an undeserved amount of their assets.

The importance of being authentic

When you don't value yourself, you can't appreciate your uniqueness. You think you're different from people because you're inferior. You believe that in order to be valuable, you need to be like them. When you don't value yourself, you exaggerate other people's qualities. Their behavior, their way of speaking, their gestures, and everything about them confirms their superiority. From your point of view, their differences are an indication of their advantage. You think they're different because they're better than you.

The fact that every person is unique doesn't make anyone superior to anyone else. Our differences show that everyone is singular and special. Beauty dwells in the uniqueness and not in the sameness. Sameness is boring. If you try to be like other people, you'll be a sheep. Instead of being original, you'll be a copycat. Your value resides in your difference.

Celebrities have a powerful influence over people. Many people think that a celebrity is superior to them, and they try to be like their idols. That's why people wear the same clothes or the same haircut as their idols. They think that if they talk like their idol, they'll be important. The desire to be like their idols shows how people think that everything they are is bad, while everything their idols are is good. Instead of celebrating their own individuality, they despise themselves.

Look at yourself to see if you aren't suffering from that. See if you're imitating people so you can be important. Do you make the same gestures, speak the same way, or wear the same clothes other people do? If you are, you're turning yourself into a carbon copy of someone else rather than being yourself.

The problem with imitating people is that you lose your own authenticity. Instead of celebrating your uniqueness and appreciating your differences, you become a replica. You're neither yourself nor them. You become an actor, because you're trying to be something you're not.

You can't escape yourself. You can't be what you aren't. If you're an introvert, you'll never be extrovert, and vice versa. Accept yourself the way you are and rejoice in your individuality. Your traits are just as important to other people as theirs are to you. You might be so used to your own characteristics that you don't see how interesting you are, but others do.

Instead of trying to be something else or someone else, you need to be yourself. The more you're yourself, the more other people will admire you. Instead of being ashamed of your differences, realize that your differences are the reason you're attractive to others. What draws people to you is the fact that there's something in you that doesn't exist in anyone else. You're unique.

Praise addiction

If you feel inferior, you hate the idea of being common. You assume that by being common, you're just another person. You think that to be special, you need to be better. When you're in a group of people, you want them to notice you. You think that if you aren't treated better than anyone else, you're inferior. As a result, you try to show off. You make jokes, speak loudly, and brag about yourself so people can see you're one of a kind.

The craving for attention causes anxiety. Instead of relaxing and enjoying other people's company, you're always concerned about how people see you.

You ask yourself, "Do they think I'm cool?"

If they pay attention to you and laugh at your jokes, you feel over-excited and tell yourself "I can't believe it! This is awesome. They think I'm cool!"

You keep telling jokes and bragging about yourself. They react positively and you feel even more excited. You may even get to the point of becoming hyper.

At the same time, you're wondering, "How much longer can I deceive them?"

You're afraid that you might say or do something wrong that will cause people to reject you. It makes you critical of yourself, and you're always worried about doing something stupid.

When you crave being in the spotlight, you feel disappointed if people don't notice you. You go home thinking that you're nothing and that no one likes you. However, when you value yourself, you don't have the need to show off. You aren't worried if people don't notice you. You know you're important, anyway, so if they don't give you attention, you don't take it personally. You're relaxed and can enjoy being in a group of people without worrying about whether they like you.

Being too concerned about people noticing you makes you selfish. Your focus is constantly on yourself, so there's no room for turning your focus outward toward other people. When you overcome the necessity to be noticed, you care about people. When you're in a group, you want to make sure everyone is feeling good. You give them attention, you value what they say, and you make them feel important. As a result, you aren't stressed, because you aren't worried about how they treat you.

The more inferior you feel, the more you want to be praised. You compensate for your lack of self-esteem by seeking people's approval. You try to show off so others can see how good you are.

Wanting to be praised is an addiction. If you feel inferior, you live in a constant search for approval. The drawback is that if you don't get the praise you expect or if you're criticized, you feel frustrated. The more addicted to praise you are, the more disappointed you'll be.

When I started preaching, I was extremely dependent on people's opinions. I went to the church lobby after a sermon, waiting for compliments. If people complimented me, I'd be excited about it for the rest of the day.

It's a waste of time to seek people's praise. Being praised won't heal an inferiority complex. The solution for your inferiority complex is inside you. When you seek people's approval, you're looking for the solution in the wrong place. You want them to approve of you, because you don't approve of yourself.

It's nice to be complimented. Although I don't crave people's praise anymore after I preach, I tell you that I delight in being praised. However, if I'm not praised, I don't feel sorry for myself. I don't need people's approval to shape my self image. I derive my strength from inside and not from other people's opinions.

Wanting to be praised makes you anxious. You're always afraid of messing up and of being rejected. As a result, you can't enjoy your performance. When I started preaching, I feared people's rejection so much that I wanted to either hide behind the pulpit or to run out of the church. It was the same with playing the piano. I couldn't have any fun because I was afraid of making a mistake and of being rejected. Playing with other musicians was even worse. I always thought that I'd wreck the whole performance.

That has changed a lot. A short time ago, I had the opportunity to play at an engagement party with three other musicians. I had a lot of fun! Not being concerned about people's approval let me focus on the music and enjoy the beauty of it. The interesting thing was that I got a lot of compliments.

When you're addicted to praise, you become overly excited about getting it.

You ask yourself, "How can someone dumb like me do anything right?"

You go home and you remember all the compliments as if it were a dream. You can hardly believe you deserved them.

On one occasion, I received a lot of applause and compliments after a concert in a church in Rio de Janeiro, Brazil. I got so excited that I couldn't sleep that night. The moments kept passing through my mind. I remembered all the compliments. It was like a dream. I couldn't believe that I had played so well and had made such an impression on people. However, the most ironic part of it all was that I was the only person out of 300 people who didn't believe in me! While everyone was impressed with me and my talent, I doubted myself.

When you believe in yourself, you don't feel overwhelmed by people's applause. You receive it naturally, because you know you're deserving. You're not the last one to believe in yourself—you're the first. If you're rejected, you don't feel disappointed, either. You know that you're capable, so you try to learn from your failure and do better the next time.

According to research, ninety percent of people fear public speaking more than anything else. They'd rather die than speak in front of an audience and face the possibility of being rejected. However, rejection is a myth. The only real rejection is your own rejection of yourself. If you aren't worried about people's opinion, you can do anything in public and not be stressed.

Craving people's applause makes you nervous. You make silly mistakes because of your anxiety. The less your craving for applause, the better you perform. Not yearning for applause let you be relaxed and focused. You perform better, and then you get applause. Therefore, the secret to getting applause resides in not craving it.

Pride is a defense mechanism

When you accept people's humiliation, you become defensive and gain revenge by humiliating them back. Then you start a competition. They humiliate you, you humiliate them, they humiliate you, and so on. That vicious cycle of humiliation can be seen in many arguments. People argue to prove that they aren't inferior to another person and try to put them down. They insult, accuse, curse, and scorn in a futile attempt to recover their self-esteem. While they try to defend themselves, they're humiliated by the other person. They end up more humiliated than before.

When you get revenge, you have the intention of stopping people from humiliating you. Unfortunately, that isn't what happens. When you react, people react back. Then a chain reaction is established.

To end the cycle of humiliation, you need to attack the problem at the root. As you can see, humiliating other people to make them respect you is ineffective. If you value yourself, you'll never feel humiliated by others. Then you won't feel the urge to humiliate people in return.

It's a waste of time to try to prove your dignity. You can't get back what you didn't lose in the first place. People don't have the power to humiliate you, so you don't need to worry about recovering what you didn't lose. It's also a waste of time to seek revenge. You can't get revenge, because other people's dignity isn't in your hands. You can't touch their worth.

Instead of arguing with people to prove your dignity, you need to respect yourself. By getting back at them, you won't fix the problem—you'll just bring it to a whole new level. You don't need to show people that you aren't inferior to them. You just need to convince yourself that they can't put you down.

Pride attracts pride. If you humiliate other people to get even, they'll humiliate back. Humiliation can't end humiliation. If you want people to respect you, you need to respect them. Even if they try to put you down, value them. By treating them with dignity, you end the cycle of humiliation. If you don't play the game, there's no competition.

Most people are receptive to a respectful approach. If you counteract their disrespect with respect, they react positively. However, there are people who resist any peaceful approach. They're so immersed in their *victim* mentality that they can't see it when you value them. They like to feel humiliated, even though it makes them suffer. As a result, they'll humiliate you, even when you respect them. In any case, don't sink to their level. Keep on respecting them, even if they try to put you down. You don't respect them because of them, but because of you. If you try to get even, you'll suffer, because you'll believe they can put you down. Then you're going to give them the power to humiliate you. By not getting even, you make their attempts to humiliate you unproductive.

When you're proud, you think that you must value only those who value you. If someone doesn't value you, you think you have the right to humiliate them. Respect should never be a response. You don't honor people because they honor you, but because it's the right thing to do. Every person deserves to be valued, even if they don't value you.

If you really appreciate other people, you always appreciate them. You value them when they value you, and when they *don't* value you. However, if you tend to humiliate people when they humiliate you, you don't ever value them. If you're proud sometimes, you're always proud.

Pride is the opposite of love

To compete is a consequence of not loving. Love and valuing are intimately connected. When you love people, you'll never have a superior attitude. You'll never try to show that you're better than they are. On the contrary, you'll seek to make them feel special and to do everything in your power to show how important they are. You won't try to cause them to feel ashamed or inferior. You won't make fun of them, nor will you make them look ridiculous. You'll be careful to not touch their past wounds, causing them to wallow in their lack of dignity. Instead, you'll try to heal their wounds with your acceptance and respect.

When I worked as chaplain at the Pio XII Hospital in Rio de Janeiro, which was part of Igase, Inc., I had the opportunity of meeting the president, Dr. Milton Afonso. I wanted to ask him to help me buy a keyboard. When I went to his office, I was nervous. I was the chaplain of the smallest of his hospitals, yet there I was, waiting to talk to the president. He was kind, and his conversation was so pleasant that I didn't feel as if I was standing in front of the president. It felt as if he was a close friend.

I thought, "It seems as if I'm the president and he's the chaplain of the smallest hospital."

Although Dr. Milton Afonso was the president of a great company, he was full of love and respect. He never said or did anything that might make people embarrassed. He didn't take advantage of his position to prove his superiority.

You need to have a good self-image and expect the best from people. Don't assume they want to humiliate you. Try to see the best in every person. When they say something, seek their goodness. Listen to people in a positive way.

The tendency to expect the worst from people comes from not believing in yourself. When you don't have a positive self-image, you think that other people want to put you down. However, when you value yourself, you look at people in a different way. You stop judging them and don't distort their intentions. You quit thinking they have a bad purpose in mind. You have faith in them and you believe in their friendship.

Have you noticed how scared you are when someone tells you they want to talk to you? Right away, you want to know what's the matter, and if the person delays talking with you, you make negative assumptions. Why do you assume the worst? Why not expect something good? When you see people positively, you stop thinking they want to humiliate you. You believe in their love.

Learn not to take humiliation personally

In any communication between humans, there are two messages: verbal and non-verbal. The verbal message is the material part of the communication, while the non-verbal message is the abstract part. The non-verbal message is loaded with feelings, and changes the meaning of the verbal message. It may be positive or negative, depending upon the feelings involved.

Every time someone talks to you, they're conveying those two messages. In some cases, the abstract message is negative. Sometimes, along with the communication, people try to put you down. In order not to feel humiliated, ignore the humiliation part and just pay attention to the message. You must clean out all the negative feelings and listen to the real stuff.

For example, let's say your wife complains that you got home late, but when she talks to you, she tries to make you feel ashamed for not letting her know.

Behind that message, you hear her saying, "You should be ashamed for not calling me."

In order not to feel humiliated, ignore the shame part of the message and respond to the real stuff. In other words, apologize and tell her that next time you'll let her know. Don't try to defend yourself. Don't accuse her of not trusting you. If you don't feel insulted, you'll be able to answer in a respectful way.

The secret to not taking things personally resides in acting as if you're a bystander who is watching from outside and analyzing everything without being emotionally involved. That can work especially well for couples. Sometimes, when they talk to each other, they unconsciously try to put the other person down. For example, a wife asks her husband to put his shirt in the closet in an impertinent way. In such a case, what the husband needs to do in order not to take it personally is not to pay attention to the subliminal message of disrespect and focus only on putting his shirt in the closet. By doing so, he won't take her comments personally and thus not feel insulted. He can then understand his wife instead of being angry at her.

When you're proud, you humiliate yourself

When you humiliate yourself, you're a divided person. It's as if there are two different people inside you—the master and the slave—and every time you fall short of your expectations, the master berates the slave, making you feel ashamed. Every time you act foolishly or do something wrong, you hate yourself. You're your own worst enemy.

Before everyone else has the opportunity to put you down, you do it yourself.

That division is a result of your childhood. There were people in your past, such as your parents, siblings, or teachers, who unintentionally humiliated you. When you did something they disapproved of, they degraded you. You absorbed their humiliation to the point that you no longer need them to humiliate you, because you picked up where they left off! As a result, every time you think you do something wrong, you hate yourself.

You tell yourself, "You should be ashamed. How can you be so stupid? I'll never accept you when you're this flawed."

Then the slave feels embarrassed and tries to defend itself by saying, "I'm the victim! I didn't know I was doing something wrong. It wasn't intentional."

The master replies, "You should have known it was wrong."

If you have pride in your heart, you're the first victim of your pride. Before you humiliate anyone, you humiliate yourself. Then you try to defend yourself against the master who lives inside you. However, the master insists on putting you down and making you feel ashamed. You live in constant conflict.

When you overcome your pride, you break that internal division and become whole. You aren't in conflict with yourself anymore. You don't despise or judge yourself. You don't feel embarrassed about your own humiliation. You don't need to make excuses. You aren't a slave or a master.

2.
Symptoms of Pride

There are many symptoms of pride. Below is a list, some of which have already been discussed in the previous chapter. They can be divided in two different groups, *interior* and *exterior*.

Interior: What you do to yourself to be superior. They represent your internal struggles for becoming a person worthy of praise.

1. **Putting yourself down.** Your main intention when you put yourself down is to get people's praise. You think that by degrading yourself, you'll change for the better. This approach is fruitless. Humiliating yourself in order to become superior will only confirm your feeling of inadequacy. If you put yourself down, you'll stay there. The only effective method to gaining your dignity is by respecting yourself.

2. **Accusing yourself.** You're hard on yourself, scolding and punishing yourself for not living up to your standards. You want to do everything right so you'll be admired.

Exterior: The work you do outwardly to deserve honor and recognition.

1. **Wanting to be the center of attention.** Every time you're in a group of people, you try to get attention in order to feel important.

2. **Making jokes.** You try to attract attention by making jokes. You want people to admire you by thinking that you're a funny person.

3. **Bragging about yourself.** You talk about great things you've done, trying to impress people. You might tell tall tales, just for the sake of being recognized.

4. **Being popular.** You try to be the coolest person in your group.

5. **Gossiping.** You criticize other people to prove that you're better than they are.

6. **Being jealous.** You refuse to accept that some people are better than you in some respects. You think they want to put you down. You confuse superior skills with superior value.

7. **Being competitive.** Instead of thinking of people as equals, you think of them as competitors. You seek to prove that you're better than they are. Your outlook on life is win-lose. You want them to lose so you can win.

8. **Taking things personally.** In everything people say, you think they're making fun of you. You're always feeling rejected and unappreciated.

9. **Being revengeful.** You try to defend yourself by humiliating people. Every time you feel they've insulted you, you try to get back at them.

10. **Looking for status.** You try to get into a position in which you think you'll get respect and honor. For example, you try to get knowledge, education, social status, or wealth in order to impress people.

11. **Getting material things.** You buy things that you think will impress people, such as a nice car, or a big house.

12. **Wanting to be rich.** Being rich can be a blessing, as long as you don't want it just to be superior. Sometimes, you try to sell the image that you're rich to impress people. You dress in nice clothes, eat in fancy restaurants, and drive expensive cars to call people's attention to you.

13. **Being sarcastic or ironic.** You're scornful to people in order to feel superior to them.

14. **Seeking power.** You want to control people. You think that by being in a position of authority, you become superior to those you're controlling.

Part Three
Loving Yourself

1.
Love is a Principle

The most important quality you need in order to master yourself is love. Loving yourself and others will make you whole. To love someone is to have a positive image of that person. If you love yourself, you'll never put yourself down, because you'll have a deep respect for yourself. Love is also connected to believing. When you love yourself, you expect the best of yourself. Therefore, loving, valuing, and believing complement each other. If you love, you value and you believe, but if you don't love, you neither value nor believe.

People who see love as a feeling are ruled by their impulses. If they feel like loving, they'll walk a thousand miles, but if they feel like hating, they'd do anything to get revenge. That's why many marriages that start with intense passion end up colder than liquid nitrogen. People who say the most beautiful words and make the most spectacular promises can turn bitter and callous in just a few years. They want to do everything in their power to destroy their partner.

When you love, you're guided by principle, not by your feelings. You may feel like getting even, but if you live by principle, you're going to take the higher route. Even if the other person has harmed or deceived you, you do the right thing. You never sink to their level.

People who love by feeling are dependent of other people's actions. If people treat them well, they return their kindness, but if people mistreat them, they get even. They alternate between love and hatred. They lack congruency. They act according to the situation, or even worse, act according to their judgment of the situation.

When you love by principle, you don't depend upon other people's actions in order to love them. You depend solely upon yourself. You don't love them because of *them*, but because of you. If you love sometimes and hate at other times, you don't love at all. Love is a decision you make. If you have integrity, you keep your promises. If you have promised to love someone, you'll love that person forever. If you've made a promise and you can't bring yourself to fulfill that promise, you don't have character.

Every promise you make to other people is ultimately a promise you make to yourself. If you make a promise and don't keep that promise, you deceive yourself. You end up losing respect for yourself, because you don't know if you can keep your word.

When you have integrity, you fulfill the promises you've made in the past and live by principle. Every lover makes promises. There are many promises lovers make in the heat of passion, but only one they make before the altar and before God. However, when you have integrity, you treat the promises you made in the heat of the moment just like you treat the one you made before God. You don't need documents to sign or witnesses, because you keep your word.

There are many ways to break promises. You break a promise when you hate, when you gossip, when you abuse, when you get payback, or when you betray. You might say you broke your promise because the other person didn't fulfill their part. However, there's no excuse for breaking promises. Remember, every promise is ultimately a promise you make to yourself. You'll certainly find many excuses to break promises, but your subconscious mind knows the truth. You can justify your broken promises to everyone but your subconscious mind. If you lack integrity, your subconscious mind will disapprove of you, and you won't find rest.

Many people lie to themselves. They try to convince themselves they're right when they get payback, have an affair, hate, or rip off their spouse in a divorce settlement. If that's your case, you'll never convince yourself. You may convince the law and other people, but your subconscious mind will eat you alive. You'll never respect yourself, because you don't have character.

You might object by saying, "Didn't you tell me that you're valuable no matter what you do?"

You're right. Even if you don't have integrity, you're still valuable. However, lack of integrity is a symptom of not valuing *yourself*. You can't separate integrity from self-esteem. When you really value yourself, you'll be a person of integrity.

You might ask, "How can I love someone who has used, betrayed, and ripped me off?"

If you're a person of integrity, you'll love them. If you love, you might divorce, but you still love.

"This is complete nonsense," you might say, "If I divorce, it's because I hate the person."

That's not true. If your divorce is full of hatred, you don't love by principle; you're controlled by your feelings. You might divorce, but you keep them inside with your hatred.

A common way of breaking a promise is having an affair. When some people don't "feel" like loving anymore, they look for someone who might spark that feeling again. They're always looking for an exhilarating experience. They feel the same obsession they felt with their partner in the beginning of the relationship. They call it love, but it isn't love—it's simply passion. They can't love that person if they don't love their partner. They don't love the new person, because they don't have integrity. They're hurting that person, their spouse, and ultimately, themselves. Their love is focused on themselves. They're only using the other person. Later on, they'll do the same thing to the new person, because their love isn't strong enough. Love doesn't lie. If you have to hide something from your partner, you don't love them.

Jennifer was married to Marius, but she wasn't happy. For nine years, she tried to change Marius, until she gave up. She wanted to leave him, but she couldn't take care of herself. Her father had given her everything when she was a kid. She didn't have to work to help the family, and so she expected to get everything from Marius. If she got separated, she wouldn't be able to live on her own, and she didn't want to work. She started dating different guys, expecting that someone would take care of her so she could leave her husband. She lied to Marius, saying that she was going shopping or meeting a girlfriend. She'd even use the grocery money Marius gave her to spend on her boyfriend. Marius couldn't understand why the money disappeared so fast. He worked sixty hours a week, only to help Jennifer spend it on her boyfriend.

That problem is very common among dependent people such as Jennifer. When a person receives everything from someone else and doesn't have to give anything back, they take it for granted. They have everything, but they're still unhappy. Worst of all is when a person lives at the expense of another and still thinks they have the right to betray that person. Such a person doesn't have any idea what love is.

If you've suffered from an unfaithful spouse, learn to value yourself. It's common for people who have been betrayed to place the guilt on themselves. A few days ago, I was talking to a man who pitied his wife for betraying him. He didn't even understand the concept of self-respect. Everyone makes mistakes, but that's no excuse for a partner to sleep around. If a spouse betrays another, it's because they don't have character.

When you love, you love forever. It isn't possible to love today and hate tomorrow. When you love, you don't stop loving for any reason. What people do to you doesn't matter—you continue loving them.

The Greeks had three different words for love: *agape, filein,* and *eros.* They separated love as a feeling from love as a principle. Agape was used for love as a principle, while filein was used for love as a feeling. Eros was the word used for sexual love.

Filein is the love we have for the people we relate with. When we spend time with people, we develop a filein for them. Agape is the love we have for every human being. We *agapaw* (the verb form of agape) our friends, our relatives, strangers, and even those who hate us and hurt us. That's the mystery of love. You can't *filew* (the verb form of filein) someone who harms you, but you can agapaw them. When Christ prayed for his enemies, "Father, forgive them, for they do not know what they are doing," (Luke 23:34) he was exhibiting agape. Although he wasn't passionate about his persecutors, he still loved them as a principle.

When we're able to make the distinction between agape and filein, we understand the essence of true love. To love unconditionally, we need to subject our feelings to principles. We must place agape above filein.

You can love a spouse who betrayed you, you can love your business partner if they were dishonest, you can love the man who raped your daughter, and you can love the terrorist who killed innocent people. You can't love them in a filein way, you can't be passionate about them, but you can love them in an agape way.

If you can't love the people who hurt you, you're still emotionally dependent. They have power over you. You give them the authority to hurt you and to make you sad. You might divorce the spouse who betrayed you, but you can't forget what happened. The years go by, and you're still full of bad memories, anger, and sadness. You put the man who raped your child in prison, but you wish he was dead.

Once I talked to a woman who had divorced her husband. She got so mad while talking about him that a vein in her temple looked like it was going to explode. She said that he'd destroyed her life and damaged her children. She had separated from her husband on the outside but still carried him inside through her anger.

If you want to find the strength to leave a spouse who has betrayed and abused you, you need to love that person. By loving as a principle, you'll be able to let it go.

To love as a principle, you need to have dignity. When you don't have dignity, you see love as a weakness. You think that if you love someone who hurts and betrays you, you're foolish. If you don't get even, you feel as if you've degraded yourself.

For many years, I had that dilemma in my own mind. I wasn't sure if I should get payback or let people walk all over me. If I got revenge, I felt as if I was a bad person. If I was passive, I felt weak. I wavered between the two extremes, but I didn't feel good about either one. Finally, I found balance through loving as a principle. I learned how to forgive with dignity. I didn't feel weak anymore, because I learned to counter evil with love.

Many people have to face that dilemma. A soldier who has seen terrorists killing a woman who had dedicated her life to saving others, or innocent children, may be tempted to sink to his enemy's level and vent his frustrations and anger with cruelty. However, if he's governed by principles, he'll be able to love. He'll face brutality with respect because he has integrity.

When you have integrity, you do the right thing in any situation, even when people aren't looking at you. If you don't have integrity, you look around to see if no one is watching to decide if you can do something without being caught. You tell the truth only if it favors you. If you think that saying a lie might avoid pain, you aren't telling the truth. When you have integrity, you do the right thing, whether you're in public or alone. You don't try to hide anything, because your life is an open book. You don't have two faces.

I could hurt my daughter inside my home and no one would ever know. I could abuse her psychologically and hurt her self-esteem, but she couldn't prove anything, because the wounds wouldn't be exposed. However, if I have integrity, I'll be as nice to her at home as I am elsewhere. I'll treat her like a princess and guarantee that she sees our home as a heavenly retreat where she finds love.

When you have integrity, you never take advantage of your position of power. As a parent, you might get your children to do what you want by force. You can humiliate them and tear down their self-esteem. They can't confront you. They're little and you're big. However, if you have integrity, you're going to respect them as if they were strong enough to confront you. You'll treat them with the same respect you'd treat people who were more powerful than you.

As a boss, you could look down on your employees. You could take advantage of them and make them work long hours for little pay. However, if you have integrity, you'll reward them. You'll value their efforts and compliment them on their accomplishments. You'll make them feel proud of themselves and you'll pay them more than required by law.

As a soldier, you could punish your enemies. You could torture, abuse, and rape, and no one would ever know. You have the power and you're in control. However, if you have integrity, you'll love them and treat them better than they'd treat you. You'll overcome evil with good.

The expression of love

Love is an emotion that expresses itself, and when it exists, it manifests in some way. It's impossible to imagine someone full of love being sullen, distant, and mean. Love is like a river whose waters can't be dammed. If you try to block the flow of water, it will find another way. When there is love, it overflows naturally, and it isn't possible to stop its flowing.

Love doesn't express itself solely through magnificent deeds. Sometimes when walking down the street, I see a billboard declaring in bold letters: "I love you, Mary!" Obviously, the person responsible for that billboard wanted to find an alternative manner of demonstrating the depth of their love. However, love is generally shown through small daily actions, such as smiling, touching, complimenting, hugging, and saying, "I love you." Although those small gifts don't seem extraordinary, they're the ones that really count. In other words, if someone who professes to love you doesn't do the little things but pays for a billboard to declare a great love for you, it wouldn't mean anything to you.

Love is learned during childhood

People learn to love through their relationship with their parents when they're young. The love they receive from their parents is the love they give to others. One day, I was visiting the house of one of my college buddies. Ten years had passed since the last time we'd seen each other. He was married and had two children. I noticed how affectionate he was with his wife and kids. His home was a peaceful and happy environment. Suddenly, the telephone rang, and he picked up and started speaking to the person in a loving tone. That seemed strange to me, and I was trying to figure out who could that person be. Could it be a woman he was having an affair with? A few moments later, I found out that he was talking to his father. Then it made sense to me. I understood the origin of the affection and respect he had toward his family. He had a father who loved him and because of that, my friend loved his wife and children.

Children who weren't loved by their parents have relationship problems when they grow up. They'll project their hatred toward other people and they'll have difficulty believing that someone might love them.

About eight years ago, I was in a bank in Brazil where an old woman was with her daughter, trying to make deposit in an automatic machine. They were arguing about the correct way to make the deposit and I was shocked by their lack of respect for each other. I realized that it wasn't a rare occurrence. It was a habit that had originated during the daughter's childhood. The daughter was treating her mother the only way she knew how. The only kind of relationship she'd ever known was one of disrespect, and she was returning the favor. Parents' love for their children is an investment. They'll receive as much as they give.

Children think that everyone is like their parents. Even when they become adults, they project their parents' image onto other people. If their relationship with their parents was a good one, they'll feel comfortable about others and will trust in their love. However, if their relationship with their parents during childhood was a bad one, they'll fear others and will have difficulty relating to them.

If you had a turbulent relationship with your parents during childhood, your spouse and your children are the ones who will suffer the consequences. All the hatred and grief that stayed in your heart will be unleashed on your family. Although the scenario has changed and the people who surround you will be different, you'll distrust your spouse and your children and think that they'll hurt you, just as your parents did in your childhood.

The biggest problem that will arise due to your parents not loving you is that you won't love yourself. As a result, you'll have the same attitude toward yourself as your parents had toward you. If your parents accused you, you'll accuse yourself. If they held you in contempt, you'll hold yourself in contempt. If they were rude to you, you'll be rude to yourself.

If you didn't learn to love yourself, you won't be able to love others. If you accuse yourself, you'll also accuse others. If you abuse yourself, you'll abuse other people. Your relationship with others will reflect the kind of relationship you have with yourself. It's impossible to love people and hate yourself. Either *you love yourself and everyone else*, or *you hate yourself and everyone else*.

The relationship between love and faith

Love and faith are inseparable. It's impossible to love someone without believing in that person. To love other people, trust in their love for you. Only when you believe that other people love you are you able to love them.

If you think that others don't love you and that they're against you, you won't love them. Your distrust will cause you to hate them and to become detached from them. Faith leads to love, while distrust leads to hate. The more you believe, the more you love, whereas the more you distrust, the more you hate.

When you believe that people love you, you treat them well. You're thankful for their affection and seek to return their love. But when you think that people don't love you, you mistreat them. You're rude and cold, because you believe they're your enemies. The secret to being friendly and to treating people well resides in believing in their love.

Faith has the power to attract good things. When you believe that people love you, you attract their love. They correspond in direct proportion to your belief in their love. If you assume people are against you, you mistreat them, and as a consequence, they mistreat you.

Happiness is a consequence of love

You can't be happy if you don't love yourself. It's impossible for you to live in a state of bliss while you're in conflict with yourself. Happiness is a result of unconditional love. You need to accept yourself. You must forgive yourself on a daily basis. If you're mad every time you commit the smallest mistake, you make your life miserable. Remember, happiness doesn't come from perfection.

Unhappiness is also caused by an inability to love others. When you don't love other people, you get mad easily. Any tiny error or flaw is a motive for you to be mad and to want revenge. Such impatience and irritability steals your joy and makes you suffer.

Studies have shown that an inability to forgive is a major cause of sadness. Being a victim doesn't bring you any joy. To be happy, let go of the past and forgive everything people did to you. When you forgive other people, you don't make them happy, but you do make yourself happy.

In addition to forgiving other people, you need to forgive yourself. Don't obsess over your mistakes. Let go of the past and live in the moment. Instead of looking back to what you did wrong, think about what you can do right—now, in the present.

When you don't love yourself, you look for happiness in the wrong places. You try to be happy by indulging in food, sex, drugs, or excessive work. Beneath all those obsessions is an attempt to compensate for a lack of love. In other words, you try to escape the pain you're feeling for not loving yourself. The only problem is that you're never satisfied. You eat lots of food and you're still unhappy. You get high, but after that, you feel empty again. You have sex, but then you feel alone and insecure.

Those things do nothing to alleviate your sadness, so you do them even more. You become obese because you eat too much. You have traditional sex and other forms of sex but you still feel empty. You double your dose of drugs, but the unhappiness is still there.

As you can see, all of those obsessions are destructive, not only for you, but for others as well. By eating too much, you suffer the risk of heart attack or stroke. When you indulge in sex, you can contract one of numerous STDs, and if you're married, you could end up divorced. Drug addiction could lead to organ deterioration, particularly your brain, resulting in death.

While you try to make up for your unhappiness, you become even more unhappy. You feel sad because you can't control your impulses. You criticize yourself, which makes you feel worse.

To overcome addictions, you need to realize that love is what makes you happy. If you want to reach a state of bliss, you need to accept yourself. You can't find happiness in material things. Contentment is a state of mind, and it can only be achieved by loving yourself.

Love is responsible

When you love, you're responsible. To be responsible is to think about the consequences of your actions in your life and the lives of others. You don't want other people to suffer, because you love them. As a result, you avoid making decisions that could bring bad consequences. You put people's feelings above your own.

There's a consequence for any action, good or bad. Many of the ordeals you face in life are the result of a bad decision taken by you or by someone close to you. For example, Nathan got HIV because of his promiscuous lifestyle, and as a result, he infected Scarlett, who was oblivious to his promiscuity. Because of his irresponsibility, he essentially killed himself and his wife.

It's important that you think before making decisions. Think about the consequences. Don't make a decision if you don't feel comfortable with it. Think about how every decision might impact those you love.

Consider your actions and their impact upon each person involved. If one person may be harmed by the results of your decision, then it's not a good decision. For example, a taxi driver in Brazil drove a woman and her daughter from the Galeão airport to a hotel in Rio de Janeiro. After leaving the woman, the taxi driver found her purse with $5,000 in currency. The woman's daughter had to have surgery, and they'd come all the way from Germany for the operation, so she was desperate when she realized that all her money had been left in the taxi.

From the taxi driver's position, it would have been an opportunity to get a big amount of money that could help himself and his family. The possibility of being caught by the authorities was almost nonexistent, since the woman didn't have his license number. Nevertheless, the man didn't think only about himself. He didn't want to benefit at the expenses of others. Therefore, he returned the woman's money—without accepting a reward.

Some people don't like to think about the results of their actions because they're slaves to their desires. When they want to do something, they're so anxious to do it that they don't think, but when bad stuff happens later, they regret their decisions.

There's an intimate connection between love and maturity. Being mature means not being controlled by your impulses. When you're mature, you're careful about the decisions you make and analyze every possible result. When you're immature, you act on your impulses. If you want something, you're willing to do whatever it takes to get it, even if you know it might be destructive to you and to others.

The power of visualization

Many problems you're facing right now are the result of negative images you registered in your mind. You tend to repeat the same patterns and behavior that you've seen. For example, if you saw your father abuse your mother when you were young, that negative image was stored in your subconscious mind. Although you were outraged by your father's attitude, the memory may affect your relationship with your wife. You may repeat the same pattern of your parents. Then, when your wife does something you disagree with, you may want to hit her, just as your father hit your mother.

If you want to change your destructive behaviors, change the negative images you've stored in your subconscious mind for images of love, respect, and compassion. You must see yourself looking at your spouse with kindness and speaking words of encouragement. By constantly focusing your mind on images of love and acceptance, you can break the curse of the past and have a wonderful relationship. When you start to visualize something positive, you're able to reproduce that positive visualization in your actions.

Reading a book is all about visualization. When you read a book, you imagine yourself in many different states. For example, when you read about love, you imagine scenes of love. You see yourself being polite to your spouse, your children, and your co-workers. You think about how you'd treat them if they were disrespectful to you. You practice loving in your own mind. When you're confronted by tough situations, you act according to the rehearsals you have inside of you. When someone insults you, you know it's not worth it to insult them back. You're not prompted by feelings of revenge. You call upon your most noble values to find the most respectful way to respond to them.

It's natural to visualize while you're reading. Reading is like watching a movie. When you read, you see a movie in your mind. Those mental pictures are powerful in transforming you, but to get the most from it, you need to practice visualization, even when you're not reading. I like to practice visualization when I'm running, taking a shower, or driving. I imagine many different situations and how I'd respond to them. I think about the words I'd say, the tone of my voice, my body language, and my facial expression.

Practice is the secret to perfection. I play for a band in a church two times a month. Our leader is dedicated to doing the best possible job. We practice two or three hours every Friday night. Then, before church on Saturday morning, we practice half an hour more. Then, when it's time to praise, it's not only praise—it's also a show.

If we want to love, we need to practice loving inside of our minds through our visualization. Imagine every possible situation you may have, especially tough ones, such as when your boss is harsh to you, your teenager disrespects you, or your spouse insults you. Think about different approaches you might take, and about how you can love without losing your self-respect.

The problem is that many times we rehearse in our minds scenes of confrontation, disrespect, and harshness. We imagine how we could be more insulting to someone who has put us down, and when we get a bad result, we think the problem was that we weren't tough enough. So we rehearse again, become even more abusive, and get an even worse result.

If you don't practice positive visualizations, you'll always have negative ones. Positive visualizations are the result of deliberate decisions. Choose to focus your mind on positive images and thoughts. And if you stay at it long enough, you'll create a habit. Then it won't take as much effort as before.

Symptoms of not loving

When you don't love, it shows in a variety of ways. It's important that you know the symptoms so that you can work to overcome your lack of self-esteem and reach your maximum potential. Below is a list of symptoms.

Difficulty loving yourself

1. **Inferiority complex.** You assume that you're inferior to other people and you don't value yourself. When you put yourself down, you don't love yourself. There's an intimate connection between loving and valuing. One doesn't exist without the other. You can't love yourself and feel inadequate. The more you love yourself, the more you respect and value yourself.
2. **Not having faith in yourself.** When you love yourself, you believe in your abilities. You think you can achieve your dreams, and as a result, you have power.
3. **Feeling guilty.** When you don't love yourself, you scold and reject yourself every time you make a mistake.
4. **To abuse yourself.** When you don't love yourself, you live an internal war. You're never satisfied with yourself and always have a reason to scold yourself.
5. **Being irresponsible.** You have self-destructive behavior. You take actions that damage your life.
6. **Not caring for your health and fitness.** You eat junk food, don't drink enough water, sleep badly, and don't exercise.
7. **Drug addiction.** Smoking, drinking alcohol, and using drugs are symptoms of not loving yourself.
8. **Mediocrity.** Not seeking to improve and grow. Lack of interest in learning and getting good grades at school. When you don't love yourself, you become stagnant. You don't feel a desire to invest in yourself in order to become successful.

Difficulty loving people

Everything you do to other people, you're doing to yourself. Harming people is an indirect way of harming yourself. That's why being dishonest and not having integrity is self-destructive. You reap what you sow. That's why the biggest fulfillment in life is helping people. By loving others, you not only get a positive response, you feel good about yourself.

1. **Not doing a good job.** Some workers tend to do their best only if they're well treated or rewarded. They give only if they receive. That's not love's way. When you love, you give first and you keep giving, even if you don't receive. When you do your best without expecting anything in return, you get rewarded, because even if you don't get a reward, you feel a sense of integrity that's usually *better* than a reward.
2. **Being rude.** When you're rude, you reveal your lack of self-love. You mistreat other people because you don't have self-respect.

3. **Being resentful.** Acting like a victim and not wanting to let go of the past. Holding grudges is a direct consequence of not loving oneself.

4. **Being revengeful.** Retaliating or craving other people's misfortune is a symptom of not loving oneself.

5. **Acting irresponsibly.** Making decisions without thinking about people's desires. Taking actions that aren't in other people's best interest. When you love others, you always take them into consideration. Everything you do and every decision you make, you think about the consequences. You want the best for them, as well as yourself.

6. **Dishonesty.** When you make business deals you know will damage other people, you're acting contrary to love. If you have integrity, you want people to profit as much as you. You look for a solution that's good for everyone involved.

7. **Lack of integrity.** You don't follow through with your word or you lie. You break promises, not realizing how much you hurt others. The problem is that you lose their confidence and end up hurting yourself more than you hurt them.

8. **Engaging in criminal activity.** Criminals have a lot of hatred inside, and in some cases, they don't feel bad about hurting others because they think other people don't love them, either.

9. **Belligerent attitude.** Being willing to fight, either verbally or physically, whenever you feel insulted.

10. **Warlike.** The reason there are so many wars in our world is because people don't love. Although authorities and leaders always have reasons for their acts of violence, behind most of their reasons is a lack of love. When there's little love, there's also little respect for other people's lives.

11. **Racism.** Lack of love has always been the cause of racism. There have been wars between races because people can't value their differences. Instead of celebrating diversity and valuing others, people tyrannize and take advantage of them.

12. **Religious Intolerance.** Although love is at the core of almost every religion, many wars and atrocities have been perpetrated in the name of God. Leaders justify their intentions by saying it's God's will. Some of them even call their violence a "Holy War." Every terrorist organization in the world is based on religious beliefs and supported by believers. Some of the most belligerent countries in the world are those in which religion and state are one and the same. Some countries live involved in constant civil war because of religious differences. When

people use God's name to justify their belligerent attitudes, they become persuasive. They deceive themselves into thinking that they're being religious when they're being anything but. The problem lies not in religion, but in people who see God as being like themselves. They transfer their own image to God, thinking God wants them to abuse and destroy. They can't see that in order to find God, they need to abandon hatred and intolerance.

2.
Emotional Detachment

When we don't love ourselves, we can't believe that other people love us. If we don't love ourselves, why should they? We think that they see us as we see ourselves. We degrade ourselves, so we think they degrade us, too. To believe that other people love us, we need to love ourselves, to have a positive image of ourselves, and to believe that we deserve love.

When we don't believe that other people love us, we're incapable of seeing their love. We take their feelings for granted. When they do good things for us, we either ignore what they do or we think they're trying to get something from us.

They say "I love you" and we reply "Okay, what do you want?"

When they say something, we think they're trying to hurt us. We see everything they do through a negative lens. We're always expecting the worst, so everything becomes the worst.

If we're incapable of accepting love, we pull away, become withdrawn and distant, and don't express our love in return. We're not enthusiastic about being around others. How can we be, if we erroneously assume that they don't love us? Instead of enjoying their company, we become uncomfortable and defensive. We desperately try to get them to love us. Every action we take and everything we say is focused toward getting their approval and proving that we're worthy of being loved.

The biggest problem is that when we don't love, we hate. If we don't believe in other people's love, we're defensive, sarcastic, abusive, controlling, and revengeful.

You can see how many negative emotions arise as a consequence of not loving yourself. When you don't love yourself, you don't believe that others love you. You don't love them in return, you treat them unkindly, and you end up becoming defensive and reactive. When you don't love yourself, you unleash a chain reaction of negative feelings. What's the end result of becoming defensive and reactive? You actually end up attracting the negative emotions and behaviors you have attributed to those surrounding you. You can't fathom that they could possibly love you, so you unconsciously encourage their rejection. When people react to your defensiveness, you interpret their behavior as proof of their lack of love for you. Your negative impressions and actions toward them eventually result in their defensiveness and disapproval, which begins a self-fulfilling prophecy and a vicious cycle.

To end the cycle, you need to attack the problem at its source. Everything stems from your not loving yourself. Therefore, through healing yourself, you'll ultimately heal your relationships. When you learn to love yourself, you'll believe that others love you, and you'll love them in return.

We become distrustful of other people's love in our childhood. The more we're abused by our parents and other people, the less we love ourselves and the less we believe in their love. When we're children, we unconsciously assume that everyone is like our parents. If our relationship with our parents is negative, we think that every other relationship will be the same, and we'll replicate our personal relationships according to our parents' standards.

Our family cat, Nephthys, is a great example of learned detachment. We found her on the street. She'd been abandoned by a family that had moved away. She hid every time she saw people. When my daughter, Carolina, went to pick her up, Nephthys scurried into the bushes. Carolina crept closer and waited for Nephthys to become distracted. When she saw that Nephthys wasn't paying attention, she quickly picked her up. When Nephthys came to our house, she was very distant and completely avoided us. She hated being picked up. With time, she began to feel more comfortable with us, to the point that now she doesn't want to leave our side. She trusts us and is friendly with everyone.

The more abused you were in your childhood, the more difficult it will be for you to be intimate with people. Like Nephthys before we brought her home, you'll hide in the bushes, afraid of being hurt.

There was a Japanese soldier who was on an island at the end of World War II. When the war ended, leaflets were thrown from airplanes to announce that the conflict was over. The Japanese soldier thought they were merely decoys being used to draw him out from his hiding place, so he remained hidden. He managed to survive, living a simple life until he was found many years later. He didn't believe the conflict was over, and wasted much of his life thinking the war was still going on. While he could have been enjoying freedom and all the comforts of civilization, he lived like a hermit on an island.

That's similar to what happens to people when they didn't have a secure attachment to at least one person in their childhood. When they become adults, they assume that the war is still going on and continue fighting. They remain emotionally isolated on their islands, believing that nobody cares for them. They fear rejection, so they remain emotionally unavailable and don't take risks, never enjoying the benefits of a relationship. They live an emotionally starved life, surrounded by potential love.

To establish deep connections, we need to believe that the war has ended. We must move past our trauma and choose to live in the present. We need to let go and allow for a new, nonjudgmental view of others.

How can we do that? How can we let go of the past and truly believe that we deserve love? By loving ourselves. We can't reverse time and repair our past relationship with our parents, but we can learn to love ourselves and fill our own love tank. We have the solution—and it's within us.

The barrier caused by emotional detachment

When we disconnect from people, we in turn cause them to disconnect from us. It's not that they want to disconnect. They're responding to our limit setting. They can't force us to love them. They can't be intimate with us if we want to remain distant. If we build a wall around ourselves, they're obliged to accept it.

When I was young, I was starving for love! I had a deep emptiness and I wanted to be loved. I entered in relationships with girls with an unconscious desire to find the love I hadn't received during my childhood. However, I couldn't believe that they loved me. I was afraid, embarrassed, and uncomfortable, so I became distant and cold. There were layers and layers of grudges, fear, and hatred that kept my love from flowing. You can guess what happened. The girls didn't feel my love and felt alone and abandoned. My relationships lacked intimacy, so they gave up on me. I'd attempt one relationship after another and was unsuccessful, again and again. I thought the solution would be to find the right girl. However, the problem wasn't with the girls. I was the one who couldn't trust, love, or open up.

When you're emotionally detached, you tend to put the blame for the failing relationship on your partner. You believe that they created the distance, but you're blind to the fact that you've initiated the dance of separation. Then you try to fix them. I vividly remember my conversations with my girlfriends in the past. I'd attempt to convince them that they didn't love me. I'd lecture them specifically on how to love me. I wanted to change them, but I didn't realize that I was the one who needed changing.

Intimate connection between two people is only established when both of them open to each other entirely. In a relationship, one can't do it alone. It's not necessary for the other person to love us in order for us to love them. I may love you, even if you hate me. However, I can't be connected to you if you hate me. I can love you, but I can't connect, because your hatred prevents me from getting closer. As a result, I love you from a distance. I wish you well, I care about you, I support you, and I help you, but I feel alone.

Before begging for someone's love and attention, look inside yourself to see if the lack of connection is stemming from your detachment. Identify any fear or distrust that might be making you distance yourself. You must break down the walls you've built around yourself that prevents people from getting close to you. It's only when you've knocked down the walls of distrust that you can enjoy full intimacy with others.

Another reason you detach from people is because you don't believe in your capacity to love. When you have low self-esteem, you think that you're incapable of having a relationship. You don't believe that somebody could find true happiness in a relationship with you. You rationalize that someone is better off without you. Therefore, the best way to keep others from suffering is by not having anything to do with them. You need to believe in your ability to love. You have what it takes to be in a truly happy, healthy relationship.

Love is not a bargain

When you're emotionally detached, you see love as a trade. You think that you shouldn't give love if you don't receive it. As a result, you want to feel loved before you love. If you don't feel loved, you keep waiting.

When you aren't emotionally detached, you don't wait until you're sure someone loves you. You make the first move. You take the initiative. If you don't get a loving answer, you keep on giving. You aren't motivated by love. You see love as a principle. You love, regardless of whether you're loved or hated.

The problem with waiting to feel loved is that you might not even recognize it in the first place. If you don't feel loved and you distrust people, you may very well misinterpret their actions. You see them through a dark lens, so you falsely believe that they wish you harm. Then you seek revenge for an imagined offense.

To be able to love others, we need to stop making assumptions, judging, and being suspicious. Their wrongs are almost always a figment of our imagination. When Osama Bin Laden launched his insane attack, killing some 5,000 people, I wondered how he could believe that all of those people were evil. What he didn't realize was that by thinking they were evil, *he* became evil. When you make assumptions and judge people, you become what you think they are. You hate them because you think they hate you.

When you see love as a trade, you seek revenge. If you feel hurt, you hurt in return. To love, you need to make a deliberate decision never to retaliate. You're never right when you get even. Love isn't a trade. You don't love other people because they love you. You love them because you *choose* to.

Love is constant, unchanging, and eternal. If you truly love others, your love will never change, regardless of their feelings and actions. If you aren't capable of loving others when you're mistreated, you don't truly love them.

Fear of suffering

Another reason you're not open to love is because you fear rejection. You think that if you love people and they don't love you back, the disappointment will be too devastating to endure.

The more you avoid suffering, the more you suffer. You think you can't handle rejection because you believe you're too sensitive. However, withholding your feelings won't prevent you from suffering. In other words, the more you love, the less you suffer, and the less you love, the more you suffer.

Love is strong. People who love aren't afraid to take chances. They take the initiative because they don't expect rejection. They believe in other people's love, so they don't fear a negative response, so they're able to handle any possible rejection.

If you protect yourself from pain, you build a wall around yourself. If you're too protective, you won't enjoy the privilege of a full connection.

To overcome the fear of rejection, you need to learn to love yourself. When you love yourself, you don't seek other people's love, you seek to love. You aren't afraid of rejection because you have nothing to lose. Your love tank is full, and you're truly happy. You're not disheartened by rejection because you're whole. If someone says no to you, there will be hundreds more who will say yes. You're on a planet with more than six billion people, so when someone says no to you, find someone else. It isn't worth suffering someone's rejection when there are so many people willing to love you. If you must value reactions, only value the reactions of those who treat you well and are responsive to your love.

Emotional detachment causes selfishness

When you're emotionally detached, you tend toward self-centeredness. You don't believe that anybody would be interested in a relationship with you, so you isolate yourself. As a result, you focus inward instead of outward. You make your plans and decisions without taking others into consideration. You disregard them because you assume they have no interest in sharing their lives with you. You even believe that you're doing them a favor when you don't include them in your plans.

Other people *are* interested in you and they want to support you. If you open up to them and allow them to participate in your plans and decisions, you'll realize how honored they feel when they become part of your life.

I realized that in my early projects. I feared telling people about my dreams and goals because I thought they'd ridicule me and wouldn't want to help. I thought I was on my own and could only count on myself, but as I grew emotionally, I started believing that others could be interested in helping me. I became bolder in talking to people about my ideas and dreams. I saw that people became excited about them and would then open up about their own dreams. Then we'd encourage and support each other.

On one occasion, I was with a couple friends who played with me in a band, and I talked to them about my desire to have a worship service in a church every month. I thought they wouldn't be interested in playing with me, so I didn't bother inviting them. However, since I didn't invite them, they invited themselves.

They told me, "We're willing to play with you and support you in whatever you want to do. Just tell us what you're going to do and we'll be there for you."

I was shocked. They were willing to help me more than I was willing to believe they wanted to.

Make a decision to share your ideas and plans with people. Share them with your family first. Tell your spouse, your kids, and your parents about your plans. Make them part of it. Let them take part in the decision. Accept their input and be open to their ideas. Don't feel rejected if they disagree with you about something. Maybe they will see something you can't see and their viewpoint will benefit your idea. Their input may be just what you need to make your plans successful.

After you talk to your family, talk to your friends and co-workers. Get them to give you new ideas and ask them to support you. Some of them will just encourage you while others will want to work with you to make your dream come true. You'll realize that people feel proud when you believe in their friendship. Even if they don't share your dreams, they may want to help you, just for the privilege of having your trust.

If you're emotionally detached, you might also think it's a waste of time to give yourself to people and help them. You think that you wouldn't get anything from supporting them. You believe that to be successful, you need to focus only on your dreams and not get involved in other people's dreams.

Because of that, many people abandon their family completely to focus on their own goals. They think it's a waste of time to give attention to their family. As a result, they don't get their family involved in their goals. Selfish people aren't very successful. The more connected you are to your family, the more successful you'll be. The more you give yourself to them and the more you get them involved in your life, the more leverage you'll have.

By being selfish, you lose more than you gain. There are many people who realize their dreams, but have a broken marriage, rebellious children, and alienated friends. When they sum up their wins and losses, they realize they're in the red.

When you're selfish, you think that if you put people above everything else, you're going to fail. You're wrong. The formula of success is to put other people *first*. There's no better motivation than helping other people. If you have a strong connection with other people and you genuinely love them, you'll empower yourself to become successful. Every human endeavor is related to other people. Your victories in life will depend on how often you're able to establish deep and genuine relationships with others.

For many years, I dreamed about writing this book, but I could never bring myself to do it. The best idea that came to me was to get my daughter Carolina involved.

You might ask yourself, "How could a 14-year-old girl help write a book?"

However, I can tell you that Carolina was the best English teacher I ever had. On my own, it would have taken a long time, and it wouldn't have been very good. No publisher would have accepted a book with such a huge number of English mistakes, but with Carolina's help, this book came to be a reality.

What would have happened if I hadn't been close enough to ask for her help? What if I had been divorced and had abandoned her? What if I hadn't believed that she was able to help me? This book speaks about relationships, and this book is the result of relationships—one of them being between Carolina and me.

If you want to be successful, invest in relationships. Many problems you've encountered with clients or co-workers may stem from your unwillingness to invest time and resources into establishing close connections. Get to know other people, become involved in their lives, and support them in their goals, and see what a harvest you'll reap.

3.
Longing For Love

Children who didn't feel loved by their parents have an empty tank inside. They're thirsty for love. They dream about someone who'll love them and give them everything they want. They even make a mental image of that person—like Prince Charming or an angel.

When the age to find a partner comes, they look for that special person. They find someone and transfer the mental image they've formed to them. They feel obsessed about that person and can't think about anything but them. They may go to work or school, but they aren't really there, because their mind is on their special someone. They become distracted. All their conversations center on the object of their devotion. They always want to be with them, and everything else comes second. They don't care about losing their job, flunking school, or missing appointments.

That obsession is proportional to their love tank's emptiness. If the emptiness is too great, the obsession is very intense. There are people whose obsession is so extreme that they become irresponsible. They don't care about anything else except being with that person. They completely lose their self-control.

Obsessed people will cross all boundaries to fulfill their burning desire. They'll even go to the point of forsaking their principles. Megan was a religious woman whose mother had been very promiscuous. She vowed never be like her mother, but after her obsession with Jonathan, her husband, faded, she found another man to be obsessed with and had an affair for three years before abandoning Jonathan.

People who have an empty love tank live off a dream. When they find someone, they project that dream on the person and fool themselves, thinking they're the special person they've been dreaming about. They can't see the person as they are. That obsession usually lasts about two years, though there's no specific time.

Christian was obsessed with his wife, Carol, for about ten years. Carol never loved him and said up front that she didn't want to marry him, but he wouldn't take no as an answer and begged her to marry him. She gave him a lot of trouble. Their honeymoon was a tug of war. Right after marrying, Carol wanted to go back to her parents' home. She always complained about Christian and told him bluntly how much she hated him and how she'd like to leave him. After they'd been married for nine years, she started having affairs.

She told Christian, "Face it, you've lost me."

Christian tried to convince himself that the marriage was over, then went from one extreme to another. He switched passion for anger.

It doesn't matter how long you've been obsessed, it'll end. Dreamers become more and more disappointed with their special person until they finally decide to release them. Then they project the mental image they got from their parents onto that person, along with all the anger they've kept inside.

It's hard to know when the obsession ends and the disillusion begins. It happens gradually. The person who longs for love feels disappointed when their partner doesn't fulfill their dream. However, they keep dreaming and waiting for their spouse to give them what they want. They try to change the other person to fit the image of the dream they've held in their mind.

While the dream fades away, the person who longs for love switches back and forth between moments of passion and anger. When they feel disappointed, they feel angry—and begin to hurt their partner. The greater the obsession, the greater the anger and abuse.

Little by little, the dreamer stops dreaming until they become completely cold and defensive. They threaten to abandon their partner, and every word that comes from their mouth drips with disdain. They forget all the promises they made and can't understand why they fell in love with such a loser. While they would have done anything to be able to have sex with that person before, now they wouldn't do it to save their lives.

Then they meet another person who gives them attention and respect. That person seems different then the loser they have at home, and might be the special person they've truly been looking for. The obsession begin again. Although they know they shouldn't abandon their spouse for the new person, they can't say no. The obsession is too strong to control. They think about the impact of a divorce on their children and their lives, but they can't stop themselves. They act crazy.

If you feel obsessed about someone, you don't love that person. Love isn't obsessive. It's a calm and serene feeling, even though it's deep and strong. Real love doesn't know extremes. It doesn't go from obsession to hatred. It doesn't fade away, but remains forever.

Passion is irrational. People who feel obsessed don't love someone because of their character. Usually, they love someone who's as empty as they are. They feel attracted to people who are also looking to fulfill a fantasy. They feel obsessed about each other—until they begin to hate each other.

The problem resides in expecting too much from other people. You become angry and resentful. When you expect too much, you'll get frustrated. Expecting too much is like not loving enough. To love others, you need to expect less. You must see them as human beings, not as mythic gods. They have problems and flaws that you need to accept.

When you don't expect too much from others, you don't get overly disappointed when they make mistakes. When you meet someone, you don't fool yourself into entertaining the notion that they're perfect. Even if you can't see their flaws in the beginning, you know they exist.

Karen told me about how she was attracted to John. She didn't look at his appearance or his charm. She saw in him a man of integrity; someone who she could trust. There was no obsession and no dream. They married and were happy. There were no big expectations and no demands. They simply accepted each other.

When Karen decided to date John, she didn't feel anything for him. However, she knew she could love him. Her certainty was based on his character. A man like John was worth loving. When you find a person of integrity, you can't help but love them. The reason is that when you find a person of integrity, you find love. Love and honesty go hand in hand. If you're guided by obsession, you may end up loving a bad person who won't love you and will eventually hurt you.

Many people think they don't love someone because they don't feel passion. When the obsession fades away, they think about abandoning their partner. They don't see their love because they're looking for an obsession.

Love is a choice you make. Passion isn't love, because when it strikes, you don't have self-control. You're carried away by the obsession until it ends. When you're obsessed, you don't make decisions, passion decides *for* you. When you love, you do things of your own free will. You don't please the other person because you feel a burning desire to do it, but because you deliberately choose to do it.

Love comes from your integrity. If you're a person of character, you aren't controlled by passion, but by principles.

Passion is selfish. When you're motivated by passion, you think about your own feelings and desires. You do anything that pleases you. You use the other person until you become tired of them. If you feel like being with them, you stay with them, but if you feel like abandoning them, you leave them.

When you love, you do things out of responsibility. You don't do things because you feel like doing them, but because you want to make your partner happy. You spend time with them, you're supportive, and you listen do them because you want them to feel nurtured and loved by you.

Love is focused on others. When you love, you want people to feel as if they're important to you. Look at the following examples:

1. **You love watching TV when you get home, but your wife likes to talk to you**. She feels much better when you spend quality time with her. Therefore, before watching TV, you talk to her for half an hour. You make sure that she feels as if she's the most important thing in your life.

2. **Your husband has dinner at night with his staff**. You'd prefer stay home and relax, but all of the other spouses will be there, and you know your husband would feel out of place if he was alone. You go because you want to support him in his career. You want him to feel that what's important to him is also important to you.

3. **Your child has a soccer game at school and invites you to go there to watch her play.** Although you don't understand anything about soccer, and you'd prefer to stay at home or work, you go because you're aware of the positive impact it will have on her self-esteem. You oppose your own desires to do something that's important to her.

When you're selfish, you don't care about other peoples' feelings. It doesn't matter how they feel, as long as you're pleasing yourself. When you love, you take other people's feelings into account. You're not obsessed about doing what pleases you. You're able to renounce your desires to make them happy.

That's one of the major differences between real love and passion. When you have passion, you please people out of your own burning desire. You don't please them because you want to make them happy, but because you want to make *yourself* happy. When passion fades away, you forget about them. Real love is focused on others. When you love, you please others because you want them to feel important. You make their happiness *your* happiness.

When you love, you stay balanced. You don't sacrifice your job or your studies because of the objective of your affection. You don't step all over other people to please your partner. If you're irresponsible toward your activities when you're obsessed, you'll be irresponsible to your partner when the passion is over. You'll abandon them, just as you abandoned your work and your study. You'll step all over them, just as you stepped all over other people.

One fundamental difference between passion and love is that passion strikes quickly and hard. It's like the flu. When you get flu, you have a sudden weakness and pain all over your body. You don't feel it coming little by little. Passion is as abrupt as the flu. You don't choose to be passionate. You're just get carried away by your obsession.

Yet love is a gradual feeling. First of all, you choose to love, and then you keep choosing every day. You nurture the feeling, you feed it day in and day out through dedication and commitment, and you watch it grow stronger and deeper. Since it's the fruit of a choice, it isn't obsessive. However, it's so strong that nothing can destroy it.

Solomon said, "Love is as strong as death, its jealousy unyielding as the grave. It burns like blazing fire, like a mighty flame. Many waters cannot quench love; rivers cannot wash it away." (Song of Solomon 8:6,7)

If you aren't obsessed about your spouse and you feel as if there's nothing left, I invite you to experience true love. To do that, take the following steps:

1. **Make a decision to love your partner.** Remember that love is a *choice*. Love doesn't choose you, it's you who chooses it. Make a decision to love the other person, regardless of their flaws. Renew your decision to love every day and stick with it.

2. **Discover what pleases your partner and do it for them.** If they want you to talk with them, to clean the house, to go to the market, to help take care of the children or go for a walk, do it—for their sake. Don't feel frustrated for not doing what pleases you. Don't claim that you're being nice out of great sacrifice. Feel the happiness that comes from making your partner happy.

3. **Engage in a constant search for growth.** Educate yourself about love. Read books about family and marriage, go to family and relationship seminars, and seek counseling. In seminars I've participated in or directed, I've realized that the greatest numbers of couples who go to such seminars are the ones who

are doing well. The majorities of couples who are doing badly don't go to such seminars and don't seek improvement.

The cycle of intimacy

The younger a child is, the more dependent they are. They always want to be around their parents. I remember I once got lost from my parents when I was a child. I got desperate. I looked for them everywhere until they found me. When I was nine years old, I went to school for the first time alone. I was living with my adopted parents, Stuti and Jandyra, and it took thirty minutes to get from Campo Grande to Santa Cruz where they lived. I took the wrong bus and ended up lost. I was afraid and crying, and a number of people offered to help me. I told them I was lost and they helped me call home. Stuti finally came and took me home.

When Carolina was little, she hated when I entered the bathroom and closed the door. She stood outside the door, crying and knocking. Children don't like to be alone, because they're aware of their dependence. They know they can't survive by themselves.

Emotionally starved people resemble children in that aspect. They're insecure and dependent, and always need to be with their partner.

When I was fourteen, I fell in love for the first time. She was a year older than I was. Although she was attracted to me, she didn't express her feelings, hoping that someday I'd express mine. She even felt hurt when she talked to me, because I seemed to be in another world. My tank of love was empty, so I became obsessed. I felt myself consumed by a strong passion, so strong that I could neither sleep well nor eat properly. I felt as if I was walking on a cloud. I thought about her all the time.

She was already interested in me, so we dated. When she realized the extent of my feelings, she backed off. She became distant, to the point of avoiding me. I became depressed. I looked for her everywhere, but she hid. I wrote letters and sent her gifts, but everything I did made her feel more smothered.

When summer vacation came, I couldn't forget her. I thought about her all the time, wondering how I'd survive without her. I couldn't sleep, so I'd watch television until 4:00 a.m.

When you're obsessed with a relationship, you scare the other person away. The person who is the target of the obsession loses interest. They feel trapped. They don't have space to breathe.

Maybe they feel as if they don't have to earn your affections. You're already obsessed, so what are they supposed to do? The relationship loses its luster.

As human beings, we have a cycle of intimacy. When we love someone, we want to be close to them for a period of time until we want to pull away. It's a natural phenomenon. We stay close until we feel as if we're losing ourselves. Then we pull away so we can find our freedom.

When you're starved for love, however, you want to cling to those you love. You fear that they're going to abandon you, so you stay close to guarantee that you have them.

When you want to be with someone all the time, you make them feel smothered. They feel as if they're losing their independence, and they want to protect their individuality. When you realize they're pulling away from you, you try to smother them even more to guarantee that you won't lose them. In turn, they become even more tired of the relationship.

I lost the majority of my girlfriends when I was young because of my obsession. I was affection starved, so I wanted to be with them all the time. I'd call them every day and talk for hours. On the weekends, it was imperative that we hang out together. Eventually, they got tired of me. When they refused to talk to me or hang out with me, I was offended. I'd make them feel guilty for not giving me more attention.

Accept the other person's need for independence. Give them time to miss you. If you're always looking for the other person, you become too easy. Trust in their love for you. Believe that after pulling away for a while, the other person will feel the need to be intimate again. Then they'll come back to you.

When you don't respect the cycle of intimacy, you make the other person tired of you. Although the other person might feel excited about being with you in the beginning of the relationship, they get bored. You repel them instead of attracting them.

Susan Jeffers uses an example in her book, *Feel the Fear and Do it Anyway*. In order to not obsess about another person, you need to see your life as a grid with many boxes. Each box of the grid represents an aspect of your life. Besides your partner, you have your work, friends, hobbies, relatives, and children, but you also need time for yourself. Your obsession is a result of ignoring all the other boxes of the grid and concentrating exclusively on your partner. You act as if they were your only source of fulfillment and that if you lost them, you wouldn't have anything left. When you value all the boxes in the grid, you might lose your partner, but you'd still have other sources of fulfillment. Your life wouldn't lose its meaning, because there would still be many other things that would bring you joy.

Wanting your partner to be with you all the time is selfish. You ignore their interests. You demand that they abandon all the other things they enjoy in order to cater just to you. You don't think about how frustrated they might feel by having to renounce so many other things they enjoy to join you in all of your activities.

Before I married my wife, I always wanted her to be at my disposal. She used to practice with a musical group on Saturday afternoons. I felt jealous about that. I wanted her to be exclusively mine. She also was our church's youth director. She had to go to meetings and lead the youth program at church. Her Saturdays were full of activities. I wanted to be with her the whole weekend, preferably at her house, where no one would bother us.

When she told me that she intended to work and study, I thought she wouldn't have any time left for me. I always wanted her around. Whenever I needed her, I wanted her to be there for me.

When you love someone, you want that person to accomplish all of their dreams. You support them in their responsibilities and you're happy when you watch them do things they enjoy. You don't make them feel guilty for pursuing their goals.

Roseanne demanded too much attention from her husband, Albert. She always wanted him to stay home. She didn't want him to go to meetings and social events. She demanded that he abandon all his friends. She didn't want to visit Albert's parents, and she didn't want them to visit her, either.

If you want your partner to renounce everything only to be with you, you won't have their love. If someone loves you, they'll love others, too. If your spouse abandons their friends and relatives to dedicate themselves exclusively to you, they won't love you. They can't love you if they don't love other people.

Love isn't exclusive. If someone loves you, they love everyone. If you want to find love, look for someone who is kind to other people. If your partner loves their relatives and friends, they'll love you, too. If they're distant and antisocial, you can't trust that they'll love you.

Sometimes we think that love can be quantified. We believe that if someone loves other people, there won't be anything left for us. We want them to keep all their love for us. That's absolutely not true. Love is infinite. A person can be very compassionate to others and still love you with all of their might. The more your partner loves others, the more they love you, too.

When you're starved for love, you often demand it. You expect too much from people and aren't satisfied with what they're willing to give. You can't seize love. The best environment for love is freedom. When you try to get a hold of love, it escapes from you. Holding people too tightly causes them to pull away. When you demand, control, and manipulate people, they lose interest in you. The more you demand, the less you get. Instead of bringing people closer to you, you repel them.

People don't like it when you're too demanding. They need to have space to breathe. Neediness is an unattractive quality. The thrill of love comes from *freedom*.

The secret to being loved resides in accepting *not* being loved. If you want to be loved, don't ask for or demand it. Give people the right not to love you. Don't expect their undivided attention. Don't make it impossible for people to satisfy you—be appreciative of what they give you.

When you think someone is a prince or princess, you tend to act as if they're above you. You're unworthy of their love, because they're so much better. However, when you think another person is superior to you, you distance yourself from them. If you believe that person is superior, it's as if you're a common servant and they're royalty. It's impossible to have a relationship with someone so far above you. When you don't hallucinate about them, you'll be closer to them. You'll realize that they're only a human being and there are no social barriers between you and them.

Accept people's differences

When you're starved for love, you think that everyone has to agree with everything that you say. If they have a different point of view, it's treated as the highest insult. It's hard for you to accept that they have different values and different beliefs.

You'll never find someone who has the same set of beliefs you have. Your beliefs and values are influenced by your environment, the country where you were born, your parents' religion, the way they raised you, the schools you frequented, everything in your past influenced who you are today—that and the information being endlessly pumped by your DNA through every neural pathway in your body.

Now, imagine that someone else had a completely different life. In addition to their physical inheritance, they lived half a world away, with completely different ideals and religious beliefs. They couldn't agree with your every word because they're so different. Even if you were born in the same country and had the same religion, that person would still have different values.

However, when you're starved for love, you have difficulty accepting that people think differently. The idea that someone doesn't share your opinions seems preposterous, so you want to impose your values onto them. If they resist, it's as if they've insulted you. You argue about it so you can prove you're right.

If someone else had your obsession about making people agree with them, yet they had different values, can you see how it would end badly? They'd be just as attention starved as you, and they'd be offended when they learned about your differences. You'd going to argue over every little thing, both of you devout in the belief that your view was the right one.

If you think that in order to be happy in a relationship, you need to make another person agree with you, you will set yourself up for frustration. If they had the same values as you, your relationship would be quite dull. The thrill of a relationship resides in its differences. The excitement in meeting someone lies in knowing that person will be different than anyone you've ever met.

Differences of opinions and values are helpful. The fact that people see the world differently gives you a different perspective. When you're making important decisions, fresh perspectives can help.

Feeling inferior causes you to fear separation

Another problem with being starved for love is that you don't believe other people love you. You think they're around you because they feel sorry for you, and you think they'll abandon you at a moment's notice. That fear of separation distracts you from enjoying the relationship.

You can't be happy with someone while you're stressed over losing them. Happiness in a relationship is a consequence of believing that you deserve to be loved. You need to consider yourself attractive and capable of fulfilling another one's necessities.

If you think someone's going to leave you, they could do just that. Like attracts like. When you fear losing someone, you send subtle signals that make them want to leave you. Fear damages relationships. When you fear losing someone, you act controlling and demanding. You cling to them as if to make sure they're still there. Unfortunately, such an overly controlling attitude causes them to become distant and withdrawn.

The best way to attract another person's love is to believe in yourself. Believe in your capacity to love and to make another person happy, and believe that they love you, too. Faith has the power to attract what you believe. The best way to get love is to believe that you deserve it.

Being starved for love causes jealousy

When you think you don't deserve to be loved, you fear that your partner will find someone better than you and leave. As a result, you hound them to reassure yourself that they're not cheating on you.

Jealousy is a result of not valuing yourself. When you're jealous, you think you're the lowliest, most disfigured person on the planet. You think that everyone else is better than you, so why *wouldn't* your companion leave you for someone so much better?

Your low self-esteem makes a negative impact. Your partner is influenced by your self-image. They'll see you according to your negative self-image. If you consider yourself unattractive, they'll think you're unattractive. However, when you have a positive self-image, your partner will think good things about you. You must recognize your virtues and value the good things you do for your partner.

When you're jealous, you also don't trust your partner. You don't believe in their love for you and view them as treacherous. You live in constant fear that they might be involved with someone else. If they talk to someone, you think that they're flirting, and if they're five minutes late, you assume they were out on a date.

Unfortunately, when you think they're cheaters, your partner will be inclined to cheat on you. People duplicate what you expect of them. If you think they're bad at remembering to wash the dishes, they'll forget to wash the dishes. When your partner realizes that you think good things about them, they'll do everything in their power to live up to that expectation, as well. However, when they realize that you have a bad image of them, they'll again try to live up to that. They feel that they shouldn't be loyal to someone who doesn't value their loyalty. When you're jealous, you feel a need to hound them to be sure they're not cheating on you. The problem with being demanding is that it causes your partner to long for freedom.

My friend Mary's husband was notorious for being jealous. When she went to work, he followed her to make sure she wasn't meeting another man. She was often startled when she got on the train and he got on, too. She felt trapped by her husband. He'd literally been fired from jobs because he'd stalk her instead of going to work. Her husband's controlling attitude gave her the incentive to divorce him. He didn't lose her because she left him for another man—he lost her because of his jealousy.

You deserve to be loved

When you're starved for love, you believe you don't deserve a good person. You think that no talented person would ever be attracted to you, so you end up dating losers. Your motto is: "hey, good enough! It's better to have something than nothing."

That was the case with Molly. She dated a guy who had serious problems. He was a moody man who beat her, even before they got married. He was unfaithful. She'd even caught him out on a date with another girl. He had a bad relationship with his parents. Her family wanted her to end the relationship, warning her about the damage he could inflict, but she didn't listen, because she thought she deserved him. She married him—and the rest is history. He became increasingly more violent, inconstant, and unfaithful until it got so bad that she finally left him.

Many people have unhappy marriages because they don't believe they deserve a good person. They know the person they're dating is treacherous, but they keep making excuses for them. As a result, they bring sadness and grief into their lives. That's why it's important to value yourself and believe that you deserve a good partner. You don't have to put up with a disrespectful, violent, unfaithful person just because you might be alone.

Affection starved people think they're unable to endure solitude. They don't think they can endure the pain of not having a partner. They think the suffering caused by being with a bad person is better than the suffering of being alone. However, it's not true. It's better to be alone than to be with someone who hurts you. You've been alone before, and you can do it again. You can handle being alone because you have your own love. Although you may not have a partner, you have yourself, and if you love yourself, you can be happy.

The difficulty of valuing other people's love

When you're starved for affection, you despise those who love you. You think that a talented person would never love you, so if someone likes you, you think they must a loser. In your imagination, people are fine, as long as they don't start liking you. The moment that they fall in love with you, you no longer think they're special. Someone who doesn't like you instantly rises above someone else who does.

That's why many married people are unfaithful. When they realize that they've already "conquered" someone, they don't value them anymore. They like putting moves on people who wouldn't give them the time of day. It's a sort of competition. They think that if a person doesn't like them, it's because they're superior, so they try to conquer them because it makes them feel important. Then, after they conquer *that* person, they lose interest and go find someone else to conquer.

When you aren't starved for affection, you're able to value people's love. You think you deserve to be loved, so you don't despise them when they like you and you appreciate their loving actions.

The selfish love

Happiness isn't the result of having a partner. No one can make you happy if you're unhappy. Instead of being happy, you'll bring unhappiness into your partner's life and then there'll be two unhappy people. Your sadness isn't the result of not being loved by other people, but of not being loved by yourself.

Happiness comes from loving yourself. When you're unhappy, you could marry the person of your dreams and you'd still be unhappy. To be happy with someone, you must be happy without *anyone.*

Your unhappiness is also harmful to your partner. When you're unhappy, you have a shadow that surrounds you. You're no fun to be around and you dampen everyone's mood.

Finding happiness is the wrong motivation for seeking a partner. Be interested in giving, not receiving. Your major desire must be to nurture and to make the other person happy.

Happiness is a side effect of making other people happy. Happy people are those whose greater goal resides in making others happy. Those who focus on others instead of themselves find the greatest pleasure in life. They're interested in other people's well being instead of their own. When they make other people happy, they make themselves happy. They live life with passion and enthusiasm.

Trying to be like a child

If you didn't fill your love tank during childhood, you'll want people to love you as if you were a child. You'll become stuck in your infancy, trying to get the attention your parents didn't give you. Then you'll get frustrated when people don't treat you like a child.

Here are the characteristics of a child:

1. **Children speak in a sweet and tender way.** When you long for love, you may speak like a child because you want people to be mellow and careful when they talk to you.

2. **Children are funny and playful.** They like to make jokes. When you're childish, you want to play all the time. You have a difficulty taking things seriously. Whenever you talk to other people, you want to entertain them. You use it as a way to attract people's attention. The child inside of you feels great when people laugh at your jokes.

3. **Children aren't responsible.** When you're childish, you don't like to take responsibility for anything. You act as if you were naïve or innocent. If you do something wrong, you try to convince people that you didn't know how to do it right. You were only the victim. They shouldn't make you responsible for something that's beyond your ability to handle. They can't treat you as an adult, since you're only a child.

4. **Children place fun above responsibility.** If they don't have someone to give them direction and structure, they spend the

whole day watching TV, playing video games, chatting on the Internet, or playing outside. When you're childish, you don't like to work or to have responsibilities. You prefer to play. Work is a burden to you. You can't wait to go home and have fun. If possible, you have fun while working. If you don't have anyone to watch you, you chat on the Internet or play with your colleagues. When you leave work, you go play or go home to watch TV.

5.   **Children want to be served.** If they aren't taught the value of giving, they want to be the center of the world. When you're childish, you want people to give you everything. You think they're strong and capable, but you're weak and worthless, so you want them to serve you. You don't realize that they may be tired or need your support. You think they're powerful and can handle everything without your help, so you're comfortable watching them work like crazy while you're having fun. You think it's their responsibility to provide for you. You don't feel financially responsible. If you work, you think you have the right to keep all the money for yourself and not help your partner with expenses. You'd rather not work and get everything from your partner.

6.   **Children need to be guided.** They like adults to make decisions for them. I can see it with my piano students. Sometimes, when I ask them to decide which song they want to play, they say they don't know. They want me to decide for them. They think that since I'm the adult and the teacher, I have the knowledge required to decide. When you're childish, you want people to make decisions for you. You think that serious things aren't for you. You can't choose between right and wrong, so you leave all important decisions to your partner. You don't want to be involved in planning the budget, how much money should be saved, or how much should be spent on recreation. You like to feel that your partner is controlling and guiding you.

Now here are the drawbacks to acting like a child. Let's examine them, point by point, to see the disadvantages:

1.   **Children speak in a sweet and tender way.** When you speak like a child, people think you're pretending to be something you're not. They think you want to be treated better than anyone else.

2.   **Children are funny and playful.** When you play all the time, people get tired of you. They realize that you don't like mature

conversation and may resort to talking in a rough way to snap you out of it and to start taking things seriously.

3. **Children aren't responsible.** If you don't take responsibility for your actions, people lose confidence in you. They don't trust you because they can't hold you accountable.

4. **Children place fun above responsibility.** The problem with having fun all the time is that people regard you as being irresponsible. You don't move up the ladder at work because you aren't reliable. You don't develop and don't learn anything new because you want to have fun. Instead of spending some of your free time reading or getting an education, you entertain yourself. You become easily bored and unhappy. You think that in order to be happy, you need to play all the time. As a result, you lose balance.

5. **Children want to be served.** If you expect people to serve you, you make them feel used. You become a burden to them. They think you're selfish, so they want to get rid of you. On the other hand, you feel incapable and inferior. People are strong and competent while you're weak and useless.

6. **Children need to be guided.** This is frustrating for those with whom you relate. When you don't take part of the decision process, people feel alone and abandoned. Imagine how your spouse feels for having to make so many important decisions without your input. When you marry, your spouse expects that you'll be in their same level. They suppose that you're a wise person who can judge between right and wrong and is willing to take part in important decisions.

No mature person wants to treat you like a child. An adult will encourage you to be an adult. They'll treat you as an adult because they want you to grow. They'll also do it because they love you. They don't want to treat you like a weak and irresponsible person. They want to raise your self-esteem. They want to show you how strong and capable you really are.

Being a child distances you from your partner, increasing your loneliness. If you're a child, you're below them. As a result, you make them superior to you. However, when you see yourself as an adult, you feel closer to them.

The only people who want to treat you like a child are needy ones. They'll be attracted to you, because they're as desperate for love as you are. They'll recognize your childish attitude and want to be with you, because they think you'll treat them like a child, too. However, they're as empty as you are. They don't love themselves, so they're unable to love you. They will come to you not to give love, but to receive it.

Step Four
Forgiving Yourself

1.
Good Comes From Love

There are two major causes of guilt. One is our *past mistakes*. When we don't love ourselves, we tend to remember our past faults and condemn ourselves for the same mistakes, over and over. We don't get to a point when we think we've already paid the price. We punish ourselves infinitely for our faults. Another cause of guilt is *the mistakes we commit on a daily basis*. The less we love ourselves, the more fault-finding we are and the harder we punish ourselves.

I have some unpleasant memories from my past that resurface once in awhile. When I was studying theology, the university's choir had an important performance for about 5,000 people. A great musician who was music teacher at the university asked me to play a song that he'd composed and arranged for the choir. I was honored, but I was busy with my theology courses, so I didn't practice the song as often as I should have. I didn't go to the choir rehearsals or ask the music teacher to help me learn the song. When the performance day arrived, the auditorium was packed. I played the introduction and the choir started to sing. In a little while, I got lost and I couldn't find my place. I single-handedly ruined the choir performance, and what should have been a moment of glory turned into pure chaos.

Another mistake happened when I was seven years old. At that time, I had a tendency to fight with other boys to prove myself. On one occasion, I was at church when I punched another boy in the mouth. I hoped the boy would retaliate and we'd have a good fight, but he didn't fight back. His mouth started bleeding and I realized that I'd broken his tooth. I regretted it instantly. Even though I eventually had an opportunity later in life to apologize for my mistake, the memory of that act haunted me for many years.

Many of us suffer from our memories. The years pass and we keep reminding ourselves of our mistakes. We wish we could go back and fix them, but it's impossible. As a result, we condemn ourselves for the rest of our lives. We judge ourselves, we find ourselves guilty, and then we condemn ourselves. We wish we didn't remember our unpleasant memories, but every now and then, they come back. To make matters worse, other people remind us, too. Family members are especially good at that.

One way of getting rid of such memories is to make an inventory of all the good things you've done. Make a list of 100 good things you've done in your life and then think about them. Any time you remember a mistake, go back to your list and think about the good things you've done.

Besides your past mistakes, there are the ones you commit on a daily basis. For example, yesterday I was going to play at a birthday party that had been scheduled for 1:00 p.m. I just needed thirty minutes to get there, so I left home at 12:30, thinking I'd be there on time, but as soon as I got on the freeway, I encountered horrible traffic. I tried a detour, but got lost and had to go back to the freeway. I arrived at the party an hour late. If that had happened a few years ago, I would have chided myself for not leaving home early enough to avoid any problems.

In order not to beat yourself up for your daily mishaps, at the end of each day, make a list of things you've done right throughout the day and then be happy about them. When you compare your mistakes with the things you've done right, you're going to realize that there were many more rights than wrongs.

Here are a few things we might accuse ourselves for:
1. Being late
2. Forgetting something
3. Not spending more time with your family
4. Being impatient or losing your temper
5. Not doing a good job
6. Not studying for a test
7. Procrastinating
8. Eating too much
9. Drinking, smoking, or using drugs
10. Lack of physical activity

The list is endless. We could spend forever trying to come up with things that make us upset with ourselves. The problem is that even while we accuse ourselves, we make the same mistakes, over and over. We think that our criticism should fix our faults, but we continue to fail. Time goes by, but we're still imperfect, so we're disappointed and wonder when we *will* be perfect. When will we get to the point where we don't make mistakes anymore?

Feeling guilty is unproductive. We don't get any practical results by accusing ourselves. The more we accuse ourselves, the more mistakes we make. Accusations also steal our joy. Feeling guilty is one of the major causes of unhappiness. Fatigue, physical diseases, and nightmares are a result of self-disapproval. Some people even get to the point of committing suicide because they can't accept their mistakes.

Taking responsibility vs. feeling guilty

It's important that you understand what I mean about feeling guilty. I don't want you to think that you should ignore your mistakes. Denial isn't the solution. My goal isn't for you to ignore your mistakes and convince yourself that there's nothing wrong with what you're doing. My goal is for you to recognize your mistakes, yet still love yourself.

There isn't anything wrong with recognizing your mistakes. It's actually helpful to admit your mistakes, because it's the only way to overcome them. However, there's a difference between feeling guilty and taking responsibility.

The first basic difference is that when you feel guilty, you don't love yourself. You beat yourself up. However, when you take responsibility, you love yourself, you accept yourself, and you forgive yourself. The second basic difference is that when you feel guilty, you don't believe that you're able to overcome your mistakes. You think you'll never change. On the contrary, when you take responsibility for your mistakes, you believe that you can overcome them. You value your progress. It doesn't matter how many times you fail—you get up and try again.

Feeling guilty is destructive. It makes you unhappy and keeps you immersed in your faults. However, taking responsibility for your mistakes is positive, because it gives you the strength to overcome your failures and to become a better person. The objective of this section is for you to look at your mistakes in a more positive way. Don't try to escape from your mistakes. Look at them and make the best of them. Your past mistakes are a tremendous source of knowledge and power. Instead of condemning yourself, be thankful for the mistakes you've made. They helped you understand how you can take advantage of your past failures in order to get better results in the present and in the future.

Overcome guilt by loving yourself

The major problem with guilt is that when you feel guilty, you don't love yourself. Your mistakes make you be disappointed with yourself, and you reject yourself. To overcome guilt, you need to be able to love yourself, despite your mistakes. You need to look at your mistakes without punishing or condemning yourself.

There's power in loving yourself. You can't overcome your faults if you don't love yourself. The more you hate yourself, the more mistakes you make. Hatred is an evil feeling, and when you hate yourself for your wrongs, you end up failing even more. Your failure is directly proportional to how much you hate yourself. The more you reject yourself, the more you fail.

Actions are a consequence of feelings. Behind a good action is a good feeling. To fix your actions, first fix your feelings. Go inside your heart to find out what makes you act the way you do. That's why your motives are more important than your actions.

More important than changing your actions is changing your heart. You can't be perfect while you have hatred in your heart. That's why you don't get anything out of beating yourself up. It's impossible to overcome hatred with hatred. If you want to be a better person, you need to love yourself. By loving yourself, you're healing the problem at its source.

If you're constantly accusing yourself, judging yourself, and condemning yourself in order to be perfect, you don't have the right motives. You may do the right thing, but for the wrong reason.

When you understand that perfection comes from the heart, you'll see how important it is for you to clean your heart. The first step to becoming a better person is to stop accusing yourself. You need to have pure emotions. Be more patient with yourself and forgive yourself. You must look at your mistakes and not reject yourself. Don't be ashamed of your failures.

Goodness is a consequence of love. Your ability to do well is directly related to how much you love yourself. To do things right, you need to love yourself first. Being good *inside* is the first step to being good outside. When you love yourself, you're being good inside. Then the outside comes naturally. By loving yourself, you're empowering yourself to do what's right.

Loving yourself is also necessary in order to be good to other people. You can't love people if you don't love yourself. You can't be good to them if you aren't good to yourself. Beating yourself up in order to treat other people well is fruitless. The more you condemn yourself for mistreating people, the more you'll mistreat them, because when you condemn yourself, you don't love yourself. By accusing and rejecting yourself, you're harboring hatred in your heart that will eventually manifest itself.

One of the major problems in relationships comes from blame. When you blame someone, you reject them and harbor resentment. You may get to the point of abusing them verbally and physically because of their mistakes. Even murder is a result of not accepting other people's faults. The tendency to blame people is a consequence of blaming yourself. You do unto the others as you do unto yourself. You abuse yourself because of your mistakes, so you abuse everyone else. When you learn to forgive yourself, you're able to forgive others. The more you love yourself, the more you love them.

It's illogical to condemn yourself for what you've done to others. By beating yourself up for having wronged them, you're making yourself do the same thing, over and over. If you mistreat yourself for having mistreated people, you'll mistreat them again. It becomes a vicious cycle in which you mistreat people for having mistreated you, and then you mistreat yourself for having mistreated them. The first thing to do in order to treat other people better is to forgive yourself for having wronged them. By forgiving and loving yourself, you'll give yourself the power to be a more patient and kind person.

When I was a child, I learned that we feel guilty because of our mistakes. I always thought that in order not to feel guilty, I had to be perfect, but after meditating and reading many books, I discovered that it's the other way around. I found out that mistakes are caused by feeling guilty. The more we accuse and blame ourselves, the more we do what's wrong.

Do you want to be a better person? Do you want to overcome your faults and do what's right? Start by forgiving yourself. Stop beating yourself up. Forgive yourself for what you've done in the past. Be patient with yourself, and don't reject yourself when you do something wrong. You'll realize that by loving and accepting yourself, you'll become a better person. You'll radiate love in every direction. You'll accept people as they are, and you won't nitpick.

Guilt is a side effect of not valuing yourself unconditionally

You condemn yourself because you think your mistakes make you inferior. You believe that to be valuable, you can't do anything wrong. However, your value isn't dependent on how good you are. Doing what's right doesn't make you important. You're important no matter what. Being evil or good doesn't alter your value. You don't need to reach perfection to be valuable. If you think that way, you're going to seek perfection for the rest of your life, and you'll neither be perfect nor value yourself.

To be a good person, you need to value yourself. You need to be able to look at your mistakes and not feel ashamed. You must maintain a good self-image, even when you do something wrong.

If you don't value yourself because of your mistakes, you also don't value yourself because of other reasons. For example, if you don't accept your faults, you also won't accept yourself if you're poor, sick, or unemployed. Accepting yourself unconditionally will not only help you forgive yourself, but also to accept your entire being. You'll be more satisfied with yourself. You'll look in the mirror and be happy because you exist. You won't want to be somebody else because you're happy with yourself.

You can't be nice to people if you don't value yourself. If you don't value yourself, you can't value them, and as result, you can't be good to them. Goodness is a result of valuing people. To be a righteous person, you need to value other people unconditionally. The more you value them unconditionally, the more you're good to them.

Perfection comes from making mistakes

Although it may seem strange, I assure you that flaws are the path to perfection. You can't be perfect without making mistakes. I've seen it with my piano students. Ashlee had problems with reading notes and tempo. I had to study each song measure by measure with her. First, she counted the beats wrong. Then, when she'd repeat the measure to fix the counting, she got a note wrong. When she did it again, she got another note wrong. When she finally got all the notes right, she'd mess up the tempo again, but Ashlee didn't take her mistakes personally. She was patient with herself, and so was I. After a year and a half of studying the piano, she no longer has to go measure by measure, and she gets both the notes and the tempo right much faster than before.

You weren't born perfect. Everything in your life requires practice and learning. You need to learn to be a good spouse, to be a good parent, or to do a good job. When you marry, you know you're going to make mistakes. You'll say hurtful things, you'll be disrespectful sometimes, and you'll be unappreciative at other times. If you have a child, you'll make even more mistakes. You may give them too much food, you may be too harsh, or you may spoil them. Although you want to do your best, you'll still fail sometimes. When you get a job, you'll be awkward in the beginning. You may even need someone to help you.

I went to the bank one day and was greeted by a teller who had just started. Although I was in a rush, I had to stay with that teller for about twenty minutes, because she had to get help from another person three times. However, I was helped by that same teller a few days later, and I could see how much she'd improved.

The path to perfection is through mistakes. Mistakes teach you more than doing it right. I want you to see your mistakes in a completely different light. I want you to look at them as opportunities for learning. Instead of beating yourself up every time you make a mistake, think about the lessons you can learn. Make the most of your mistakes. Think about what you can do to improve instead of accusing yourself. Look at the situation in a positive way.

When my daughter was having problems at school, I was desperate. I accused my wife and felt hopeless. Then I invited my wife to read parenting books and to go to counseling. That brought awesome results, since it not only helped us in our relationship with our daughter, but also to better understand each other.

It's a waste of energy to beat yourself up because of your mistakes. The energy you spend accusing yourself would be much better spent seeking a solution. If you have marriage problems, don't tell yourself you're inept—seek a counselor, read a book about marriage, and above all else, love yourself. By focusing on the solution instead of the problem, you'll solve your problems much faster. If you have problems at work, talk to someone with more experience or read books related to your profession.

What you are is a result of your genes and your childhood. If you're angry, impatient, eat uncontrollably, or are a sex addict, it's because of some problem from your past. You can't criticize yourself for things that happened to you that you had no power to control. You can't do anything to change your past, but you can do something to change your present. Instead of accusing yourself, look for a solution.

You aren't a slave to your past. You don't need to continue suffering from it. Your life is in your hands, so do something. There are plenty of resources waiting for you. For any problem you have, there are hundreds of books that can help you overcome that problem. The amount of help is so overwhelming that in addition to overcoming your problem, you could even become an authority on it. Can you imagine that?

In my own case, I had incredible problems in my childhood that caused trouble with my wife, my daughter, and my job. Then I started meditating and reading books, and now I know so much about my emotions that I'm helping you right now.

You can change from being the worst spouse to the most caring and loving one. You can change from being a dictatorial parent to being the kindest one. You can change your anger and become a patient person.

Forgive other people

When you love, you don't harbor resentment in your heart. You forgive people while they hurt you. When my brother, Carlos, was graduating from medical school, he had a number of invitations to send out. There were a small number of fancy ones and a greater number of simpler ones. My father was afraid that there weren't enough fancy invitations for all his closest friends and relatives. Without a doubt, Oraci and Jandyra Stuti had to receive one of the nice ones, because they were the ones who had raised me when I was a child. But they were close friends of Moises, one of my father's brothers, who got a simpler invitation. One day, Moises was visiting the Stutis, and they ended up talking about my brother's graduation. The Stutis showed Moises the invitation they'd received from my father. When Moises saw the invitation, he felt humiliated. He got mad at my father for not sending him a fancy invitation. Not only did he not go to the graduation, but he also didn't speak to my father for many years. If he had to visit the Stutis, he'd first call to find out if my father was there so he didn't bump into him.

How long does it take *you* to forgive people? Do you harbor resentment in your heart for a long time?

We tend to think love is fickle. We think that it's normal to love now and hate later. We go back and forth between love and hate. When people treat us well, we love them, but when they mistreat us, we hate them—but real love isn't fleeting. When you love, you don't stop loving, you love forever.

If you harbor resentment, you don't love completely. You need to get to the point where you don't feel angry at other people anymore and forgive them instantly. You won't take minutes, hours, days, weeks, months, or years to forgive them—you'll forgive them right when they hurt you.

2.
Believe in Your Goodness

You accuse yourself because you think you can't do anything right. There's an intimate connection between feeling guilty and not believing in yourself. You are what you think you are. If you think you're a jerk, you'll be one. You'll make yourself do things that fulfill your expectations. If you think you're evil, you'll carry out your self-imposed prophecy.

Your subconscious mind believes everything you think, whether it's right or wrong. If you tell your subconscious mind that you can't do anything right, it will believe what you say and will act upon that belief. If you're always messing up, it's a sign that you've being telling your subconscious mind negative things.

To be a good person, you need to believe in your own goodness. Tell yourself that you're a nice person, that you're full of good intentions, and that you can do what's right. Crowd your mind with positive thoughts about yourself. Expect the best of yourself. You have the power to be whatever you think you are, so expect the best of yourself to bring out your best qualities.

Be especially careful about what you tell yourself when you make a mistake. People often say things like "I'm hopeless," "I'll never do anything right," or "I'm stupid" when they make mistakes. Don't indulge in negative comments when you fail. Instead, tell yourself that you're a good person, getting better every day, and that you *will* overcome your faults.

Usually, it's when you make mistakes that you discourage yourself the most, when you're angry at yourself. However, it's in moments of failure that you need your own love and faith most. On those occasions, you must encourage yourself and believe that you're getting better. Forgive yourself, even if you make the same mistake again and again. Think that you're getting better, and you'll eventually overcome your flaws.

There isn't any flaw that can't be overcome. No one is a lost case. Even the worst criminals can change if they look for help in the right place. If you find yourself repeating the same wrong patterns of behavior, you need to change your approach. You may be looking for the solution in the wrong place.

Trust that you can make good decisions

Thinking that you're a bad person makes you insecure. You doubt your ability to choose between right and wrong. You think you're incapable of making a right decision.

The problem with not trusting your wisdom is that you become indecisive. You hesitate because you're afraid to make the wrong choice. You mull over a decision and you never reach a conclusion.

The solution is to trust your gut. You must believe that you're mature and capable of making right choices. You'll attract what you think. If you think you're unable to make the right decision, you'll only fulfill your negative expectations, but if you have self-confidence, you'll get good results. Your confidence will help you make the right choices.

Another reason you delay decisions is because you can't accept yourself if you make a wrong choice. You're so hard on yourself that getting a bad result could possibly end in self-flagellation. You keep thinking so you can guarantee that you'll make the right choice, but postponing decisions too long is a problem in itself. You lose opportunities and get into trouble when you put off decisions too long.

When you have to make a decision, you need to believe in your wisdom first. Trust that you're mature and wise. You can make the distinction between right and wrong. Second, you need to take responsibility for your decision. After you decide, don't look back. Accept your decision and go forward. Don't criticize yourself in case it turns out to be wrong.

Don't tell yourself, "I knew I was going to screw up. I never do anything right."

No one's perfect. Even the most successful and wise people make mistakes. They sometimes make poor choices and get bad results. The only difference between them and others is that they don't lose faith in themselves. They don't write themselves off as stupid. They learn from their mistakes.

When you don't think you can make a good decision, you ask for other people's opinions. You assume they're wiser and more mature than you and by following their counsel, you'll get a better result. You're easily influenced by other people's thoughts. Any input they offer is enough to make you change your mind.

Other people are no better than you. They're as mature and capable of making a good decision as you are, and you can ask for their input, but you mustn't be prone to following their opinions. Sometimes, their advice will be wrong.

You may be inclined to blame them for giving you bad advice, but you're the one who made the final decision. It was you who listened to them, and it was you who followed their opinions. Take responsibility for your decisions. You could have chosen to follow your gut instead of following someone else's advice.

Don't always think you're wrong

When you feel guilty, you think that you're always wrong. Even when you've done something right, you doubt yourself. You're so influenced by the idea that you're a bad person that you find fault in everything you do.

When you're nitpicky with yourself, you believe everything bad that other people say about you. You accept their accusations because *you* think you're a bad person. Although it's good to recognize your mistakes, be careful about going to the other extreme. Don't accept every criticism people make. There's a difference between recognizing your faults and being overly critical of yourself. Recognizing your faults means to be humble and to accept that you're wrong—when you actually *are* wrong. When you're overly critical of yourself, you think you're wrong, even when you're right.

Be aware of people who are looking for a "scapegoat." They don't like to take responsibility for their mistakes, so they try to find someone they can accuse. If they realize that you're willing to take the blame, they'll happily blame you for everything.

Don't let people criticize you and make you wrong. If you fall into the trap of taking the blame for everything, they'll accuse you even more. They won't be worried about how you feel.

Don't allow people to step all over you, even when you're wrong. Don't give them room to humiliate you. You can recognize your mistake and apologize, but don't wallow in your faults. Don't act as if you're so horrible that you need to die a slow and painful death. You can recognize your mistakes while keeping a sense of dignity.

You're the one who sells your self-image. When you think you're a bad person, you convey that to others. They see your lack of confidence, distrust you, and expect you to do something wrong. Then, when something bad happens, they're willing to think that you're the culprit.

When you believe in yourself, you send a positive message. You radiate waves of self-confidence through the air that people sense subliminally. They feel your self-belief and trust you. Even if you do something wrong, they're not harsh in their accusations because they know you're a serious person.

Although it's good to recognize your mistakes, you mustn't exaggerate them. If you forget to take out the trash, don't spend the next six hours brooding over it. The problem with exaggerating your mistakes is that you think you're a monster. Be realistic about your faults. You need to know when you're making things worse than they are. One way to know is when you're being sentimental. When you're sentimental, your thoughts always end in an exclamation.

You think things such as, "I'm such a bad person!" "That was so dumb!" "They'll never let me live it down!" or "I'm such a jerk!"

Perfection doesn't come from demanding

Have you ever demanded that you overcome a fault and then do it all over again? Maybe you've been doing that your entire life. You feel powerless and hopeless.

You can't force yourself to be a better person. While you demand perfection, you'll never overcome your imperfections. You want to force yourself to do what's right because you don't think you can. The simple act of forcing shows a lack of faith in yourself. If we really trusted in yourself, you wouldn't demand perfection.

There's a difference between demanding and having self-control. When you demand, you don't believe in yourself. You think you need to force yourself because you imagine you can't do the right thing spontaneously. However, when you have self-control, you believe in yourself. You trust that you're able to do the right thing.

Forcing is sentimental, while self-control is rational. You don't get a good result when you demand, because you're being emotional. Your thoughts end in exclamations that show how powerless and hopeless you feel. By using them, you're already expecting that you won't be able to overcome your faults. When you have self-control, you don't exclaim, so you aren't sentimental. You confidently think, "I can do this," "I can change," "I'm responsible," and "I'm in control."

Another thing that distinguishes demanding from self-control is the use of the phrase *have to*. When you say you *have to* do something, you're exhibiting doubt. You don't believe in yourself. When you have self-control, you say, *I will*. By using this expression, you show that you have no doubt that you can do something. Look at the following examples of *have to* vs. *I will* statements:

"I have to be more patient with my children." vs. "I will be more patient with my children."

"I have to stop judging people." vs. "I will stop judging people."

"I have to give my spouse quality time." vs. "I will give my spouse quality time."

"I have to get to my job on time." vs. "I will get to my job on time."

I will is powerful, while *have to* is weak.

From now on, if there's something you want to do, don't say "I have to do it."

Say instead, "I will do it."

By using *I will* instead of *have to*, you'll empower yourself to be all you want to be.

Believe in other people's love

When you feel guilty, you think other people don't love you. You assume they have the same perception of you as you do. You don't accept yourself because of your mistakes, so you think others don't accept you, either.

If you feel guilty, you think you deserve to be punished because of your mistakes. When you do something wrong, you expect other people to be mad at you. You're unable to believe that they still love you as before.

When you feel guilty, you have a negative image of other people. You think they're incapable of forgiving you. You see them as judges who will punish you. You expect them to be hard on you because you're hard on yourself. You punish and beat yourself up every time you make a mistake, so you expect them to do the same.

The problem with thinking that people are upset with you is that you become distant. You think they want to punish you, so you hide from them to avoid punishment. Your fear of rejection causes you to steer clear of intimacy.

When you think other people want to punish you, you get mad at them. You become disappointed with them because you think they don't want to forgive you. You hold your feelings back and you aren't as loving and caring as you could be.

I had that problem when I married. Every time I did something I thought was wrong, I was so hard on myself that I thought that my wife would never forgive me. I believed that she was so upset with me that she'd abandon me, so I became distant and cold.

When you detach yourself because you think someone is upset with you, you raise the problem to a new level. You make two mistakes. You're wrong in your actions and you're wrong in your feelings. The biggest mistake you can make isn't material, but spiritual. In other words, doing something wrong isn't as bad as becoming distant. When you disconnect out of the fear of rejection, you're making the biggest mistake of all. You're withholding your love.

The solution is to forgive yourself. When you forgive yourself, you're able to believe that the other person forgives you. You don't think the person is upset with you, so you aren't afraid of punishment. You can apologize and trust that the other person will forgive you. You don't hold yourself back for fear of being rejected.

Don't allow your mistakes to keep you from other people. Believe in the power of love. There's nothing so bad that it can't be forgiven. No matter how badly you've wronged someone, trust in that person's ability to forgive you. Don't feel ashamed, and don't think you don't deserve to be loved. Give yourself to them without fear.

When you feel guilty, you don't believe in your ability to love. You expect that you'll hurt people because you're a bad person. However, you need to believe in your ability to love and to make people happy. You have everything you need to fulfill others. Don't hold yourself back in fear of making them unhappy. Trust in your love and your goodness.

Accusing yourself to be loved

When you think your mistakes prevent you from being loved, you want to overcome them so you will be loved. You demand perfection from yourself and beat yourself up so other people will love you.

You don't need to be perfect to be loved. Love is unconditional. When other people love you, they accept you as you are. Expecting yourself to be perfect will neither make you perfect nor get other people's love. Although you criticize yourself, you'll continue making mistakes, and you won't feel loved.

The problem isn't that people don't love you because of your mistakes, but that you don't believe in their love. When you think you don't deserve to be loved, you find reasons to justify why other people don't love you. When you believe in other people's love, you don't see any reason that would prevent you from being loved.

If you do good things in order to be loved by others, you aren't doing good things for the right reason. Doing good things to be loved is selfish.

You're thinking about yourself and not about others. True goodness is doing the right thing because of other people and not because of yourself. When you overcome guilt, you'll focus on people instead of yourself. Your main objective will be to make them happy.

Approval addiction

Another reason you accuse yourself is to get people's praise. When you're addicted to approval, you fear doing something wrong and being rejected. You always want to be right so you can always be praised.

When you do the right thing in order to be praised, you're being selfish. Your focus isn't on other people, but on yourself. Goodness is *real* when it's focused on others. Doing things right in order to get praise has no value. What if you aren't praised at all? What if, instead of being praised, you're rejected? Will you do the wrong thing so you'll be praised? You need to do the right thing because it's *right*. If you're praised, that's okay, but if you aren't, be satisfied with the fact that you've done the right thing. Your main goal needs to be the certainty that you've done right.

Doing something right doesn't always cause you to be praised. Sometimes you do what's right and you're condemned. It's impossible to please everyone all of the time. Instead of trying to be perfect to get people's approval, you need to overcome your approval addiction. In other words, you need to approve of yourself. If you accept yourself just the way you are, you won't worry whether other people agree or disagree with you. Although you'll respect other people's opinions, you won't be a slave to their approval.

Perfectionism is a consequence of feeling guilty

When you're a perfectionist, you're nitpicky. You want to be perfect, so you worry about little things that aren't important. You have a set of rules that's impossible to follow. You get frustrated because you can't reach your vision of perfection. Then you get stressed and worried because you're spending too much energy on small things.

When you're a perfectionist, you demand perfection from others, too. You apply the same rules you have for yourself and then smother them with your expectations. You criticize them every time they do something you consider to be wrong and exhibit constant disapproval. They feel frustrated because they can never satisfy you.

Guilt is a result of an inferiority complex

You accuse yourself because you don't have a good self-image. When you have a positive self-image, you believe in your goodness and your ability to do the right thing. When you feel guilty, you think everyone is better than you. You exalt other people and depreciate yourself. You think other people are always right and you're always wrong.

No one is perfect. Other people fail, just like you do. You're neither the worst person of the world nor the best. You're just a normal human being who sometimes makes mistakes and sometimes does the right thing. Making mistakes isn't your exclusive domain.

When you think other people are better than you, there's a wall between you and them. They're in heaven and you're in hell. It makes it impossible for you to be intimate with them. In other to feel connected to others, you need to believe that you're equal to them. Stop thinking they're good and you're bad.

When you think that other people are better than you, you feel ashamed. You think they're focusing on your faults and that they despise you. You feel as if they have the power to read your mind and to discover your errors. You feel uncomfortable when you're around them. However, other people aren't paying attention to your faults. They're so occupied with their own lives that they don't have time to think about your mistakes, and if they think about you, they think about what you're thinking of them.

By thinking that other people are better than you, you become naïve about them. Sometimes you get involved with dishonest people, but you don't realize it, because in your mind, they're perfect. You can't imagine that they'd hurt you. You're so naïve that you don't complain when they step all over you. You think they're right when they hurt you because you deserve to be punished for your mistakes. They harm you, yet you apologize to them.

Some people stay in abusive relationships because they think they deserve to suffer. They're attracted to abusive partners. In their imagination, if a person was really good, that person would punish them. Therefore, they exalt in those who, in their view, have the courage to hurt them—and they continue to stay in the abusive relationship.

Even if you have faults, other people don't have a right to hurt you. Your mistakes aren't a justification for their wrong actions.

Having inflated expectations of others causes you to be upset with them. You don't expect them to wrong you, so if they do, it's the end of the world. When they make a mistake, you're outraged and resentful. Your unrealistic expectation causes you to hate and crave for revenge.

You ask yourself, "How could they do something like this? Aren't they perfect?"

When you realize that other people are no better than you and that they're capable of making mistakes, you're more patient. When they fail, you aren't so disappointed and you're more capable to forgive. You aren't appalled by their failures because you haven't exaggerated their holiness. You consider them to be normal human beings who can fail. Although they're capable of doing what's right, they can also do what's wrong.

Don't think that other people want to humiliate you

When you think that people are perfect and you aren't, you think they want to show off. If they criticize you, you think they're trying to prove they're better than you. You take the criticism personally. Instead of fixing your mistake, you focus on the humiliation, then justify yourself to prove that you aren't inferior.

One way you might defend yourself is by criticizing them back. You show how good you are and how bad they are. You exalt yourself and put the other person down, but your defense might cause an argument. When you criticize them back, you may humiliate them. Then you both begin to criticize each other to put each other down, and neither one of you will want to stop the argument, because stopping would mean losing.

If you don't feel humiliated by criticism, you don't have to defend yourself. You can explain yourself in a respectful way. You don't want to accuse the other person so you can prove that they aren't better than you. You might even recognize your mistake with dignity and self-respect.

Badmouthing is a way of defending yourself

You talk about people behind their backs because you're trying to prove that you're better than they are. You want other people to believe that you're flawless. It's a form of competition. You talk about them because you feel inferior.

You don't overcome your feeling of inferiority by talking about people. It only shows how inferior you feel. The solution to an inferiority complex isn't accusing people, but believing that your mistakes don't make you inferior. Making people wrong won't make you feel any better.

Talking about people reveals your low self-esteem. You do unto others as you do unto yourself. You despise yourself because of your mistakes, so you despise them, too. If you loved yourself, you wouldn't criticize others.

By talking about other people, you make yourself wrong. When you gossip to your friends, they fear that someday you'll gossip about them. They don't trust you. What you say may be true, but when you talk about people, you're wrong. Talking about people is cowardice. You talk about them behind their backs because you don't have the guts to say things to their face. By fearing the other person's reaction, you act dishonestly.

Gossiping is a bad habit, and the best way to overcome it is to quit, once and for all. If you don't have anything good to say about someone, don't say anything at all. Avoid the company of other people who like to gossip. If you listen to them, you'll be tempted to do the same thing. If you can't get away from them, stay quiet. They'll feel embarrassed, so they'll stop gossiping. Over time, they'll realize that you don't like listening to gossip, and they won't do it anymore.

Feeling guilty makes you sensitive

When you feel guilty, you're sensitive to your faults. You have difficulty accepting your mistakes, so you pretend they don't exist. You don't want to recognize your flaws because it causes you pain. You're always finding new and improved ways of denying your imperfections.

The reason you avoid your mistakes is because you don't love yourself unconditionally. You think that in order to love yourself, you need to be perfect. Then you criticize and condemn yourself every time you make a mistake. Self-disapproval causes you pain and to avoid the pain of self-accusation, you escape through denial.

One method of denial is to act like a victim. You find an alibi to justify your mistake. For example, let's say you're late to your job and you blame the traffic. But at that time of the day, traffic is always bad. The solution would simply be to leave home earlier. Another example is if you're speeding when it's raining and the car slides and crashes. You blame the rain, but the problem wasn't the rain—it was your speeding.

When you feel guilty, you become talented at finding excuses. You don't even realize it anymore. It becomes so natural that you end up believing your excuses.

Another way to avoid the pain of recognizing your mistakes is through amnesia. Jefferson, who had cheated his wife, told me that he met a woman in a restaurant and took her home, but he didn't know how he ended up with her in bed. Jefferson had dumped the images of his sexual relationship with the woman in his subconscious mind to avoid the pain caused by remembering the incident. The problem was that the woman got pregnant and called Jefferson to assume the paternity.

Smith was married and had one son and two daughters. He was going with his family for a vacation trip in a beach. He was speeding, lost control of the car, and hit a tree. His wife and one of his daughters died. His son became paralyzed, and Smith was taken to the hospital in very bad condition. The only who didn't suffer much from the accident was his daughter, Alicia. Later, when people tried to get information about the accident, Smith couldn't recall the crash. He'd hidden the images from the crash in his subconscious mind to avoid the pain caused by its memory. That kind of amnesia doesn't have a physical reason. It's a resource used by a person's mind to avoid feeling guilty.

Some people put up an expression of innocence and pretend not to be responsible for what they do. They act like naïve children who don't know what they do and don't have any bad intentions. They make terrible mistakes, like being dishonest, gossiping, or hurting people, but when they are confronted, they pretend to be naïve so people won't hold them accountable.

The problem with not taking responsibility for your mistakes is that you don't grow. You can't overcome your mistakes unless you recognize them. The mere act of admitting to yourself that you're wrong is proof that you're overcoming your errors. Recognizing a mistake is an act of courage and love. By taking responsibility, you're accepting yourself, and that acceptance can help you overcome your faults.

Sensitivity can also damage your relationships. It might be hard for you to be confronted by your spouse on some issue. When your partner tries to tell you that you're wrong, you take it personally and defend yourself by being mean. You think your spouse is trying to put you down.

Mary had problems taking responsibility for her mistakes. She got very upset with John, her husband, over little things.

When John told her that she'd forgotten to turn off a light, she retorted with, "If it pains you so much, turn it off yourself."

Sometimes, he tried to talk to her about some behavioral problem of their daughter, but Mary felt as if John was accusing her of not being a good mother.

Overcoming sensitivity is very helpful to communication. When you don't feel guilty, you can talk freely about problems in your relationship without taking it personally. You don't feel humiliated when other people point out your mistakes, because you love yourself unconditionally.

Accusing people to escape feeling guilty

Another method of escaping guilt feelings is by placing the guilt on someone else. You justify yourself by saying you were the victim of someone else's mistake. Someone's wrong actions forced you to do what you did. The problem with placing the guilt on someone else is that you transfer the pain from yourself to the other person. Although you don't like being accused, you accuse someone else. You make another person suffer for something they didn't do so you won't suffer.

Placing guilt on someone else is dishonest. When you don't take responsibility for your faults, you show weakness and lack of integrity. By not taking responsibility for your mistakes, you lose other people's confidence. They may end up accusing you more so you can recognize your mistakes. Recognizing a mistake is an act of honor. If you take responsibility for your mistakes with a sense of dignity, people will respect and accept you better than if you place the guilt on someone else.

Step Five
Anger Management

1.
Anger Management

Ninety percent of your anger is a result of your childhood. You think you're angry at people today, but you're really angry at the people who hurt you in the past. You've accumulated a lot of stuff in your mind since childhood, so when anyone does anything you disagree with, that stuff comes up, and you overreact. You're not angry at them, but at all that stuff. You take out the anger you feel for eighteen years of abuse on someone who's completely innocent.

Cornelio was a boy who suffered abuse from his parents. On one occasion, he was visited by his cousin Fabricio, who was taking a vacation with him. Cornelio was about seven years old, while Fabricio was about eighteen. Fabricio realized that Cornelio had low self-esteem, so he teased him and made fun of him, day in and day out. He didn't realize it, but he was adding to all the resentment Cornelio had built up over the years.

One day, Cornelio got his stepfather's gun and walked to the kitchen where everybody was except Fabricio. He told them that if Fabricio didn't stop bullying him, he'd shoot him. His mother's eyes became wide and she was terrified. She walked to him slowly and took the gun out of his hand. After that, Fabricio stopped teasing him. As you can imagine, no one was happy about Cornelio's attitude, and he was criticized by his family for a long time.

That anger problem didn't end with Cornelio's childhood, but remained inside of him. He's the type of person who keeps things inside, so for a long time, his anger was latent until it resurfaced. He was so impatient and irritable that he couldn't bear himself. His wife and his children were the main targets of his wrath.

When you look at Cornelio's story, you notice that the anger inside of him didn't disappear with his childhood. It resurfaced years later. Although he thought he was angry at his family, he was really angry at his parents for what they had done to him in his childhood.

That's why our anger is usually out of proportion. We become outraged about things that aren't important. The problem isn't that we're outraged for what people did to us, but for what our parents did to us in the past. What someone does to us in the present is the drop of water that makes our glass overflow.

Unfortunately, the people who suffer the most from our anger are the members of our family. It's because they're the most similar to our parents. They're the ones we depend on emotionally. Our subconscious mind can't tell the difference between our parents and our spouse and children. The subconscious mind thinks everyone is the same, and therefore guilty.

Imagine that you weren't hurt in your past. Imagine that your parents were perfect and that you felt completely loved and accepted in your childhood. Think about how your present relationships would be different. Things that used to annoy you wouldn't bother you anymore. You wouldn't blow a gasket over little things. Instead of exaggerating what people do to you, you'd be calm, centered, and nice.

To reach that state of mind, stop acting as if everyone's a carbon copy of your parents. You need to see other people as they are. You must also realize that your parents weren't what you think they were. As a child, you thought they hurt you on purpose. You thought they knew what they were doing and that they could have been nicer if they'd wanted to be. However, they didn't know what they were doing, so they couldn't change their approach. They acted the same way their parents did. You were part of a cycle of abuse that had been going on for generations.

To change the cycle of abuse, you need to make a conscious decision.

Tell yourself, "Enough is enough. It stops with me. I won't pass this on to my children."

That's exactly what I decided. I hurt my wife and my daughter for years until I said to myself, "Enough is enough. I believe I can be a different person. I won't allow my problems of the past get the best out of me. As of now, I will be a more patient person."

I want to invite you to make the same decision. It doesn't matter how much hatred you've harbored inside. You can change and become a better person. You can be patient, nice, respectful, and kind. You just need to believe that you can be transformed and then do the work.

Anger is a habit

If you're an angry person, it's because you've lived with an angry person in your past. You didn't have a good role model. You were exposed to someone who was either angry at you or at other people. You saw that person abusing and disrespecting others, day in and day out. Consequently, you copied their attitude, thinking anger is a normal way of reacting.

Anger is a habit. You're angry because you learned to be angry. Then, after you created the habit of being angry, you repeated it on a daily basis. However, you can get rid of the habit. You just need to believe that you can act differently and picture yourself in a different way. Develop a mental image of being patient. Visualize yourself being calm when people mistreat you or make mistakes. If you keep thinking about yourself being polite, eventually you'll convince yourself that you *are* polite. You'll develop a new role model. You'll create the image of a patient person in your mind to replace the negative role model you've had since childhood. You'll start acting according to that new role model and develop a new habit. The old habit of being harsh and impolite will be traded for one of being calm and nice. You'll become a new person.

Repressed anger and unrestrained anger

There are two types of anger: repressed and unrestrained. Some people repress their feelings to avoid hurting others or for fear of revenge. Others explode over the smallest things. Both types of anger are destructive and cause unhappiness.

I suppressed my feelings since my childhood. I avoided expressing my anger because I didn't want to hurt people. I thought about how I'd feel if someone lost their temper with me, so I didn't want to lose my temper and wound others. I either suppressed my feelings or I expressed them in a careful way. As a result, I didn't communicate my message in a way that would help me get the respect I wanted.

One reason you may suppress your feelings is because you fear rejection. If you get mad at someone, you think they won't love you anymore. You keep your anger inside, and it turns into resentment.

The problem with suppressing your feelings is that they don't go away. They stay inside you, making you unhappy. Sometimes they manifest in the form of health problems, such as headaches, ulcers, allergies, and heart disease.

Another problem with suppressing anger is that people will feel it anyway. Although you may not abuse them verbally or physically, you withhold your love. You become cold and distant. As a result, people notice that you resent them.

It's impossible not to express your feelings. Speaking is only one way of doing so. You convey anger through your body language, and even your silence. Absence of feelings is equal to hatred. If you don't show your love, other people conclude that you're angry at them.

If you don't hurt people by saying something, you hurt them with your coldness and distance. Your detachment and lack of involvement causes them to feel abandoned. You can be in the same room and be emotionally closed off.

Eventually, there will be a day when you'll blow up. You'll yell, throw things, or even resort to violence, hurting people much more than if you'd just told them how you felt when you disagreed.

Unrestrained anger

The other extreme is unrestrained anger. There are people who wear their hearts on their sleeves. They act as if they have no self-control whatsoever. Whenever they're upset, they convey their anger in the most disrespectful way. They may even pride themselves on their sincerity. Nevertheless, they hurt people's feelings and damage their relationships.

Joaquin was the elder of a church. He had a problem with unrestrained anger. Unfortunately, because of the nature of his position, he had a lot of involvement with people. He had to make announcements and sometimes preach. If someone made an observation he took a dislike to during the announcements, he'd berate them in front of everyone. Understandably, everyone got mad at him, but he reacted as if someone had done him a great injustice. He didn't realize that by doing the right thing the wrong way, he was still wrong.

That approach, unfortunately, has been praised by many pillars of psychological society. They think that if you react to being hurt, you'll be happy. There are even sessions in which people yell or hit a pillow. However, none of those approaches is effective in eliminating anger or making people happy.

For a long time, I thought that would help me. On one occasion, I was upset with a bus driver in Rio de Janeiro, Brazil. It was during Carnival, when dancers and spectators were in the streets. I was at a stoplight, and when it turned green, the bus turned and smashed into my car.

I waited to see if the driver would come and talk to me. He didn't. I left my car and entered the bus so I could talk to him.

When I got in the bus, someone yelled, "Get your car out of the way!"

The bus driver told me to get off the bus, but I snapped, "You can shove my car into the sidewalk. I won't leave until the police get here." Then I turned to the passenger who was backing him up and said, "If you want to defend him so much, you can stay here and testify for him."

I was proud for having expressed myself, but I had confused abuse with courage. I didn't know how to communicate my feelings without being rude and disrespectful. I thought that by being harsh, I was being strong. I believed it was a normal response. However, my overreaction didn't help me feel better. I just felt powerless.

Although expressing your anger is a step in the process of overcoming it, it isn't the solution. If you disagree with somebody, you have the right to convey your feelings. You don't need to hold your discontentment inside for fear of rejection. Yet you don't have to explode, either. You can communicate your message in a positive way that doesn't degrade the other person. That balanced way of expressing your feelings is called *assertiveness*. When you're assertive, you have authority without been rude. Although you're firm, you aren't harsh. You speak in a way that doesn't hurt.

To be assertive isn't the same as being wimpy. Some people convey their meaning carefully because they fear rejection or they don't want to hurt other people. By being too cautious, they don't get the respect they want. People don't take their message seriously. When you're assertive, you have a sense of dignity. People feel your self-confidence and respect you. You have respect toward yourself and toward others.

Self-loathing

There are two major causes for being angry. The first is other people. We get angry at somebody who mistreats us or makes fun of us. The second is our day-to-day experience. We get angry because we're late for work or because we trip and fall.

There's always an external reason for our anger—something doesn't go as planned or someone defies us. However, the real reason for our anger isn't external—it's our inability to love ourselves unconditionally. We attribute our value to what happens to us, such as getting to work on time or being respected by people. However, if we value ourselves unconditionally, people can mistreat and make fun of us, we can trip and fall, or be late for work, but we won't feel angry. We'll be calm, no matter what happens, because we never feel inferior.

Anger is the result of thinking our value is in other people's hands. We get angry because we think that when they mistreat us, we become inferior. To overcome anger, we need to realize that people don't have power over our value. They can't humiliate us. If we value ourselves, we never get angry at people.

You can overcome your anger. Maybe you thought that to have a peaceful state of mind, everything had to be perfect, things had to go smooth, everything had to happen exactly as you planned it, and everyone has to be nice to you. However, if you place your emotional state in other people's hands or on what happens, you'll never be happy because you can't control people or what happens. You can't force people to be nice to you, and you can't change circumstances that are out of your control.

Although you can't control things outside of yourself, you can control how you react to them. You can feel worthy, no matter what happens to you. You have power over your emotions. You just need to choose to value yourself in any situation. It's not what happens to you, but the *meaning* you give to what happens to you that counts.

For example, if your boss scolds you in front of everyone and you think it's humiliating, you're going to be angry. You didn't get angry because your boss scolded you, but because of the meaning you gave to the situation. You got angry because you felt degraded.

To get rid of your anger, you need to change the meaning you give to what happens to you. When your boss scolds you in front of other employees, don't think the situation is degrading. Perhaps your boss was the one who felt humiliated, so he scolded you. Perhaps he had a personal problem that caused him to be angry. Find a meaning for the situation that isn't against you, but in your favor. By the same token, if you trip and fall, don't think it's embarrassing. If you don't attach shame to falling down, you won't feel angry when you stumble.

Anger is a result of perfectionism

To overcome anger, you need to lower your expectations. If you expect too much from life and people, you get mad easily. For example, if you think that in order to be happy, people need to do everything you ask, you're going to get angry a lot, because they can't always do what you tell them to. By the same token, if you think that in order to be happy, people need to agree with you every time, you're going to be upset a lot because they're going to disagree with you in various situations. It's impossible for them to agree with you on everything, because they don't value the same things.

You may think that in order not to be angry, everything has to happen exactly as planned. For example, you have thirty minutes to drive to work, lunch is at noon, and you have an appointment at 3:00, and at 5:00, you're going home. However, there's a traffic jam and you spend an hour instead of thirty minutes getting to work, which makes you angry. Then there's a meeting scheduled for 11:00 that's delayed thirty minutes and you have lunch at 1:00, which makes you angry again. The person who had scheduled the appointment calls and says that he can't come today, and you spill water on some important papers and spend thirty minutes salvaging everything you can. You keep getting mad because nothing goes according to plan.

To overcome anger, you need to lower your expectations and accept things as they are. Life is full of surprises, and things don't always happen as you expect them to. When you create a schedule, you need to know beforehand that some things won't occur as planned. If you aren't such a perfectionist, you'll be happier.

You also get angry at people because you expect too much from them. You have certain standards that need to be met in order for you to accept someone. You create an ideal human being and then you try to fit people in that model, but no one fits, because they have different standards, so you get angry because you expect them to be different. If you want to overcome anger, you need to lower your standards.

A good standard for happiness is "I'm happy because I'm alive."

Wow! If that's all you need to be happy, you'll always be happy.

For example, if you get to work late, you remind yourself, "Yes, I'm late, but I'm alive."

A meeting starts late and you have lunch an hour later, but you remind yourself, "I may be late for lunch, but I'm alive."

To overcome anger in your relationships, you need to lower your expectations about people, too. For example, your standard may be "My happiness will depend on having lots of friends and loving them unconditionally." First, if you love people unconditionally, you'll have lots of friends. Second, you'll be happy all the time, because no matter what they do to you, you'll love them, anyway.

Sometimes you get angry at objects. When I was a child, I once got very angry at a table. I was walking and hit myself on the table, and it really hurt. I punched the table and hurt my hand. Getting mad at objects is kind of weird, isn't it? You can get mad because you buy a pair of pants, and the first time you wear them, they split. You get angry about the faulty craftsmanship. You're not angry at people, but at objects. If you aren't angry at someone, who are you angry at? Are you angry at a stone, a table, or a chair? You're really angry at no one but yourself. In fact, every time you get angry, you're angry at yourself.

The same thing happens when someone offends you. Before you get angry at them, you get angry at yourself. When they mistreat you, you think that you deserve the mistreatment because you're inferior, and you get angry at yourself. Then you get angry at them because they made you be angry at yourself. You want payback. The secret to not being angry at people or objects is not to get angry at yourself. If you don't feel humiliated when people mistreat you or when things happen against your will, you don't get angry at yourself, and then you don't get angry at anyone else. It all boils down to loving yourself unconditionally.

Anger's a two-way street, one to the inside and one to the outside. When you get angry, you're angry at yourself and at people or objects. You hurt people and yourself at the same time. Your hatred not only affects people, it also affects you. If you overcome your anger, you're at peace with people and with yourself. You not only stop hurting others, but you also stop hurting yourself.

Anger is the result of being too sensitive

You're angry because you think you're unable to face adversities. When people say something remotely insulting, you get mad. Even if they make an innocent joke, you feel offended.

A woman once asked a felon why he had killed her husband, and he answered, "Because he laughed at me."

You can see that the felon was pretty sensitive. The mere fact that a man had laughed at him was enough reason to be outraged to the point of killing him.

When you get mad, you're making a big deal out of something superfluous. If you're driving down the freeway and someone cuts you off, is that enough reason to be upset? Up until now, you may think that it is, but think about this. A man caused a terrible accident that killed a couple. He got very angry because the couple had cut him off, so he followed them and cut them off, causing them to crash and die.

When you're too sensitive, you see things out of proportion and give unrealistic meaning to adversities. You get angry when you could just laugh. Your children are afraid to talk to you because you think the most innocent joke is an insult. You give importance to things that aren't very important—or simply aren't important at all.

I've seen that kind of attitude between parents and children. A mother made her daughter sell the bike she'd just gotten because the daughter flunked a test. A woman poured a pan of hot water on her husband because he'd come home late from work. He was taken to the hospital and died from third degree burns.

If little things like being cut off on the freeway are enough to make you outraged, you're making yourself vulnerable. You're getting mad over little things because you think you're too sensitive. However, you are what you think you are. In other words, you're frail because you *think* you're frail. On the other hand, if sensitivity is fruit of your imagination, you're stronger than you think you are. You can face other people's disapproval, you can trip and fall, you can be cut off in traffic, and not be angry if you think you're strong.

Sensitivity is caused by your difficulty in valuing yourself. You're sensitive because you attach value to the things that happen to you. The more you feel inferior, the more pain you feel. Your anger is proportional to your fragility, which is proportional to your inferiority complex.

When you value yourself, you're strong. You don't get mad easily because you have dignity. Your self-confidence is like a shield that protects you against the bad things that happen to you. Even if people think about hurting you, they can't, because your self-esteem protects you. If you want to be a stronger person, you need to value yourself unconditionally.

The more sensitive you are, the more people can hurt you. Have you realized that when you have an open wound, you keep bumping into it? It's like a magnet. You don't seem to bump anywhere but there. Or have you ever noticed that when you drop buttered bread, it always seems to fall with the buttered side down? When you're too sensitive, you're buttered. It's as if you tape a piece of paper emblazoned with "hit me" on your back. People sense your fragility and hurt you.

I suffered a lot in my childhood because of my sensitivity. My peers sensed my vulnerability and thrived on bullying me. My poor self-esteem made it fun to them. They liked to see me sad.

When people realize that you don't get hurt easily, they don't provoke you. They don't want to waste their time nagging you when they realize you won't get mad. The secret to not being hurt by people is being emotionally strong. The less fragile you are, the less you get hurt. Think that you're capable of facing people's rejection, and you'll be as strong as you think you are. Don't feed your sensitivity. When people attack you, don't feel sorry for yourself.

Anger makes you unhappy

Angry people are unhappy. They're easily annoyed because of their perpetual bad temper. Anger is the closest relative to pain. When you're angry at someone, you're suffering because of what that person did to you. You want them to change the way they treat you so you won't suffer anymore.

Anger is a wound to the soul. You're angry because you have an open wound in your heart. Every time someone touches that wound, you feel the pain, and you suffer. When you're angry at someone, you're hurting yourself. Although you may hurt another person with your anger, you hurt yourself more. Sometimes people aren't even aware that you're angry at them, but you suffer from your anger, anyway.

Itamar was an angry man. He felt as if everyone was after him, and he resented them deeply. He was also angry at Janet, his girlfriend, because he felt as if she was his worst enemy. He criticized her and her family, considering them to be a bunch of hypocrites. As a result, Itamar was always unhappy.

When you're angry at other people, you suffer more from your anger than from what they do to you. You're the biggest victim of your anger. By overcoming anger, you'll be happy. Love is a source of happiness. When you love, you don't feel angry. You don't suffer from your anger. People can't make you suffer, because no matter what they do to you, you can't stop loving them.

Anger is caused by pride

When you're proud, you long for praise and compliments. You want to receive special treatment because it makes you feel superior. However, when you're insulted, you become angry. Your anger shows your frustration for not receiving the special treatment you crave. Instead of feeling superior, you feel humiliated.

I was in a seminar put on by the company where I worked. The meeting started out amiably, with the president of the company giving employees and their wives an opportunity to express their ideas. One wife stood up and talked about how worried she was about her husband's long hours and not having enough time to be with the family. The president took the feedback personally and became angry. He told everybody that he was unsatisfied with her husband's performance and that he'd have to work even more hours if he wanted to avoid being fired. The wife started crying and all the families were stunned by the president's lack of self-control.

The president felt as if he had to be treated special because of his status. He didn't like getting negative feedback because it wounded his personal importance. He wanted to be praised and complimented by his subordinates.

The more praised you want to be, the angrier you get when you aren't. To overcome anger, give up the need to be honored. Be humble and accept that people won't always give you special treatment. The more humble you are, the less irritated you'll get when people don't praise you.

2.
Love Overcomes Anger

When you're angry, you want to get even. You want to do something that hurts another person. Even if you control your anger and don't get payback, you expect them to be punished in some way for what they did to you. Revenge is a waste of time. If half of a forest is on fire, firefighters won't burn the other half so the fire will die faster. It doesn't make sense to fight fire with fire. If you want to fight fire, you use water.

Getting even is trying to overcome hatred with hatred. Instead of extinguishing other people's hatred, you fuel it. If you want someone to be nice to you, you must not get payback. The best weapon is love and all of its variants, such as forgiveness, patience, and respect. When you use weapons of love, you're throwing water on the fire. When you return the offense, they're even more offended, and they hurt you even more. As a result, you end up angrier than before. The best revenge is love.

Put yourself in other people's shoes

To overcome anger, you need to put yourself in other people's shoes. More than ninety percent of the time, people mistreat you because of themselves and not you. They hurt you because of emotional wounds from their own past.

Usually, people don't realize what they're doing. When they mistreat you, they can't see they're doing it because of their past wounds. They think you're the cause of their anger. They're not aware that they're transferring their past images to you and doing unto you what they felt like doing to their parents in their childhood.

Although people aren't aware they're putting anger on you, you're aware of how they feel. You've carried the wounds from your own past for a long time that have caused you to be angry at people and to hurt them, so you can understand others. You can face their rudeness without taking it personally. You're able to empathize with them without getting even.

When you get even, you aren't innocent anymore. By getting payback, you become like those who hurt you. The order of occurrence is irrelevant. It doesn't matter if you hurt the other person *after* they hurt you. What matters is that you've hurt them, so you're no longer innocent. You can't justify your anger by saying someone mistreated you first.

Believe in other people's love

Anger is the result of the negative image you have of others. You get angry at them because you think they're against you and want to hurt you. Instead of seeing them as friends, you see them as enemies.

To overcome anger, you need to believe in other people's love. You must expect the best from them and believe that they want you to be happy. You have the power to attract what you expect from others. By having a positive image of them, you invite them to treat you well. When you believe in others, you send positive messages through the air like radio waves. People sense your belief and they treat you according to your expectations. By believing in people, you become friendly. You treat them according to what you think of them. Therefore, the better the expectation you have of them, the better you treat them.

You deserve to be loved

You get angry at others because you don't love yourself. When you don't love yourself, you're unable to believe that other people love you. You distort their actions for the worst. Everything they do seems to confirm the fact that they don't love you. The problem isn't that they don't love you; it's that you think you don't deserve their love, and you think they see you as you see yourself.

When you're angry at someone, you aren't angry at them, but at the image you've projected unto them. You see them like you see yourself. If you don't like yourself, you'll think that they don't like you, either. You're not angry at them, you're angry at yourself.

To overcome anger, you need to have a better image of yourself. By loving yourself, you'll be able to believe that other people love you. You won't distort their actions for the worst. You'll respect and love yourself, so you'll believe that they respect and love you, too. When they say or do something to you, you won't take it personally.

The solution for anger is loving yourself

Your anger reflects the difficulty you have loving yourself. You can't love others if you don't love yourself. It's impossible to accept them if you don't accept yourself. If there's a war going on inside you, there'll be a war outside you. If you accuse, belittle, and insult yourself, you'll also accuse, belittle, and insult others. You'll do unto them as you do unto you.

The best way to know what happens inside you is to compare it to what happens outside you. It's hard to enter your heart to know what's going on in there. When you mistreat people, you realize that you aren't at peace with yourself. Your anger shows that you have a conflict inside your heart. You abuse them because you abuse yourself.

If you want to overcome your anger, you need to start overcoming the anger you have toward yourself. By loving yourself unconditionally and forgiving your mistakes, you can love and forgive others. You need to accept your own anger. Instead of beating yourself up for your anger, forgive and love yourself. By having a positive attitude toward your shortcomings, you'll be able to look at other people's mistakes without being resentful.

Anger is a symptom

Anger isn't a problem—it's a symptom. The problem isn't outside you, it's inside. The real problem is hatred. If there's hatred inside your heart, it's going to manifest itself in some way. You may try to hide your hatred for a while because you fear the repercussions of your anger, but it's going to surface eventually. It may appear through physical problems.

Hatred doesn't happen the moment you get angry at someone. It's constant. Even when you're calm, the anger is inside you, just waiting for when you're provoked. When someone mistreats you, they stir up the hatred inside you and you get angry.

You may think that you hate people only when they hurt you, but that's not true. You hate people all the time because you have hatred in your heart. If you didn't have hatred inside of your heart, you wouldn't ever get angry at people. No matter what they did to you, you'd love them all the time.

You may think that other people are responsible for your anger. You get angry at them, because they hurt you. You mistakenly assume that if people always treated you well, you'd never be angry. You try to change them so they don't hurt you, but other people aren't responsible for your anger. You don't have to change people—you have to change yourself. How people treat you doesn't have anything to do with your anger. Even if they were perfect, you would be angry at them. Trying to change people so you don't get angry is the same as trying to quench your thirst by taking a shower. Water poured outside of your body can't solve your thirst unless if you drink it. If you really want to overcome your anger, you need to go inside yourself. You need to get rid of your hatred. When you love, you'll never get angry at people.

Robert was married to Monica, but separated temporarily from her. He rented an apartment close to Monica until they decided what to do. To make him jealous, Monica told him she was waiting for her ex-husband, Richard, to spend the next weekend with her. Robert got very angry at Monica and determined to resolve the issue with her. He was willing to kick Richard out from the house if he came. When he got to Monica's house, his friend, David, who Monica called to help in case Robert became too upset, was standing in front of the door to prevent Robert from entering Monica's house. Robert was determined to talk to Monica, so he shoved David out of the way. David collided with a window, breaking the glass and injuring his hand. Monica called the police and got a restraining order against Robert. The interesting part is that Richard wasn't even there. She had made up the story to provoke Robert to find out if he still loved her.

A few days later, Robert said he wasn't that violent. He said it had been Monica who'd caused his anger. If she hadn't provoked him, he wouldn't have gone out of control.

Robert's experience exemplifies the case of most angry people. They blame their anger on the ones who mistreat them. If everyone was nice to them, they wouldn't ever get angry, or so they say, but no one is to blame for someone's anger. If you get angry, it's hatred that's to blame. If there was no hatred, there wouldn't be any anger. The solution for not getting angry is to eliminate hatred. Love isn't fickle. When you love, you always love. If you want to overcome anger, stop blaming other people. Don't try to convince them that they have to be nice to you so you won't get angry at them. Make a decision to love them unconditionally.

Anger is the opposite of gratitude

Anger is a way of complaining. When you get angry at someone, you show them that you disliked something they did to you. Anger is a complaint and a request for people to act differently. You demand that they don't treat you the way they did before.

When you're angry, you don't see the good in others. You become so addicted to complaining that you're unable to recognize their good actions, and you take them for granted. Even their good deeds are considered flaws. You distort everything in your mind because you don't believe in other people's love.

Your anger makes you ungrateful. Instead of complimenting others, you complain. Instead of thanking them, you get mad. People lose the motivation to do good things to you. They think that trying to please you is pointless, because no matter what they do, you'll never acknowledge it.

If you want people to do good things for you, you need to acknowledge their goodness. Stop complaining and be thankful. Instead of criticizing, give them compliments. Thankfulness is a powerful motivator. To get people to do more, be grateful for the little things they do. People like to give when they feel appreciated.

Love attracts love

Anger is an attempt to get love through hatred. To make them treat you well, you hurt them. You can't attract love through hatred. Hatred attracts hatred, while love attracts love. If you want to be loved, you need to love. By getting even, you only make matters worse. You'll never get people to love you if you insult and offend them. The best way to change people's attitude toward you is through respect. Be patient, be nice, be willing to forgive, and you'll be surprised at how much love you get. The secret to being loved resides in loving. If you can't overcome hatred by loving, there's nothing more you can do. If, after you love someone, a person insists on mistreating you, don't think that getting mad and seeking revenge will make them love you.

Edward and Kellie were headed for divorce. Kellie was disappointed with Edward because he'd been unfaithful. She'd already left him and had gone to a friend's home to make her final decision. Edward didn't want to divorce Kellie, so he decided to talk her into getting back. During the conversation, Edward got mad because Kellie wasn't agreeing with him, so he slapped her. That was the last straw. They never got together again.

Had Edward been patient with Kellie, he might have gotten her back. However, he wasn't able to control his emotions. He blew his last chance because he wanted to get love through hatred. If you want people to love you, you need to overcome your anger.

Anger is caused by neediness

You get angry because you want people to love you. When the necessity for love isn't fulfilled, you get angry. Anger is demanding. Other people *have* to love you, whether they want to or not. If they don't give you the love you want, you get mad at them. Love comes from *freedom*. It can't be forced or coerced.

If you want people to love you, you need to give them the right not to love you. Accept that they don't love you. Don't be demanding or controlling. Graciously accept what people give you. Better yet, give people the love you want them to give you. Don't focus on how they treat you or what they do to you. Think about what you can do for them. By concentrating on other people's needs, you'll forget about receiving. You'll be so occupied by loving that you won't worry about being loved. Then you'll get love.

Anger is a selfish attitude. It's an emotion directed toward yourself and not toward others. Love, however, is directed at others. When you love, you think about others and forget about yourself. When you focus on them, your needs are met. By overcoming anger, you become people-oriented instead of self-oriented. When you're people-oriented, you don't get angry because you don't focus on what people do to you, but on what you do to them. Your biggest concern is for others and not for yourself.

Anger is an obsession

Anger is an obsessive emotion. When you get angry, you have difficulty controlling yourself. You do and say things you wouldn't say if you weren't angry. Later on, you regret having done what you did and wish you could go back to act differently. You feel guilty and kick yourself. However, when someone upsets you, you get angry and you disrespect, mistreat, and hurt them all over again.

You feel as if you don't own yourself. You do things you'd disapprove of in another person. You don't need to be controlled by your emotions. Remember, you own your emotions, not the other way around. You're the boss. If you want to love, no one can prevent you from loving. Although people may provoke and hurt you, you'll be able to forgive them.

Love is a choice you make. Anger, however, isn't a choice. To be angry, you simply need to lose control of your feelings. If you don't choose to love, you hate. If you want to overcome anger, make a conscious decision to love others, no matter what they do to you.

On the other hand, self-control comes from practice. Every time you choose to love instead of being angry, you become stronger than before. Then, the next time someone mistreats you, you'll be more patient. Self-control is an emotional muscle that you develop.

Believe in your authority

People are angry because they don't believe in their own authority. They think that if they're nice, they'll be stepped on. They assume that if they're rude, people will respect them. When I worked as a chaplain, I saw that in many executives.

There was a manager who thought that the only way he could get the respect of his employees was through threatening. There was a wall between them. He was unable to be nice and authoritative at the same time. He thought that if he treated his employees well, he'd be considered wimpy. His employees disliked him so much that he was fired.

I found out how I could be kind and still get people's respect while dealing with children. When I started directing a children's choir, I lost my temper and screamed at the kids to get their respect. After three minutes, they'd start acting up again. It took months until I found the right way to treat them. The secret to my authority was that I was always calm. I'm firm with them, but I never lost my self-control. I could reprimand them and laugh with them, too. Even when I played with them, they felt my authority.

The secret to authority mixed with kindness and respect is believing in yourself. When you don't believe in your authority, you think you need to be rude to affirm yourself. If you don't believe in your authority, you'll scream and threaten, but you won't have authority. Even though people may do what you want, they won't do it out of their free will. They'll obey you only because they fear you, and you'll always have to resort to threats to get what you want.

To have authority, you need to believe that you deserve it. When you have self-confidence, you send a positive message to others. They respect you because they feel that you believe in yourself. How can you be respected by people if you don't respect yourself? How can they have confidence in you if you don't have confidence in yourself?

Authority is abstract. It isn't what you do, but what you feel. You can scream and not have authority, or you can speak softly and have authority.

Your anger is a result of thinking that other people are too strong. Because you think you're a wimp, you think you need to exaggerate your approach to gain their respect. You're rude and offensive in order to prevent them from hurting you. Therefore, anger comes from a feeling that others are too strong.

To have authority, you need to believe in other people's love. When you believe in their love, you don't think you need to be rude to get their respect. You're nice and respectful because you trust their goodness. When you trust others, you send them a positive message. It's as if their hearts have an antenna that picks up your faith. When they feel that you believe in them, they want to please you. Other people will feel loved by your faith. They like it when they realize that you trust them.

That approach is especially suitable for children. Having authority over kids is proportional to how much faith we have in them. When we believe in them, we attract their respect. Children feel hurt when they realize that we don't believe in them. They misbehave because they resent our lack of trust. Their misconduct is punishment for our not believing in them.

You get angry because you think you're wrong

Your anger is a result of your insecurity. When you're not sure of your beliefs, you feel angry every time someone disagrees with you. For example, you tell someone that you're a Democrat and list all the reasons why you believe the Democratic Party is the best. That person disagrees with you and lists all the reasons why someone should be Republican. You get angry and argue to prove you're right.

You're not angry because the other person has a different point of view. You're angry because you feel threatened by their belief. Deep inside your heart, you doubt yourself. If you really believed in yourself, you wouldn't be mad at the other person. You'd be capable of hearing their point of view and respecting it. You fight to prove that you're right because you don't believe you're right. You're dependent on other people's approval of your ideas because you don't believe in yourself.

When you believe in yourself, you give people the right to have their own beliefs. You give them the right to be wrong. Who cares if they're wrong? Do you need to be right all the time? No! You can be wrong sometimes. If you don't need to be right all the time, neither do they.

Accept that people have different beliefs. Don't feel threatened by their opinions. They don't have different opinions because they want to hurt you. They have the right to have their set of beliefs. They don't need to be a carbon copy of you.

Anger is the result of feeling guilty

Another reason you get angry at yourself is because you don't accept your mistakes. You think that in order to love yourself, you have to be perfect. Then you get angry every time you fall short of your expectations, and then punish yourself for your mistakes.

If you get angry at yourself because you err, you'll get angry at others, too. You'll do unto them as you do unto yourself. Instead of hurting yourself when you make a mistake, you need to forgive yourself. By forgiving and loving yourself unconditionally, you'll love and forgive others. As a result, you won't be angry at them anymore.

Your anger comes from your difficulty in forgiving them. You accuse yourself the same way you accuse them. Anger and accusation are twins. Every time you get angry at people, you're accusing them of something you believe they've done. By forgiving others, you'll be able to overcome your anger, but first you need to forgive yourself.

Hurry causes anger

That's why people get mad while driving. Most of them are in a hurry. When someone cuts in front of them, they tailgate them to force them to get out of the way. Usually, I don't like to drive too close to other cars. On one occasion, a driver who was tailgating me got upset because I was staying away from the car in front of me. When he passed me, he motioned to the car in front of me. He thought I should tailgate the car in front of me, like he had been doing to me.

Another example is when you're driving to work. There's an accident and you get to work an hour late. You become angry because you think about all the things you can't do because you got caught up in traffic.

Maybe you get angry at people when they don't keep up with you. I've seen that pattern many times, especially among couples. I remember how upset my mother got with my father for his calmness. When he had to travel, he got up early to organize everything. Then, when he was finally ready to go, he always needed to go to the bathroom. After he left, he remembered something he'd forgotten at home, and went back to pick it up. My mother nearly had kittens over all that.

If you're always in a hurry, you'll always be nervous and stressed. You'll think you're always late. You'll always be scolding yourself for not being fast enough. Then, when you hurry, you forget things and make mistakes. The problem is that when you're in a hurry, you strain your brain. You spend excessive energy stressing, and as a result, your brain malfunctions. The brain doesn't like to be pushed. The more you rush, the less you perform.

When you love yourself, you perform at maximum capacity. Your brain works better when it's loved. Don't rush yourself and don't treat your brain as if it was an object. Your brain lives in your body, and loving yourself implies loving your brain. Respect your limits and give your brain time to rest and restore itself. When you give your brain the respect it deserves, it rewards you with amazing productivity. A brain that's loved and respected will give you everything you need. You'll remember what you need to remember and won't be stressed and depressed.

Step Six
Believing in Yourself

1.
Words Become Prophecies

We learn to believe in ourselves during childhood, mainly through our relationship with our parents. Parents put their children down because they don't believe in themselves. They project the image they have of themselves to their offspring and think their children are as dumb and incompetent as they think they are.

If parents want their children to be winners, they need to start seeing themselves as winners. They must change what they think of themselves and trust in their own abilities. They need to develop self-confidence. When they believe in themselves, they're able to believe in their kids.

Some parents wonder why their child is rebellious, stubborn, irresponsible, or incompetent. They can't understand why their child acts so disruptively. The problem is that they expect their child to act that way. They have a bad image of the child. By thinking negatively of their child, they attract negative results.

Parents influence their kids with their negative vision. They send a pessimistic message that's captured by their children's subconscious mind. The children believe it and act it out.

Parents unconsciously communicate what they expect from their children. If they think their children are evil, their children will act accordingly. If they think their children are stupid, their children will act stupid. They treat them as if they're irresponsible, stubborn, rebellious, or incompetent. They convey it through their words, their eyes, their tone of voice, and their bodies.

If you're a parent, you can't hide your opinions from your kids. You can hide them from yourself, but not from your children. You need to change what you think about yourself. If you develop a positive self-image, you'll be able to transfer that positive image to your offspring.

The result is that your children will respond to your belief. They'll catch on to your feelings about them and they'll see themselves as winners. They'll meet your expectations and they'll respond to your faith. They'll see themselves as smart and competent.

What parents say has a great impact on their children. That's why complimenting is one of the best ways of raising a kid's self esteem. Expressions such as "I believe in you," "You're great," "You're smart," and "You can get everything in life" are tremendously powerful to make children develop a *can do* attitude.

When my daughter was about three years old, I used to go with her to the park, where there were many structures that represented a challenge for her. Sometimes I was afraid she'd fall and hurt herself. However, I hid my fear and asked her to say, "I can do it" and "I'm strong." They were the magical phrases that boosted her self-confidence. She applied the same phrases to different situations to believe that she could do other things.

Sometimes she asked me to help her climb the structures. Instead, I showed her how she could do it by herself. I asked her to step here and put her hand there, so she could climb without my help. My intention was to make her more independent. I wanted her to have a broad vision of herself and not to be limited by self-imposed boundaries.

Parents who do everything for their children fail to help them develop self-confidence. I had a friend who in her thirties didn't work and was completely dependent upon her parents. Although she was getting her second college degree, she didn't have a purpose in life. One day I was in her home and we had dinner together. After eating, she cleaned the table and started washing the dishes. Her mom took the dishes out of her hands and said that she didn't need to wash them because they had a maid who would do it. Then I understood why my friend was so dependent and insecure. Her parents had failed to help her develop a *can do* attitude. In the name of love, they were overprotecting her. They did everything for her. They thought they were doing something good, but the reality is that they were draining all of her self-confidence.

Parents need to avoid criticizing their children. Words such as "You're incapable," "You're stupid," "You're not fit for anything," or "You'll never amount to anything" may cause a child to develop a feeling of incompetence that will damage their future. Those kinds of words are absorbed by the subconscious mind of a child and they repeat it like a recorder throughout their lives. Then, when they face a test in life, they hear their subconscious mind repeating those words and they think,

"This is too hard for me," "I can't get it," or "They'll fire me because I can't do anything right."

When parents criticize their kids, they don't necessarily have bad intentions. Quite the opposite, they think their criticism will make their children prove that they're capable. However, what happens is the contrary. When parents tell their children that they're incapable, they drain their self-confidence, make them doubt themselves, and become insecure.

Since children are naïve and trusting, they believe everything their parents say. That's why parents need to be careful with their words. Everything they say will impact their children's lives. Children represent what they hear their parents say about them. Parents' words are prophecies.

As a piano teacher, I've observed the influence of parents' words on my students. The books I use to teach are accompanied by a CD. After the student plays a song a few times, I ask them to play it again with the CD. One day, a student told me that his dad had told him he couldn't play the song with the CD.

I tried to convince him that he could, but he stubbornly replied, "Daddy told I can't play with the CD."

His father had made the boy believe that he would be unable to play with the CD so he didn't believe he could.

In another case, a student thought he had a bad memory. His mother had told him that she didn't have a good memory, and that he'd gotten his difficulty of remembering things from her. As a result, he didn't believe in his ability to memorize songs, and it would take him months to memorize even the shortest pieces.

Children remember the negative beliefs their parents hold about them. They internalize their parents' thoughts about them so that when they face new challenges, they hear their parents' voices resounding inside. They don't live up to their potential because they're limited by their parents' prophecies. Although children don't like it when their parents don't believe in them, they end up agreeing with them.

The correlation between believing and feeling capable

There's an intimate correlation between believing and feeling capable. When you believe in yourself, you feel capable. You believe you're able to learn, to memorize, and to understand things. If you're a student, you believe in your capacity to understand the subjects you study. You don't feel overwhelmed and frightened by your assignments. You're confident in your capacity to learn.

When I was in the fifth grade, I had a problem with mathematics, but I was dedicated and got help from a young man who worked at the school. He was studying medicine and had a good knowledge of mathematics. I studied hard with him and learned the subject well, but when I took tests, I became insecure and afraid, which made me forget almost everything. That situation lasted the whole year, and since I got failing grades, I had to go to summer school.

Although I was only ten, I was able to think about what was happening to me. I comprehended that I was afraid and that my problem wasn't a lack of knowledge or intelligence, but a lack of faith in myself. I realized that all I had to do (besides studying) was to be calm during tests and trust in myself. I was able to control my emotions and believed that I could remember what I'd studied.

I had one more chance. I couldn't fail again. I studied hard as always, and then took the test, confident that I'd remember everything and that I'd pass. I scored 100%. That experience taught me that all I had to do to score well in mathematics was to believe in myself.

When I came to the United States, I had the opportunity to study mathematics at Hartnell College in Salinas, California. I got A's in both Algebra classes I took. Since I hadn't study math in more than twenty years, I was very rusty at the beginning. I had a hard time understanding what the teacher taught in class. To make up for all the years I'd shunned mathematics, I went to the tutorial center or to the mathematics lab and asked for help. Although it was hard, I studied between one and three hours a day outside of class. On the first test, I got 112 out of 120, and on the second, third, and fourth tests, I got 100%. The same was true on the final exam.

My experience with math taught me that there's no subject that's too difficult. The concept that math is too hard is a myth. Young people don't do well in math because they hear people saying that math is too difficult and they believe them. Parents and teachers need to stop saying that math is hard so they don't send negative messages to kids. They need to pass the idea that math is just is a subject, the same as any other.

Some time ago, I helped a boy who was repeating seventh grade for the third time. When I asked him why he was flunking, he said it was because he was stupid. I told him that he wasn't stupid, but he stubbornly believed he was. Then I asked who had told him he was stupid, and he replied that it was his parents.

He explained that whenever he and his dad worked together, his dad always said, "You're stupid, incompetent, and useless."

These words were registered in his mind so deeply that they affected the way he regarded himself. His perspective of himself was identical to his father's.

The teachers also belittled him. Instead of helping him believe in himself, they put him down. Of course, students made fun of him, as well. When parents demean their youngsters at home, they set up a cycle of humiliation that goes beyond their home. They cause their children to suffer humiliation at school, in the streets, and when they become adults. It's like black magic.

I told him, "You're not stupid. You're smart. However, you'll become stupid if you believe those lies. Don't believe people when they say negative things about you. When your father or any other person says you're stupid, tell yourself that you're intelligent. Tell yourself that you're smart and that you can achieve anything in life."

He started doing that and to my surprise, he did it out loud.

When his father told him he was stupid, he replied, "Pr. Claudio told me that when you say I'm stupid, I should tell myself that I'm smart."

I told him, "You're going to pass this year, but you need to have faith in yourself. When you study, believe that you can understand and retain the information. When you take tests, believe you'll get a good grade. Trust that you'll remember everything you've studied."

His main difficulties had been in history and mathematics. The history teacher asked the class to do an assignment, and he got the highest grade.

Then, when other students asked if they could copy from him, he replied, "Didn't you say I was stupid? Why would you want to copy from a stupid person?"

He also studied hard for mathematics, and he got 100% on the final exam. From that point on, his life changed. He enlarged his vision of himself. He'd encountered someone who had helped him believe in himself. Words of encouragement were spoken to him that entered his subconscious mind and broke the spell of defeat.

To feel capable is also necessary in other areas of life, such as the workplace. I've seen people be unsuccessful at their jobs because they doubted themselves. Their lack of trust caused them to make mistakes and ruin their opportunities. When you don't have faith in yourself, your brain doesn't work properly. Your feeling of incapacity makes you make mistakes you wouldn't make if you believed in yourself.

You tell yourself, "My mother was right when she said I was a loser. I'll never amount to anything."

The results in your life seem to confirm that you're incapable or stupid. However, they're a consequence of your lack of self-esteem. You're getting what you think you *should* get.

If you want to be a winner, you must not wait for victory to believe in yourself. You need to believe in yourself in order to become victorious. If you're not successful, the reason isn't because you're incapable, but because you don't have faith in yourself. Start believing in yourself right now. Your present situation doesn't matter. Tell yourself you're a winner. Repeat to yourself several times that you're capable, you're great, and that you have everything necessary to realize your dreams.

You also need to believe in yourself to be successful in your relationships. When you ask someone out to dinner, believe they will accept your invitation. Believe in your capacity to make someone happy. You *are* capable of loving someone. Value yourself.

You're capable of doing what's right. You must believe that you're a good person and that you're able to do good things. Don't be afraid of making mistakes. Believe in your wisdom and in your capacity to make right choices. Believe that you're responsible and mature. Trust your good intentions. Always believe that you can be the best.

Don't believe people when they put you down

When you don't believe in yourself, you're easily influenced by other people's words. You have a tendency to believe every negative thing they say about you. You allow them to put you down and you think they're right about you.

If you had parents who put you down, you're especially sensitive to other people's opinions. Although you dislike when they say you're incompetent, you agree with them, which is why you get upset with them. You're upset because deep inside, you believe they're right. If you had a different self-image, if you believed in yourself, you wouldn't be upset. Their negative words wouldn't impact you.

Throughout my life, I've met many people who told me I was incompetent or unable to do something. Some of them were well intentioned and apparently wanted the best for me. However, they weren't helping me. For a long time, I listened to their words and believed them.

One time, a minister told me I didn't have the talent to be a pastor. I told him I was reading a book about leadership to help me with my limitations. He replied that since I didn't have the talent to be a leader in the first place, a book wouldn't be of any use. At the time, I agreed with him and stopped reading the book. One year later, I questioned his words. I thought he had been wrong about me and that the book could help. So I opened the book again and read it, and it worked wonders for me! It helped me not only to be a good leader, but also to believe that I can do anything if I believe in myself. The book was *Develop the Leader Within You,* by John C. Maxwell.

Writing a self-help book was an old dream of mine. I wanted to share the marvelous things I've discovered about myself. However, I had people who discouraged me, and some of them even made fun of me. A close relative told me I shouldn't write at all. He was afraid I might get into trouble by writing something inappropriate.

It took time for me to ignore those negative words and not to allow them to stop me. I had to develop a good self-image and be independent of people's opinions. I had to create a shield of self-value that protected me from their negative words. I finally got to a point where no one could prevent me from believing in myself.

Avoid the company of negative people

Besides not allowing people to hold your attention with negative words, avoid the company of negative people. If you feel that somebody is intentionally or unintentionally trying to put you down, avoid them. Don't let dream stealers drain your energy. Seek the company of positive people. Stay connected to the ones who believe in you and motivate you.

Don't surround yourself with complainers. People who feel like victims are always talking about how everyone is against them and will steal your energy. Have you realized how much those people negatively influence those around them? When they're in a group, they create a negative ambience with their complaints. They spread their gloom and cause an atmosphere of discontent. Seek those who always have a reason to be thankful and happy.

Make your internal voice positive

The negative words that were spoken to you during your childhood were recorded in your subconscious mind, and you repeat them over and over without noticing. They become so natural that you don't realize you're putting yourself down. They may take different forms, but in essence, they say "I'm not competent," or "I'm incapable." For example, if you say "I don't like to cook," the real words inside of your subconscious mind are "I'm not capable of cooking."

Maybe your house needs to be painted and you decide to ask a professional to do it. You say you're too busy to paint it yourself or you're afraid of doing a poor job, but the actual reason may be that you feel incapable of doing a good job because you think you're incompetent.

Perhaps you see someone playing the piano and say, "I wish I could play the piano like that, but I'm too old to do it."

Although your motive may seem reasonable, the fact is that you don't believe in yourself. You feel incapable learning, so you use the excuse that you're too old.

We can find many excuses to justify our sense of incompetence. We come up with explanations for why we can't do things, but behind all of them is the assumption, "I'm incompetent."

What if, from now on, you stopped making excuses and you told yourself, "I can do anything. I'm capable, and I'll get everything I want."

You need to combat negative thoughts and exchange them for positive ones. You aren't a slave of your mind. Don't think you can't control what you think. You're able to change the course of your thoughts for the better and have a positive frame of mind.

Another kind of negative self-talk that's harder to perceive involves your feelings. You may feel incapable of learning a subject, of cooking, of playing the piano, of being a good parent, or of being a good lover. The feeling of incapacity permeates everything, though it may not be expressed in words. You just feel uneasiness and discomfort when you have to do something. You have a sensation that things are too hard and you feel overwhelmed. It seems as if everything is too difficult and complicated.

One method you can use to combat your negative self-talk, thoughts, and feelings, is to bombard your mind with positive messages. By reading or listening to self-help books, you can change your mind's programming. You have power over your mind. You can be a positive person. You just have to choose that. Reject negative thoughts and fill your brain with positive ones, to the point that it plays back positive thoughts all the time.

Here's a list of negative words and phrases you shouldn't say:

"What a loser."

"What an idiot."

"I'll never succeed."

"It's impossible."

"I don't have what it takes."

"It's never going to change."

"No one loves me."

"Everyone is against me."

"I'm never going to amount to anything."

On the other hand, here's a list of words and sentences to say every day:

"I'll succeed."

"I'm going to fulfill my destiny."

"I'm getting better every day."

"I'm capable."

"I'm intelligent."

"I'm smart."

"I'm competent."

"I have a bright future."

"I'm a positive person."

"I believe in myself."

"I'm healthy."

"I'm valuable."

"Everyone likes to be with me."

"I'm triumphant."

Intelligence isn't enough

There's a difference between what you are and what you believe you are. Like everyone else, you're intelligent. You can reach great heights and realize many dreams. However, it depends on how much you believe in yourself. If you think you aren't intelligent or smart enough, you won't have the strength to reach your dreams. You'll be shackled by the chains of your pessimism and lack of faith in yourself.

Your actual intelligence is inconsequential. How much you believe in your own intelligence is what matters. You may be a genius, but if you think you're dumb, you won't accomplish what you want. Your negative self-image will hold you back and you'll be crippled in your ability to reach your destiny.

There are many people who live in mediocrity when they could be prosperous and successful. They're defeating themselves because of their poor self-image. Many homeless people and beggars are very intelligent. Many of them live in a miserable condition because they don't believe in themselves, limit themselves, and live according to their poor self-image.

Don't worry about your intelligence. You don't need to take an I.Q. test to believe in your capability. Just have a *can do* attitude. If you want to get a degree, believe that you can get it. If you want to learn a new language, believe in your capacity to learn. If you want to open a business, trust that you'll be successful. You can if you think you can.

2.
Faith is a Source of Strength

When you believe in yourself, you have the strength to get what you want. Faith is a source of energy. If you have faith, you're strong, you're courageous, and you're powerful. Faith gives you the motivation to pursue your goals. It's the *vitamin of the soul*. You wake up every day excited about your activities, you perform tasks with passion, you initiate new projects with boldness and courage, and you aren't afraid of risk.

If you don't have faith, you're weak and don't have the motivation to pursue your goals. You're afraid to start new projects, and you feel lazy and discouraged. You don't want to get out of your comfort zone to risk something new.

The most important thing you need in order to fulfill your destiny and to be successful is *faith*. You may have money, you may have influence, and you may have talent, but if you don't have faith in yourself, you don't have the power to see your dreams come true.

People who don't believe in themselves are stuck in their comfort zone. The years go by, but they stay in the same place. They don't seek to advance, because they don't believe they can. They don't learn anything new. They're afraid to open a business because they don't have faith in themselves.

When you have faith in yourself, you don't stay in the same place. You're always progressing. You're always investing in something new. You don't hold to the status quo.

Your mind works according to your faith. If you don't believe in yourself, you don't have ideas and thoughts of progress. You assume unconsciously that it's a waste of your time to invest in your dreams, since you won't be able to reach them, anyway, so you don't give yourself the right to dream or to make plans to reach your goals.

On the other hand, when you believe in yourself, your mind is always dreaming and making new plans. Brilliant ideas are constantly bombarding your brain. You become exceptionally creative. You give yourself the right to dream and to believe that you can realize these dreams.

Faith brings action

People who believe in themselves are action-oriented. They don't live out their lives just planning and dreaming. Since they expect positive results for their plans, they want to get started as soon as possible. They act upon their dreams because of their faith in themselves. They're fueled and empowered by their sense of competence and capacity.

There's a danger in excessive dreaming and planning. If you're always dreaming and planning and you never act, it shows that you don't believe in yourself. Your dream may seem too unrealistic and too good to be true. You may think "how good it would be if" or "it would be marvelous if I could," but deep inside you don't think it can become a reality because you don't think you have what it takes. You stay in the dreaming stage and never go to action.

When you dream, take your dreams seriously. Dream about already making plans and establish a date when you'll start realizing your dream. Don't put that date too far away. If you dream about doing something more than one year from now, it may signify that you don't believe you can achieve your dream. There's a probability that one year from now, you'll postpone the realization of your dream for another year. The best thing to do is to get started *now*.

Don't wait for things to be perfect to start acting upon your dreams. Don't wait for someone to believe in you or help you, don't wait for the right amount of money, and don't wait for the ideal opportunity. Don't make excuses to postpone the realization of your dreams. Do whatever you can *now* with the resources you have. Just get started, and you'll see that the resources will come your way.

Fear is the opposite of faith

"He who doubts is like a wave of the sea, blown and tossed by the wind." (James 1:6)

While faith makes you expect the best, fear does the opposite. If you don't believe in yourself, you expect something bad to happen. If you have a job interview, you think they won't accept you, and if you get the job, you think you'll be fired.

Fear causes suffering. You become stressed because you fear defeat. If you have an upcoming test, you get nervous and worried because you think you'll fail. When you study, you're anxious because you doubt that you can learn. Then, when you're taking the test, you sweat and shake because you don't believe you can pass. Those fears may have nothing to do with reality. You may be prepared and know the material, but you still doubt yourself, and because of that doubt, you're nervous.

It may be even worse when you have to do something in public, such as speaking, singing, or playing an instrument. You have the talent and you've practiced hundreds of times, but you're still afraid. Everyone in the audience believes in you but yourself. Your lack of faith causes you to shake, your hands are cold, you stumble over the words, and you forget what you had to say. You make mistakes just because you're afraid.

Sometimes you're afraid of losing something. You may have a job, but fear losing it. You may be afraid your spouse will divorce you or that you'll get sick and die. You can't enjoy the good things in life because you're constantly afraid of losing them.

Not believing in yourself brings fear, stress, and suffering. Instead of celebrating your job, your marriage, or your health, you live in fear of losing them. Everything you do is a source of anxiety because you don't believe in yourself.

To have faith is to overcome fear and to expect the best. Don't assume against yourself. Assume in favor of yourself. Always believe that the best will happen to you, and don't be afraid that you'll lose the good things you have. You'll go into an exam believing that you'll pass. You'll make your speech, you'll sing, and you'll play your instrument confidently. You'll get good results in everything you do.

Faith vs. pessimism

To be pessimistic is to believe the worst. When you're pessimistic, you think you'll fail. You think you won't succeed because you aren't smart enough. You always expect a negative result.

The problem with being pessimistic is that you attract what you expect. If you expect the best, you attract the best, but if you expect the worst, you attract the worst. Faith is like a magnet that attracts good things, while pessimism is also like a magnet that attracts bad things. You have the power to bring to yourself whatever you believe.

If you want to have good things in your life, you need to expect the best. Faith has the power of transforming dreams into reality. If you expect the best, the best is what you'll get. If you're optimistic about your future, your future will be crowned with success. The more faith you have, the more you'll attract good things. Thus, every dream you have and every plan you make *needs to be mixed with faith.* Set a goal for yourself and believe you can reach it.

Look for the easiest way

Something that prevents people from reaching their dreams is the thought that it has to be hard. They don't like it when the process is easy and smooth. They don't feel thrilled. They like it only when it's hard, slow, and full of setbacks.

Such people have a victim mentality. People who act like victims have a tendency to value things that make them suffer. They're addicted to pain. If it's easy, smooth, and pleasurable, they try to make it hard, rugged, and full of pain. They thrive in suffering because it makes them feel superior.

Sometimes it's impossible to avoid pain. We will always encounter difficult moments on the way to success. However, we shouldn't search for pain. We always need to look for the easiest, fastest, and most pleasurable way.

If you can reach a goal in a week, don't take a whole year. A good example was this book. For more than a year, I wrote only a page or two every now and then. I realized that I was being influenced by my old tendency to do things the hard way. Instead, I decided to write the greatest possible number of pages every day. I created a motto: "Just one more." I started writing at least five pages a day, and then increased the number of pages, just to extend my comfort zone and to prove to myself that things don't have to be hard and slow.

If you can double your income right now, don't wait until next year. If you can improve your relationship with your family, don't wait for things to get worse. Now is the best time to be all you can be. Just do your best today and make the most out this day. If you make your goal to use your time wisely in order to get the best result possible every day, you'll make giant steps that will cause you to achieve your dreams much faster.

Insecurity at work comes from a lack of faith

When you don't believe in yourself, you think you have to work more to compensate for your incompetence. You work longer hours and neglect your health and family. You think that more hours will make up for your limitations. You run in all direction to avoid failure. You're a firefighter, trying to extinguish fires caused by your insecurity.

Working more hours won't do any good if you don't believe in yourself. Your lack of faith will catch up to you. Working more can't compensate for a lack of faith. When you believe in yourself, you become more balanced. You aren't stressed or afraid because you know you can handle things. You can rest confidently, knowing you'll succeed.

Don't limit yourself

When you don't believe in yourself, you don't realize how capable and intelligent you are. You're blind to your talents and you take yourself for granted. You don't see your potential. There's a gap between what you are and what you think you are.

The result of limiting yourself is that you don't reach your maximum potential. Your lack of faith holds you back. It's like the cruise control in a car. If you set the cruise control at fifty-five, whenever the car goes a little bit faster, the cruise control pulls the speed back to fifty-five. The same happens to you if you don't believe in yourself. For example, if you only believe in yourself eighty percent, that means that you'll reach twenty percent less of your potential than if you believed in yourself completely.

A symptom of limiting yourself is when you think something is too hard for you to accomplish. When that happens, you feel overwhelmed by your responsibilities, which causes you to be stressed and worried. You fear that you'll perform poorly and that you'll let other people down. That fear is caused by limiting yourself and will probably bring about the exact thing you fear.

When you limit yourself, you see your tasks as being beyond your capacity. You look at yourself as if you were too small, and you look at your goals as if they were too big for you to achieve. You exaggerate the size of your dreams, you diminish yourself, and you amplify your tasks. You have a distorted vision of yourself and your goals.

Sometimes, you may face new situations in your life that you think you won't be able to handle. I was married for one year when I learned that my wife was pregnant. Although I was already twenty-nine, I considered myself incapable of raising a child. I didn't believe in my own maturity and still considered myself a child.

To overcome your self-imposed limitations, you need to think well of yourself. The less you limit yourself, the more successful you will be in everything you do. Don't think that your spouse is too good for you, that your child is too stubborn for you to control, or that your goal is too big for you to accomplish. Don't feel overwhelmed, and don't feel that you're incapable of performing anything. Believe you can handle anything that comes your way. You're bigger than your goals and you're stronger than your problems. Nothing will submerge you if you think well of yourself.

Think big

A good way to increase your faith in yourself is to think big. Don't settle for mediocrity. Don't satisfy yourself with poor goals. Have a large vision, a big dream, and believe you can reach it.

Throughout my life, I've encountered many people who said that if they could play the piano only half as well as I do, they'd be satisfied. They considered me a good pianist and thought that being like me would be impossible. I explained that if they could play half as well as me, they'd want to play better. After all, I don't think I'm as good as I can be, and I'm still trying to improve.

I've set some musical goals for myself, one of which is to have the technique of a concert pianist. I also dream of playing jazz and improvising like the best jazz pianists. Those big dreams have helped me to be the pianist I am, and they give me the motivation to pursue my goals.

Two years ago, I was playing in a restaurant and had the opportunity of meeting Jefferson, a young Mexican man. He worked there as a waiter and had a dream of opening a business in a tourist area in Mexico where there are many other hotels. He worked about two years and saved the money he needed to open his business. Now he's enjoying his life as an entrepreneur in Mexico.

Don't set limited goals. Don't think about having a small apartment. Instead, dream about having a two-story house. If you're a student, don't be satisfied with just passing. You can get B's and A's. Don't dream about an income of $40,000 or $60,000 a year. Think about getting more than $100,000.

The problem with some people is that they think big achievements are for other people and not for them. When they think about something big, they discourage themselves with phrases like, "I don't have what it takes," or "This may be fit for other people, but not for me." They even make fun of themselves, saying, "Who am I to think something so big?" As a result, they don't take themselves seriously.

You need to have a deep respect for yourself. Don't make fun of yourself and don't criticize yourself. Whenever something big comes to your mind, don't demean yourself. On the contrary, support yourself with words of faith and encouragement. Take yourself seriously. Don't think that you're too childish or too immature to think something so foolish. Think you can reach what you are dreaming of—or better than that.

The power of visualization

"Faith is being sure of what we hope for and certain of what we do not see." (Hebrews 11:1)

Most things that happen to you're a result of your visualizations. You bring to yourself what your see in your mind. Therefore, having faith means being able to see yourself achieving something. First you must picture it in your mind. What you see through the eyes of faith, you'll attract.

We don't realize it, but our mind is always visualizing something. We're always dreaming about the future. The problem is that most of us visualize negative things. We expect our marriage to fall apart, our children to be rebellious, and our boss to fire us. We feed our mind with negative thoughts twenty-four hours a day and then get what we expect. We don't have strength to achieve anything, since we don't believe we can get it. We bring to ourselves all the negative things we see. Our marriage goes downhill, our children become rebellious, and our boss fires us.

You *can* change the course of your imagination. You can stop those negative images from coming to your mind and change them to positive ones. If you've been seeing yourself as a failure and incompetent, incapable of achieving anything, and destined to mediocrity, you can change that image to seeing yourself as a winner. You can change the course of your thoughts and have all the things you want.

You need a detailed picture in your mind of what you want. Imagine colors, smells, sensations, and sounds. If you want a house, think about its size, the types of floors, and the plants in the yard. It may be on a beach or on a hillside overlooking a beautiful valley. Imagine your children playing and you seated in the yard talking to your spouse.

Your brain has the power to make your dreams come true. That means that you can talk your brain into obtaining what you want. Positive visualization, mixed with faith, is the secret to success.

In August 2004, I started visualizing myself directing a children's choir. At the beginning, it was hard to believe. I thought it was beyond my capacity. However, I talked to Miramonte School's secretary about my vision and she believed in me. She kept encouraging me and saying I was able to do it.

When I thought about the choir, I felt excited, but it was a dream that seemed almost impossible to reach. However, I continued to visualize it and to take myself seriously. I fought against the idea that I wouldn't be able to do it. Then, in January 2005, I was invited by a pastor to start a children's choir at his church. I accepted his invitation and a month later, I started another choir at Miramonte School. On May 14, 2005, we put on a concert in which both choirs sang together. The event was successful and attracted even more children to my choirs, which already had twenty kids each. It was a dream come true. I visualized it, I believed in it, and it happened as I'd seen in my mind's eye.

I could have buried my dream in the beginning. I could have indulged the doubts that came to my mind, but I believed in myself and envisioned my dream. I mixed my visualization with faith, and they stopped being mere dreams and became reality.

To achieve your dreams, mix your visualizations with faith. When you dream, take yourself seriously and believe you can achieve your goal. Then the next step is making plans. Establish goals and schedule them chronologically. You need an order of steps to follow.

The final step is to take action. You've dreamed and you've made plans. Now it's time to act upon your dreams. Work out your plan. You must get the job done in order to get the desired outcome.

Even after realizing a dream, you need to continue dreaming. Have other visions to give meaning to your life. To stop dreaming is the same as dying while you're still alive. A person without dreams is a person without purpose, so keep dreaming and visualizing new things every day.

When I was a chaplain, I worked in a nursing home where I met many people who had lost their purpose in life. They'd stopped dreaming. Many of them were still able to work and be productive, but they felt life had lost its meaning. They considered themselves incapable and useless. They didn't believe they were still able to realize their dreams.

If you want to be successful, think good thoughts and dream good dreams. What you think and what you see in your mind is your choice. You have control of your mind and you can make it think positively.

3.
To Fall Forward

Something you can count on as you move toward success is failure. Everyone who has walked the path to victory has faced that inevitable reality. The only way out of failure is not risking. If you stay in your comfort zone and don't seek to achieve your dreams, you won't fail.

Failing is one of the best methods of learning. It's a source of experience. You discover that something doesn't work and you try another way. If you fail again, you keep trying until you find a solution. You change your approach and adapt your methods until you get the result expected or something *better.*

Have you ever noticed that when you get lost, you learn how to get where you're going much faster? One day, I was going to a church in Boston to preach when I got lost. Since I'd been in America only a few months, it was difficult for me to get help. I'd stop and ask for information, but when people tried to help me, I couldn't understand what they were saying. I just looked at their hands and I went in the direction they pointed. I drove in circles for two hours until I got to the church—after the service was over. The two hours had I spent getting to the church helped me learn the area so well that I never forgot. I failed one time—but never failed again.

I also learn about the importance of failing when I practice the piano. There are songs I have to play many times in order to play them well. I've learned to accept my mistakes. For a long time, I thought that not being able to play a song right away was my fault. I thought I might be incapable of playing certain difficult songs. However, over time, I could play pieces that I couldn't play before, so I learned that it was just a matter of practicing them until I could.

Many people give up when they face failure because they think they're incompetent. They think that if they were capable, they wouldn't make mistakes. They're very sensitive to their errors. They can't maintain a good self-image when they fail. They take failure personally

When we're babies, we face disappointments more easily. Children fall down many times until they learn to walk. I remember when Carolina was two years old and we were at a picnic for the hospital where I worked as chaplain. There was beautiful grass and she was walking on it. It was incredible how many times she fell down. She couldn't stay standing for a minute. However, she didn't show any sign of frustration. She'd just get up and walk again.

We need to relearn how to face failure the same way we did when we were children. We need to fall and get up again, without feeling sorry for ourselves. The difference between winners and losers is that winners don't take failures personally. They aren't sensitive to their mistakes and don't get discouraged or disappointed when they fail. They don't see themselves as victims. They maintain their good self-image and keep trying.

It's unproductive to mourn over your failures. When you complain and whine about your failures, you're wasting time and energy that you could be spending on trying to learn from your mistakes. Instead of assuming that you're incapable, think about how you can learn from your mistakes. Use failure to your advantage.

Thomas Edison failed more than a thousand times before he could make his lightbulb work. The secret of his success is that he didn't take failure personally. He didn't assume he was incapable. He didn't become irritated or impatient. He accepted his mistakes and persevered until he succeeded.

When you take failure personally, you become impatient. Every time you make a mistake, you get upset. You can't maintain a positive attitude, and you're unable to persevere. Small mistakes cause you to quit.

However, when you believe in yourself, you don't quit. You try one method, you try another, and you try as many methods as necessary until you get what you want.

There's no easy way to success. Many people who want to study the piano ask how long it'll take them to learn. I tell them it depends on how much time they spend practicing. Most of them quit after a few weeks or months. When they realize it's going to take time and effort and that they can't be a good piano player in just a few months, they get frustrated. They don't enjoy the process. Only a few students get to be really good piano players, because they don't take failure personally.

If you want to succeed, accept your mistakes and continue pursuing your dreams. Don't expect it to be easy and fast. Along the way, you'll fall many times. There will be times when you'll go up two steps and fall back three. Instead of being disappointed, just get up and continue. The problem isn't falling, but falling and staying down. Both winners and losers fall. The difference is that winners get up and keep climbing, while losers stay on the ground.

Persistence

When you believe in yourself, you're persistent. Take the example of this book. I first started writing it in 1989. I wrote about ten pages, but when I read it, I didn't like it. Then I wrote a different book, which I never published. In November 1998, I tried to write this book again. I typed six pages in one day and got very excited. I could see clear progress. Then I had the opportunity to take writing classes in college, which opened my eyes to what I needed in order to be a good writer. I learned that books aren't written—they're rewritten. In 2003, I went back to what I'd written in 1998 and rewrote the first chapter.

After that, I discovered the importance of reading in order to be a good writer. I started reading one or two books a week, which improved my English, made my ideas come across more clearly, and gave me even more insights. That process took sixteen years. There are some chapters I've revised six times, and some chapters I rewrote again after having revised six times.

It doesn't matter how many times you fail, don't give up. Change your approach, learn from your mistakes, but keep going. You may be closer to realizing your dreams than you think. The way to success has many hurdles. You'll fall many times. You may be tempted to think you'll never achieve your goals—but *never* give up.

You're never too old to begin

When you don't believe in yourself, you find many excuses not to pursue your dreams. One of the most common is age. You might say you're too old to learn piano, to get a degree, or to open a business.

Delia was a famous piano player in Brazil who began studying the piano in her twenties, but in only two years, she had learned enough to record a jazz CD and to travel around the country giving concerts. Sergio learned to play the piano when he was almost thirty, and besides learning to play very well, he became a fine arranger. I've had adult students who were able to learn to play the piano from scratch and became very good. One of them was Moises. He started studying the piano in his thirties, and he could play well in less than two years.

Lance Almond was a student who became a close friend. He started playing when he was sixty. He practiced every day for at least an hour.

Every week, he had at least one song prepared. He had problems with tempo, but he didn't get discouraged. He practiced and overcame that difficulty. I remember that in one of his lessons, he had to play a song with sixteenth notes, which isn't easy. He did it perfectly and I was excited to see his development. When he was sixty-two, he decided to retire and move from Salinas, California, to Ridgefield, Washington. I thought he'd stop working, since he had enough to live comfortably. However, he decided to start a new career as realtor.

Research shows that a company has a seventy-three percent greater chance of succeeding if the entrepreneur is fifty-five old. The secret is that those people have learned from their past mistakes and failures and have more maturity and experience.

A person reaches their maturity between 35—40 years of age. Most great achievers don't realize their dreams until they're forty or older. Research shows that a person reaches their maximum performance at age sixty-five. That means that age isn't an encumbrance, but an advantage.

If you're older forty, you have one more reason to believe in yourself. Your maturity and experience will help you succeed. You have an advantage over younger people. Consequently, instead of regretting your age, be thankful for all the knowledge and wisdom you've accumulated. Now is the time for you to realize your dreams!

That doesn't mean that if you're under forty you can't succeed. There's a way to compensate for your inexperience. All the knowledge and wisdom mature people have is in books. You don't need to wait until you're forty or fifty to be successful. You can learn from those who've already walked the path. When you read books, you're taking advantage of other people's wisdom. Through reading, you can learn faster and without making as many mistakes. The more you learn, the less you fail. Your path to success will be smoother and faster.

I regret not reading more when I was younger. My wife told me that if I wanted to be a writer, I should read. I was offended by her advice and proudly said that I knew everything and didn't need help from books. If I would have listened to her, I could have written this book a long time ago. If you're young, don't be stubborn like I was. Don't think that you know everything and you don't need help. It's good that you're reading *this* book, but read others, too.

It's never too late

One thing that hinders many people is the thought that it's too late to start a new endeavor. They look at the past and count how many opportunities they've wasted. They conclude that since they've failed so many times, they won't succeed. They keep regretting their past mistakes and think their situation is irreversible.

Instead of mourning the opportunities you've wasted in the past, look ahead and realize how many opportunities you still have. The positive person is always looking ahead. When you're positive, you see so many opportunities that you simply forget about your past failures. It's not worthwhile to spend time mourning the past when you can work toward the opportunities in front of you.

When you maintain an attitude of mourning and regret, you become blind to your options. You think that you can't succeed and find excuses for not being successful, but opportunities are inexhaustible. It doesn't matter how many chances you've missed, there will always be new ones. You simply can't waste all of them. Instead of looking back, focus on the present and the future. Instead of regretting your past mistakes, get excited about the chances you have right now. It's never too late.

Be thankful

When you're positive about the present, you're also grateful about the past. You see good things ahead and you also see good things in your past. You look at everything in a positive way. The present is full of opportunities and the past is crowned with victories. Even the problems you had are considered to be the steps necessary to lead you toward the success that's right in front of you.

If you're a positive person, you don't complain. You don't spend your time mourning about your past. You see the good side of everything. You look to your past in a positive way and you're able to realize how many good things have happened to you. That doesn't mean you ignore the mistakes or poor choices you've made. You've made mistakes, but you've done more right than wrong. All the mistakes you've made have given you the knowledge and wisdom you have today. The past isn't a disadvantage, it's an advantage.

To be positive about your present and your future, stop complaining. Don't feel like a victim. Don't think that the things that happened in your past have caused irreversible damage to your life. Instead of complaining, be thankful. Thank yourself for all of your hard work throughout your life. Thank people around you for the different ways they've blessed you. Be grateful for the mistakes you've made that taught you important lessons. Thank the problems that occurred in your life, because they helped you to grow and mature. Be thankful even to the people who harmed you, since they helped you grow stronger. Be grateful for everything, good or bad, because they all made the person you are today. They're the reason you're better than ever. You have a lot of experience that will help you to be successful and to attain all your aspirations.

Taking risks

One thing that separates great achievers from everyone else is that great achievers are willing to take risks. Although they realize they may fail, they don't avoid taking risks.

Taking risks takes you out of your comfort zone. For example, if you're a doctor and you work for a hospital, you might think that you'd be more fulfilled and would also make more money if you opened your own clinic. However, you might think about all the difficulties you'd encounter, the money you'd have to invest, the leadership skills you'd have to develop, and the advertising you'd have to do to attract clients if you opened a new clinic. What if the clients didn't come right away? What would you do with the employees you'd have to pay? When you consider all of these factors, you feel so stressed and afraid to fail that you may decide not to take the risk and to stay in your comfort zone.

When you get out of your comfort zone, you stretch your faith. As you face your doubts and fears, you become stronger. Taking a risk is an act of faith that brings more faith. You fulfill your dream, and it proves to you that you're capable. When a new challenge comes, you're more confident. You're more secure in taking another risk. You strength your self-confidence until you get to the point that it becomes natural to take risks.

4.
Being Independent is to be a Giver

If you don't believe in yourself, you'll think that other people don't believe in you, either. You'll project your lack of self-confidence onto them and you'll try to prove that you aren't what they think you are. You don't have to change people's opinions of you. You just have to change your opinion of yourself. If you believe in yourself, you won't seek other people's approval. You won't feel sorry because they don't believe in you. You'll be satisfied with your own approval.

When you seek other people's approval, you're trying to fix an internal problem through an external solution. Other people can't believe in you for you. They can't fix your self-esteem. You're the one who needs to believe in yourself, and you're the one who needs to approve of yourself.

There will always be people who don't believe in you. One reason is because they don't believe in themselves. When other people feel worthless and incapable, they see you as they see themselves and project their own negative self-image onto those around them.

Another reason is because they're jealous of you. They compare themselves to you and think you're superior. They can't celebrate your success because your success threatens their lack of self-confidence, so when they criticize and try to put you down, it isn't because they think you're incompetent, but because they think *they're* incompetent. They want to degrade you so they won't feel inferior to you.

When you don't believe in yourself, you exhibit an insecurity that makes people not trust you. You aren't convinced of what you're capable of, so you can't convince others. You're your best advertiser. To make people believe in you, you need to trust yourself.

When you don't believe in yourself, you convey it through your words, appearance, and actions. A cloud of negativity surrounds you. You don't show any zest or motivation. On the other hand, when you believe in yourself, you convey security and self-assurance. You spread enthusiasm and excitement. You influence people with your positive attitude. As a result, you gain respect and assurance. People feel your self-confidence and believe in you.

The more you try to make people believe in you, the less they will. If they feel that you care about their approval, they'll withhold it from you, so don't beg for their belief and don't feel dismayed by the lack it. Don't try to prove to others that you're entitled to their approval. Don't waste your time and energy trying to convince them you're right. The more you seek their confidence, the more frustrated you'll feel. If you feel the need to prove that you're capable, it means you don't believe you're capable. You're trying to prove to others because you want prove it to yourself.

You don't need other people's belief to reach your dreams. Although it's good to have the approval of others, you won't fail if they don't believe in you. Even if the whole world doesn't believe in you, you can still succeed if you believe in yourself.

When you think people don't believe in you, you feel like a victim and use that as an excuse for not realizing your dreams. You hold them accountable for your poor performance and failures. If you blame others for your failures, you'll continue feeling powerless and dependent. You'll always look for motivation in the wrong places.

If you failed, it wasn't because other people didn't believe in you, but because you didn't believe in yourself. You failed because you were looking for power in the wrong place. Instead of trusting yourself, you waited for someone else's trust. Your future isn't in other people's hands. You don't need other people to believe in you in order to thrive. If other people don't motivate you, you need to motivate yourself.

When you don't believe in yourself, you become dependent. You assume that you're incapable of facing life on your own and that you need other people's counsel, support, and help to get by. You live off them in order to feel secure. However, other people can't make you win if you don't believe in yourself. They can't go to your office and do your work for you or go to school and study for you. They can't transfer their strength to you.

Dependence is the consequence of feeling inferior

Being dependent causes you to feel inferior. You assume that other people are more capable and stronger than you. You look up to them as if they were better than you. You think they can survive by themselves, but you can't. They can take care of themselves and still help you. You feel ashamed and embarrassed, and you think you don't deserve their love and respect.

Thinking that people are more capable makes you jealous. You think you can't do what they do. As a result, you can't celebrate their success. Their victories intensify your feeling of inadequacy and cause you to think they're better than you.

When you believe in yourself, you don't feel humiliated by other people's victories and you don't compare yourself to them. They are what they are, and you are what you are. They're good at something, and you're good at something else.

You need to see people's success in a positive way. If they can win, so can you. You're as good and as smart as they are. Instead of being jealous, learn with them. Discover what's behind their success. Ask what they did to reach their goals. People like to share their formula for success. If you ask them, it's likely that they'll tell you. Then copy their methods.

Being dependent makes you feel like a burden. You think you have nothing to give. You assume that other people are better off without you. As a result, you fear losing them. You need to value what you are. You have what it takes to fulfill someone. Don't take yourself for granted. There are many things you are doing for people that you may not realize.

If you're dependent, you look at every relationship as an opportunity to receive. You think about what people can do for you instead of what you can do for them. You have a one-way relationship with them in which you expect everything while you're not giving anything. You live like a parasite, sucking away their strength and vitality.

It is incredible how much you increase your self-respect when you shift from being a receiver to being a giver. You feel capable and strong when you realize that you can make a difference in people's lives. You're amazed at your own talents and abilities.

Look for opportunities to serve. Be willing to help in any way. Offer your support and feel the satisfaction that comes from giving. Surprise people by doing unasked favors. Don't complain when people ask your help. Don't claim that they're asking too much or that they're preventing you from doing other things. Either say no or do the favor with contentment.

Always do more than you're asked to do. If your husband asks you to cook, not only cook, but also serve it to him. If your wife asks you to put the trash away, not only put the trash away, but sweep the house. Do more and better than your boss asks you to do. Surpass their expectations and go the extra mile.

Give your time

When you're dependent, you think that helping people is a waste of time. Just being with another person and listening to them makes you feel used. You think you aren't profiting from spending time with them. You don't like to talk or play with your children because you have a lot of work to do. You don't want to listen to your wife when you get home because you're tired and you need to make your schedule for the next day. You don't want to call your parents because they talk too much and you have more important things to do.

Learn to spend time with people without feeling sorry for yourself. Feel the pleasure of giving time. Schedule some time with your family. Give at least fifteen minutes of undivided attention to your spouse every day. Play with your children or read a story to them before they go to sleep.

Set aside a day of the week to be with your family and totally forget about work. Go to a park and have a good time. Be willing to make your spouse and children happy. Do everything possible to make them feel that you're absolutely theirs and they're the most important thing in your life.

Set aside a time during the week to be with your spouse. Ask a relative or a friend to be with your children so you can be alone with them, but don't make them feel as if you're doing it out of great sacrifice.

Quality time is vital in every relationship. Children feel valued when their parents spend time with them. They have a higher chance of having happy marriages, of being successful in their careers, and of not having psychological problems.

Time spent with family is an investment. You may think that in order to be successful, you need to dedicate all your time to your career, but if you neglect your loved ones, you'll end up losing instead of winning.

Be willing to be flexible. Things won't always go as planned, so be prepared for unexpected events and accept them when they come. Don't be rigid with your schedule. Learn to accept interruptions without being upset. You'll always have things to do, and you'll never feel as if all your work is done.

People are more important than things. They're the reason for everything we do. They're the end and not the means. Therefore, they're above our work and activities. We work for them and live to serve them.

In the parable of the Good Samaritan, Jesus talked about a priest who was going to a worship service in the temple and didn't want to stop and help a man who'd been assaulted and almost stabbed to death. The priest valued the service in the temple more than the man. After the priest, a Samaritan passed by, saw the wounded man, and stopped to help him. The Good Samaritan had a very different perspective. He took pleasure in helping the man. He placed the man above his endeavors.

Don't Feel Sorry for Giving

Dependent people have a hard time giving. While they're prone to receiving, they dislike giving. They think about how many things they could buy with their money. You need to learn to let it go. Give your money without feeling sorry for yourself.

Although you may feel that if you give your money, you're losing or becoming poorer, it's the opposite. Generous people are usually wealthy. They aren't dependent upon others, so they trust in their ability to make ends meet and still help others. The more they have, the more they give.

Believe that you're capable of helping yourself and still meeting other people's needs. Being financially dependent will make you feel incompetent and inferior. Being a giver, on the contrary, will make you feel capable and competent. Give to your parents, your children, and your spouse with pleasure. Don't make them feel that they're a burden to you. Don't show discontentment when you help them.

Allow yourself to be used

People tend to keep track of what they give and what they receive. If they realize that they're giving more than they're receiving, they feel used and resentful. They either stop giving or they give with a feeling of bitterness.

If you're a true giver, you won't resent giving. You won't keep track of how much you give and how much you receive. You won't feel used, because you'll be happy when you give.

If you tend to keep track of how much you give versus how much you receive, you may end up sabotaging the results in your favor. You might take the little things you receive for granted and exaggerate what you give, when it's the other way around. If you resent giving, you're not a true giver. You may give *things*, but you don't give your heart. The giving is real when it's given with happiness.

Maybe someone is taking advantage of you, but if you resent that person, you lose your right. If you give from the heart, you'll feel pleasure in giving, even when you realize the person is using you.

In some cases, if you continually give to someone who takes advantage of you, you nurture the person's selfishness. You might have to stop giving to that person so you can help them become more independent and self-confident. However, it shouldn't be a form of revenge. In any case, never withhold your love. Don't feel victimized by someone who tries to take advantage of you. You're never the victim if you value yourself. Try to understand the other person's emotions, knowing that they try to take advantage of you because they feel incompetent.

Be grateful for what you receive

When you're dependent, you take what people do for granted. You expect too much from them, so you don't value what they do for you. You demand that they do more and you complain that they aren't doing enough. To value what people do, make a list of everything they do, even the small favors. Sometimes you complain about things that you should be grateful for. Thanking and complementing are never too much.

Don't ask too much

When you feel incapable, you have a tendency to ask people's help for things you could do yourself and burden other people unnecessarily. You overwhelm them with your dependence and deplete their energy needlessly.

Joseph and Sharon were a couple who decided to remodel their home's bathroom on their own to save money. They worked together with their son and daughter and did a beautiful job. Besides saving money, they also helped their kids develop self-confidence.

There are occasions when it's better to delegate certain tasks so you have more time to pursue your dreams, but you need to avoid asking other people to do things simply because you feel unable to do them. Only ask for help when you find something that you absolutely don't know how to do or don't have time to do. Don't exaggerate your weaknesses. Take opportunities to develop your self-confidence. If you can do it on your own instead of asking, you'll increase your faith in yourself and feel more capable.

When you help someone, you're helping yourself

The best way to get people's help is by helping them. The more you give, the more you receive. When people realize how generous and giving you are they'll want to be generous with you, as well. If you're selfish and want to receive all the time, they may resent you and withhold their giving to prevent you from using them.

When you give, forget about receiving. Give solely for the pleasure of giving. If you give in order to receive, you're giving to yourself. You can tell if you're being selfish by noticing how you react when people don't give back. If you get resentful, it means your giving isn't genuine. Your frustration shows that your primary interest in giving isn't the other person, but yourself. Never regret giving, and don't complain when people don't match your giving.

Think about the other person

When you're dependent, you think that people are strong and capable and don't need your aid. You assume they're superhuman. You believe they can do everything for themselves and still help you. You don't see them as human beings. You don't realize that they have their limitations. You don't recognize that you have something to contribute. You unconsciously want to think that they're strong and independent so you can lean on them.

The ideal relationship is the one in which both people give and receive. When one person does all the giving while the other only receives, the relationship becomes unilateral. Instead of being a relationship, it's a charity. The person who does all the giving feels abandoned and feels as if they don't have a partner.

Expecting the other person to give you everything while you don't give anything back is childish. The parent-child relationship is one-way. Children can't work, cook, or make adult decisions. They can't protect their parents. However, the adult relationship is based on reciprocity. Both people are committed to support and help each other, and both have responsibilities and duties.

In a marriage, if one of the partners sees themselves as dependent on the other and incapable of giving, they're putting themselves in the position of a child and not a spouse. They don't want a spouse, they want a parent. The result is frustration from the spouse, who doesn't have their needs met. Instead, they have a child to contend with.

You have a responsibility to fulfill your spouse's needs. So stop thinking that you're incapable and incompetent and realize that you have something wonderful to contribute. Take responsibility for your role in the relationship.

5.
Have Faith in People

Faith is a universal feeling. When you believe, you don't believe in only one person. You believe in the whole world. You expect the best of everyone. You consider every person capable and smart. You think that everyone can be a winner.

You believe in people because you believe in yourself. You think they can win because you think you can win. However, when you don't believe in yourself, you also don't believe in other people. You expect them to perform poorly and doubt them because you doubt yourself.

Some people don't look great on the outside. Some are too short, too fat, or too timid, and others don't exhibit any self-confidence. Many people who have talents and potential don't exhibit an inspiring exterior. However, there are many people who became great achievers despite an unpromising exterior.

When you believe in other people, you ignore their appearance and look to the inside. You believe in what you can't see. Your faith isn't based on the exterior. You know that behind a gloomy exterior can be something wonderful that you can't see. You believe, because you have faith.

To believe in others is to have faith in them, even when they don't believe in themselves. There are talented people who don't see themselves that way, and they exude an aura of unworthiness as a result of their own self-imposed limitations.

When you believe in others, you see what they don't see in themselves. You don't agree with their negative self-image. You have faith in them, even if they don't have faith in themselves. You know that they're better than they think they are.

When you see someone who doesn't trust in themselves, you have two options. You can either agree or disagree. You can step on them and make them feel even more unworthy or you can lend a hand and make them feel valuable.

When you realize that someone doesn't believe in themselves, the natural tendency is to put them down, humiliate them, and make them feel worse than they felt to begin with. However, when you agree with that person's self-imposed limitation, you're reinforcing their negative self-image. You aren't helping them rise above their feeling of unworthiness.

When you see someone who doesn't believe in themselves, you need to disagree with them. Cheer them up and raise their self-esteem. Tell them they're better than they think they are and treat them with respect, even if they think they don't deserve it.

Avoid labeling

Labeling people is to make presumptions. You meet someone and they say or do something that causes you to have a negative impression. From then on, everything they do or say seems to confirm the negative image you've created in your mind.

To believe in someone, avoid making negative presumptions about them, avoid thinking bad about them, based on a few mistakes they've made, and be open to really knowing them. When you label someone, you hinder your ability to know them. There's a universe inside of that person that you can't touch if you've already made up your mind about them. You can't know an individual if you're judgmental.

Don't be prejudiced

Sometimes we're prejudiced and we don't know it. Women think men are disorganized. Men think women are too detail-oriented. Some members of a religion think that members of other religions are evil. People who believe in God may consider atheists evil. Atheists may think that religious people are blunt and have limited thinking. Some people think all politicians are corrupt. The list of discrimination is endless.

We develop prejudice in our childhood and it becomes so ingrained in our minds that we don't realize it anymore. For example, a woman whose father betrayed her mother may develop a tendency of thinking that every man is disloyal. When she gets married, she expects that her husband will do the same. Whenever he gets home late, she asks if he was with another woman. She complains whenever he talks to a woman. She can't see the truth because she's prejudiced.

Bigotry prevents us from seeing other people as they are. Because we have a negative image of them, we close our mind to the facts. We have a mental picture of someone and we try to fit them into that picture.

To believe in other people, we need to remove all the prejudices we've formed since childhood. We need to open our hearts to everyone. We must expect the best from them and have faith, regardless of race, status, gender, knowledge, or career.

Faith is the power to change others

When you believe in other people, you have the power to change them. People respond to what you think of them. If you think positively, you attract the best from them. They become what you expect of them.

Faith is like a magnet. It's the power that unleashes people's talent and potential. Twenty years ago, I walked into the office of psychiatrist Cesar Vasconcelos in Rio de Janeiro as a defeated person, believing that I had a health problem that prevented me from living a normal life. For 1½ years, I had quit my studies to take care of my health, and I had spent the previous four months on a farm to rest and to regain my strength. I was suffering from a self-imposed negative image that was preventing me from living at my full potential. After the second visit to Dr. Vasconcelos, I left his office with the strength to pursue my dreams. His faith in me had caused me to believe in myself.

You don't need to be a psychiatrist to unleash other people's power. All around you are people who can be touched by your faith. You can believe in your spouse, your children, or your parents and make them feel better about themselves. You can use words of appreciation and encouragement that will cause them to believe in themselves and to pursue their dreams.

In your work environment, there are people who need your motivation. Your faith in them may cause them to thrive and reach their goals. They'll become better employees if you make them feel good about themselves. You can tell them how great they are. You can inspire them with words of faith. Your belief in them will be like a magnet that will attract the talent and potential that they have inside.

Step Seven
Overcoming the Victim Mentality

1.
The Victim Mentality

When you don't love yourself, you try to substitute love for pity. You think that by pitying yourself, you'll feel better. As a result, every time something bad happens, you comfort yourself by feeling like a victim.

You say to yourself, "Poor me, why did something so bad happen to me?"

When you value yourself, you don't pity yourself or feel like a victim. You face your problems with dignity. Your love is like a shield that protects you from degrading yourself. You value yourself unconditionally.

The victim mentality doesn't cure an inferiority complex. It only denounces that you feel inferior. When you pity yourself, you aren't feeling good about yourself, but you're ashamed of yourself. Pity is an artificial answer to your lack of self-love. You deceive yourself by pitying yourself. The only real solution for your problems lies in loving yourself unconditionally.

By victimizing yourself, you suffer twice as much. You suffer for the problem and you suffer from not valuing yourself. You suffer even more from not valuing yourself than from the problem itself.

If you really want to value yourself, stop feeling sorry for yourself. Even amid adversities, keep a positive attitude and think that nothing can make you inferior. You have a choice between pitying yourself or keeping your self-respect. Changing your situation won't make you value yourself. Even if things are perfect, you'll still degrade yourself unless you learn to love yourself unconditionally. It isn't the hardships that cause you to put yourself down, but how you respond to them. The major problem you face isn't on the outside, but inside. It isn't what happens to you, but what you make of what happens to you. How you look at your problems will determine if you humiliate yourself or maintain your sense of dignity.

When you don't value yourself during the difficult times, you won't value people when they endure hardships. You'll see them as you see yourself. If you can't love yourself because of your problems, you can't love them, either. You won't give people the support they need when troubles come their way.

To become a good supporter of those who are suffering, love yourself during hard times and believe that you deserve unconditional love. Don't feel rejected by your friends and family, and see everyone as your friends.

If you don't love yourself when you have problems, you also think that other people don't love you. You believe that they see you as you see yourself, and you assume that because you don't accept yourself, they don't accept you, either. As a result, you end up suffering more. You suffer because of the hardship you're facing and because you think that other people don't like you. You feel rejection coming from everywhere. You feel your own rejection and you feel other people's rejection.

If there's ever a time when you need to believe that people love and support you, it's when you're facing a hardship. You must believe that they're interested in your well being and that they want you to be happy. The certainty of other people's support will give you the strength to endure your problems because you won't feel alone and abandoned.

People become what you expect of them. If you think they're against you and don't care about you, guess what happens? If you believe that people reject you because of your problems, you'll cause that to happen.

You treat others according to your expectations. If you think they don't love you, you treat them badly. You become detached, sullen, and sour, and you mistreat them. Your body language conveys your distrust and resentment. There's a wall between you and other people that prevents you from loving them.

Consequently, when the chips are down, when you crave love the most, you reject your loved ones. When you most need people's support, you drive them out. Then you think they're abandoning you because of your problems. However, you're creating everything in your mind and are making things happen the way you expect them to.

Have faith in other people's desire to support you. When you believe they want to help you, they come to you. They give their love because they feel that you're open to their friendship.

Give and you shall receive

When you victimize yourself, you want people to treat you in a special way. You assume they have to give you special treatment because you're facing problems. You become demanding and controlling. You manipulate others in order to get the attention you crave.

That demanding and controlling attitude usually brings the opposite. The more you crave love and support, the less you receive. People don't respond well to demanding. When they're forced to love and support you, they lose their motivation. The best way to get their support is not to demand it.

When you victimize yourself, you have a selfish attitude. Your focus is on you. You don't think about supporting others. You just want them to support you. That attitude of expectancy doesn't help you be loved by people. Because you demand love, that love is denied to you.

If you want other people's support when you're undergoing hardships, change the direction of your thoughts. Instead of thinking about receiving, think about giving. Don't focus on your own problems and difficulties. Think about other people's needs and interests. Become people-oriented instead of self-oriented. When you pity yourself, you're self-oriented. You expect people to always support and care about you. However, if you want to get people's help, you need to be people-oriented.

Don't think about what people should be doing for you. Don't resent their lack of support. Don't complain that they're not treating you the way they should. Start doing unto them as you expect them to do unto you. Help them as you expect them to help you.

There's a catch in a people-oriented attitude. If you do things for people because you expect them to help you, you'll end up not getting their support. People will catch on to your selfishness and may not support you. You need to be absolutely centered on other people and to renounce yourself entirely.

Many people complain that they do much for others who ignore them. They resent that they're good to people who don't give back. The problem is that they're directing everything toward themselves. They're giving so they can receive. In reality, they aren't giving to people. They're giving to themselves.

If you want other people to give to you, give to them. Give and it shall be given to you. If you want other people to support you in difficult times, support them during their troubles. If you need people's love and care, start loving and caring. Give them attention, send them a card, and speak words of appreciation. Let them know how important they are to you. Tell them how proud and happy you are to have them in your life. You'll be surprised how much love and support will pour into your life when you give yourself to others without expecting a return.

Don't use your problems to be loved

If you pity yourself when you're facing difficulties, you'll also want other people to pity you. You'll expect them to give you a lot of attention and support. However, real love doesn't pity. When people pity you, they cause you to feel inferior and weak. They drain the strength you need to get better. They cause you to become comfortable with your present situation.

When I was twenty years old, I looked to a psychiatrist to help me get over my depression. As I used to do with every person I encountered, I wanted him to pity me. However, he told me that I didn't have any problems at all and that I should stop taking sleep medication. Instead of pitying me, he showed me that there was no reason to be pitied. He helped me realize that my victim mentality wasn't getting me anywhere. His attitude helped me break free of my inferiority complex and become a winner.

People who really love you won't pity you, they won't see you as a victim, and they won't give you exaggerated attention when you have problems. They'll deal with you as they normally do, because they want you to be strong. They won't think you're inferior because you're facing problems.

If you don't love yourself, you resort to your problems to be loved by others. You try to find some ordeal that will draw other people's attention, cause them to support you, and make them worry about you. You want to make up for your lack of self-esteem. You think you don't deserve to be loved as you are. You assume that if you have a problem, people will care about you.

You say, "See how I am suffering, I need your love" or "If you can't love me, just pity me as I am suffering so much."

You become addicted to problems because you think there's an advantage in being a victim. You think you'll realize your dream of being loved and respected and will make up for the emptiness of your heart.

If you use your problems to attract people's love, you may become a masochist. Unconsciously, you'll want to have problems so people give you their support. When they ask you, "How are you?" you'll ramble on and on about your problems so they'll pity you.

However, you don't need hardships to be loved. You have qualities and virtues that other people like. You're unique and special. Being pitied won't fill your emptiness. People who act like victims to attract other people's attention are never satisfied.

Susan was a problem addict. When people asked her how she was, she always had a long list of problems. Things were never okay. She had personal problems, her children were always in trouble, and her grandchildren were always suffering and needing help.

On one occasion, Susan hurt her spine while working in a nursing home. She didn't get her insurance benefits and had to file a suit against the nursing home. She got paid while training for another job, but she never completed the training.

About six months later, Susan was taking care of an old couple for a living when she didn't get paid according to the agreement. She was dismissed from the job and sued by the daughter of the couple. Susan had various problems because she unconsciously liked being in trouble. She thought that by having problems she could receive the love she expected. She was always negative when people asked how she was. She could give them a list of reasons to pity her.

A person who feels like a victim unconsciously seeks problems so that they can attract other people's interest. If they don't have a real problem, they make one up. Sometimes in their craving for attention, they even cause their own problems.

In one of my seminars, a man talked to me about a problem he was facing with his wife, who wanted to divorce him. He told me that he had resorted to drinking as a way of escaping the problem. I asked if he was drinking in order to get his wife's attention, and he said yes. He wanted her to pity him and think that if she abandoned him, he'd destroy his life.

Some people go to extraordinary lengths to attract other people's attention. They starve themselves, use drugs, cut themselves, and even try to commit suicide. They want to draw someone's love so badly that they're willing to destroy themselves if necessary to get the love they're looking for. They don't understand that they won't satisfy their emptiness by being pitied by others.

If you use your problems to get someone's love, you'll never be happy. You can't be happy while you pity yourself. Even if you get other people's attention and they pity you, you won't be happy while you maintain an inferiority complex.

It's a mistake to think that your happiness will be attained when people pity you. Your happiness will come when you rise above your victim mentality. You'll be happy when you see yourself as a winner, believe that you're special, and that you deserve to be loved without having to resort to any kind of problem. You may not have everyone's attention, but you'll be happy because you accept yourself unconditionally.

The need to be superior

The victim mentality also comes from a necessity of being superior. When you feel inferior, you believe that you don't have any qualities, virtues, or advantages that others might value in you. You feel that you're a bundle of flaws, mistakes, and imperfections and that there's no hope of ever being respected and appreciated by others.

You assume that the only way to be superior is through your problems. You believe that your tribulations will attract people's admiration. If you have problems that no one else has, you have an ordeal that puts you in a privileged place. Your hardships and difficulties entitle you to be treated a unique way. You're superior, not because you're the best, but because you're the worst. You deserve special treatment because you're the most troubled and unluckiest person of the world.

Trying to amaze people with your ordeals causes you to feel even more defeated and ashamed. Even if they give you the attention you crave, deep inside your heart, you think you're nothing.

The only way out of your inferiority complex is by valuing yourself. Develop a healthy self-image and see yourself as a winner. You're lucky, you're blessed, and you have every reason to be thankful.

Acting like a victim so you can get special treatment isn't worthwhile. It's better to be ignored and be well than to be praised by being miserable. There's no advantage to being a masochist. Acting like a victim will only intensify your feeling of rejection. It will cause you to think that the only way you can be loved is to suffer. You'll think that people only give you attention because you're facing adversity and therefore don't love you at all.

If people love you, they love you in any situation. However, if people don't love you when you're well, they won't love you when you have hardships, either. It's a mistake to think that you'll get other people's love as a result of your suffering. Your problem won't change their attitude toward you.

Shane was sad because his girlfriend dumped him, so he thought about what he could do to get her back. He assumed that if he tried to kill himself, she'd pity him and would come back. However, it didn't go as planned. Although she felt sorry for him, it didn't change the way she felt about him.

You don't need to impress people to get their love. You don't have to be in a miserable condition to be cared for. You just need to believe that they love you. You waste time and energy trying to get people's pity so they'll respect you. If you open your eyes, you're going to realize that people love you as you are. You don't need to play the martyr to get their affection, since their affection is already there for you to enjoy. You just need to trust that they love you and be happy.

When you act like a victim, you become controlling and manipulative. You think that people are obligated to give you support and attention because of your suffering. Unconsciously, you use your ordeals to get their love and to force them to do what you want. You imply that your problems are their fault and that if they had acted differently, you wouldn't be in that situation.

Hurting yourself to get people's love is an indication that you don't love yourself. While you look for people's affection, you don't care for yourself. To seek other people's love while you hurt yourself doesn't make sense.

Love is a gift. When people love you, they don't need you to force them to support you. They do it naturally. If you use your problems to get people's love, they'll feel trapped. They'll resent that you're using your hardship to get their attention. Even if they give you the attention you're looking for, they may not do it of their own free will. They'll do what you want out of fear and guilt.

If you don't love yourself because of the problems you have, it's awful to be around yourself. All the love people give you isn't enough to outweigh the love you *don't* have for yourself. The love you most need in times of trouble is *your own* love. Wherever you go, there you are.

Imagine that you got sick and had to stay in the hospital. If you didn't love yourself unconditionally, you'd probably be depressed and would mourn over your disease. Now imagine a close friend comes to visit you. She shows you compassion and offers words of encouragement. She stays for an hour and then goes home. Suddenly, you're on your own again and start moping.

You think, "I'll never be healthy again. I'll never live a normal life. My life doesn't make sense anymore."

You realize that getting someone's love and attention for one hour isn't enough to help you if you're moping the rest of the time.

When you complain about your problems, you cause your loved ones unnecessary pain. They become concerned about your well being and it makes them suffer because they love you. When people ask how you are, don't give them a lot of reasons why they should be concerned about you. Let people know that you're well and that they don't need to worry about you. It's a gift for your loved ones when you don't play the role of a victim. When you assume a victor's attitude, you bring joy to everyone around you.

When you act like a victim, you're trying to be loved while you don't love. You want people to worry about you, though you aren't worried about how they feel. If you really love other people, you won't make them worry about you, you won't be a burden to them, and you won't bring them unnecessary stress and sorrow.

People don't love you because they don't love themselves

Don't take it personally if people don't give you the support you need in times of trouble. Don't think that they don't give you attention because you're inferior. If people don't give you the support you need, it's because they don't love themselves. Although you think the reason they don't care about you is because they don't like you, it's really because they don't like *themselves*. People can't give you something they don't have. It's not your problem, it's theirs.

You may think that you're at a disadvantage when people don't support you. It's human nature to think that you're losing while others are winning. Although they might look better than you on the outside, on the inside, they're not. They're suffering more than you because they don't love themselves, and if they're worse off than you, they're at a disadvantage. Remember, the worst thing that can happen to anyone is not loving themselves.

The problem isn't that people don't give you support, but the way you react to their lack of support. If you put yourself down and mourn that no one cares about you, you're causing your own suffering. You bring unnecessary pain by taking their unwillingness to help you personally. Although you don't have the power to change other people's attitude toward you, you have the power to control how you react. You can choose between taking people's lack of support personally or not.

When you take what people do to you personally, you become selfish. Instead of trying to understand their feelings, you think about how unfairly they treat you. Instead of comprehending what's behind their actions, you feel like a victim.

Acting like a victim expels people from you. When you complain, you create a gloomy environment. Your presence doesn't radiate contentment. Being around you is depressive, so you become unattractive. If you really want to draw people to you, stop complaining and start talking about all the good things that happen in your life. Be thankful for everything that occurred to you and see the bright side of every problem.

Having a victim mentality is contagious

When you have a victim mentality, you influence people negatively, and your complaining causes them to see things in the same pessimistic way. Instead of being an inspiration, you become a negative force.

It's interesting to observe the immediate influence of pessimistic people over others. For example, when you're in a long line at the bank and someone starts complaining, most other people do the same. They start criticizing the clerks, the manager, and the bank. The same thing happens when someone complains about the government. Suddenly, there's lots of negative talk about politicians, social conditions, the lack of health benefits, and so on. Complainers influence everyone with their negative attitude.

You're responsible for the influence you have on others. If you act like a victim, you cause other people to be like you and you spread your negativity to those who surround you. You need to be especially careful if you have children. If you're always talking about your problems, you'll cause people to see life in a bleak way. On the other hand, if you're always speaking about the good things that have happened to you, you'll cause people to look at life in a positive way. A winner never wins alone, while a loser never loses alone. If you choose to be a winner, you'll bring other people with you. However, if you choose to be on the losing side, you'll take other people down with you.

Being negative attracts negative people

Positive people don't like to be with those who have a negative frame of mind. They abhor negative talk and don't like to hear complaints. If you're a negative person, you'll drive away positive people and you'll be surrounded by losers.

The problem with attracting negative people is that they won't help you overcome your negative attitude. Instead of helping you become a happier person, they'll increase your distress and sorrow. When you're positive, however, you attract people who become an inspiration to you, and who will help you see opportunities everywhere. They'll become a source of motivation.

Don't compare yourself to others

When you feel like a victim, you have a tendency to compare yourself to others. You think they don't have problems and that you're the only one who's suffering. They're good and you're bad, they're happy and you're sad, they're winners and you're a loser. You judge people by their external appearance. You can't see their struggles, so you assume they're feeling great.

The problem of thinking that everybody is doing well is that you can't feel compassion. You think that people don't need your help and support. You assume that they're able to solve their problems and can take care of themselves, but you need to realize that everyone is vulnerable and undergoes difficulties and hardships. They're just like you and have problems that sometimes make them feel overwhelmed and hopeless.

Assuming that people have no problems comes from your desire for their aid. Unconsciously, you don't want to see their humanity, because it would prevent you from getting their support. A victim mentality induces selfishness because you want help, but you don't want to help.

When you realize that everyone is human, you become more compassionate and supportive. You understand that people need you just as much as you need them. You become more aware of their needs and you comprehend that you aren't in this world for the sole purpose of receiving, but for giving, as well.

Problems don't choose people. There aren't any entities whose sole purpose in life is to make a certain person suffer. Problems can occur to anybody, no matter how famous, rich, healthy, or beautiful they are. Everyone is susceptible to losing a loved one, to sickness, to accidents, and to death. Therefore, if you're facing difficulty, don't start thinking that you're suffering because you're inferior. It's just your fate. It could have happened to anyone, but it happened to be you.

Everyone deserves good health, prosperity, love, respect, and happiness. We don't always get what we deserve. Some people get the short end of the stick, and if it happens to you, it's not because of God wants you to suffer—it's just chance.

If you think other people don't suffer, you think they're superior to you. You become jealous. You can't celebrate their successes and victories because you think their victories cause you to be inferior. You start competing to show that you're better than they are. Every time something good happens to you, you use it as a way to demonstrate your importance. You may even feel gleeful when something goes wrong in their lives because it gives you a chance to rub it in their faces.

The fact that a person is doing better than you doesn't make that person superior to you. You aren't superior when you're in a better condition than the others, and you aren't inferior when you're in a worse condition.

2.
Be Optimistic

To overcome your victim mentality, you need to be optimistic. An optimistic person is one who chooses to see the good side of every situation. When you're optimistic, you're a believer. You see a bright future and always expect things to go well.

When you have a victim mentality, however, you're pessimistic. You always expect the worst. You have a tendency to think that something bad is going to happen. If you're married, you dread getting divorced. If you're employed, you fear losing your job. If you're healthy, you dread getting sick.

The reason you expect something bad is going to happen is because you think you're inferior. You think that blessings are only for those who are valuable, and that good things happen to other people because they're superior. You think you can't be blessed because you don't deserve it.

Things happen to you according to your expectation. If you're pessimistic, you'll attract problems. If you want to be blessed, expect blessings. Think that you're special, valuable, and deserve to be well. By having a positive frame of mind, you'll miraculously attract many opportunities to you. You'll be a magnet that will draw good things.

Focus on what's good

When you have a victim mentality, you focus on what's bad. Although you may be surrounded by blessings, you overlook them and concentrate on the evil. Sometimes, your blessings outnumber your problems ten-to-one, but you forget all the good things and think about that one problem.

To overcome a victim mentality, focus on good things. Don't take your blessings for granted. Recognize all of them and be thankful. Think about the blessings more than the problems, because you have more blessings than problems.

I'm not saying you should pretend that nothing bad is occurring when you have a real problem. You don't need to live in denial in order to be happy. But you must recognize that there's much more good than evil in your life. You have more reasons to be thankful than to complain. Don't allow your problems to blind you to your blessings. Value the good things and be thankful for them.

When I bought my first home, I was happy and anxious to move in. I was excited about owning a home and not having to pay rent anymore. However, something happened that blurred my happiness. One day, I went there with my daughter to drop off some things. My daughter noticed a cable dangling in the garage, and she had to jump and pull it. As a result, the garage didn't close automatically. I put two fingers in a crack in the door and pulled it down with all my strength. The crack closed in on my fingers and I could hear a splintering. The pain was excruciating. I knew I'd broken my finger, and the next day I went to the hospital to confirm what had happened.

For a while, the fact that I'd broken my finger took away the joy I had about buying the house. I'm a pianist, so it caused a lot of trouble. I had to wear a cast for more than a month. I still played without that finger, but it was a limitation. After it had healed, I realized that my finger wasn't as agile as before. I was limited in my movements.

However, when I played, I noticed that not folding my finger completely didn't prevent me from having the technique and dexterity I once had. Actually, with practice and effort, I could play even better than before.

Although the event was painful, I realized how much I had taken my fingers for granted. Being able to play the piano is a privilege! I know a pianist who lost one of his fingers in an accident, but he still plays. I can understand how he feels about not being able to do all the things he could do before. After breaking my finger, I became more appreciative of the privilege I have to play the piano with all my fingers.

You probably have many good things in your own life that you overlook. You may be taking many blessings for granted that you should be thankful for. A good way to value the blessings is to enumerate them. Set some time aside to write down a hundred blessings, even small ones. You'll realize how many good things you've taken for granted.

After you have completed your list, spend some time thinking about them. Recognize what a difference they make in your life. Be appreciative of their importance and be thankful for them. When you encounter people, talk about the good things. Share your blessings so that other people may be influenced by your optimism.

Give a positive meaning to every event of your life

When you're negative, you change the meaning of the events in your life for the worst. You think even the good things are bad. You start complaining when you should be thanking. If you have a negative attitude, you see problems everywhere. You see problems where they exist, but you also see problems where they don't exist. Everything seems to be blurred and bleak. The past is desolate and the future looks dark.

When you're positive, however, you see blessings and opportunities everywhere. You have many reasons to be happy and thankful. You recognize how many blessings you had in your past and you're confident about the future.

Your attitude affects the way you see your life. The meaning you give to events depends entirely on how positive you are. Everything seems bleak when you're negative, while everything seems good when you're positive.

When you're negative, you think that you need to change events so you can have a positive attitude. You think that you have lots of reasons to be desolate, since so many bad things have happened to you. However, you don't need to change anything but your own mind. If you change your attitude, everything will seem different. Although the conditions and situations are the same, you'll look at them in a positive way.

By giving a positive meaning to everything, you'll look at the same events in a completely different way. Things that seemed bad before will seem good. The same stuff you complained about in the past, you'll be thankful for. What appeared to be a problem will look like a blessing, and what seemed to be a misfortune will be an opportunity.

For example, you may think that you have a terrible job when many people would like to have that job. You may think your spouse is a lousy person, though everyone else thinks that they're great. You feel your children are immature and irresponsible, while your friends would like their kids to be like yours.

Things you considered bad will seem good if you have a positive attitude. If you have an optimistic mindset, you'll see the same situations and events you saw before, but in a positive way. Just by changing your attitude, you'll make your entire world look wonderful. Instead of being desolate and sad about your past, you'll be happy and grateful. Instead of being hopeless about the future, you'll be thrilled by how many opportunities and possibilities you have in front of you.

Stop complaining and be thankful

When you feel like a victim, you have a tendency to complain. As a result, everything is a motive to mourn and whine. You complain about the past and whine about the present. You complain about your job, your boss, your spouse, your children, your parents, your health, your fitness, and your car. You find reasons to complain everywhere, and if you don't have a reason to complain, you create one. You complain for the sake of complaining. You complain if people ask you how you are doing, and if they don't ask you, you complain, anyway. You complain because you want people to give you attention, to be worried about you, and because you want to feel loved.

The opposite of complaining is being thankful. To be thankful, you need to change your attitude of complaining. Be grateful for the same things you complain about. Realize that everything that happens to you is a reason to be thankful. Even the bad things that happen are reason to be grateful.

If you're a positive person, you'll realize that the bad experiences you've faced in your past brought a seed of a blessing. Even the problems you faced were a source of immeasurable lessons and experience. You'll also realize that by taking advantage of the troubles you've undergone in the past, you've become more mature, stronger, and better prepared for the future.

To be thankful is so powerful that it can change your present and your future for the better. You'll overcome depression by being thankful. You'll become happy, excited, and will face life with enthusiasm. You'll also transform your future by being grateful. Your ability to recognize the many blessings that come on your way will help you see the opportunities in front of you. Being thankful will help you become more prosperous and successful.

I want to invite you to taste the power of being thankful. Stop complaining and be grateful. Take a look at your list of blessings and start being thankful. Thank yourself for your hard work. Thank people for the difference they've made in your life. Be thankful for all the events that have happened to you. Thank God for his constant presence.

Be thankful even for the bad things. Thank yourself for your failures, since they made you be greater than you were. Thank the misfortunes and adversities you've faced that caused you to learn and grow. Thank the people who hurt you, since they helped you develop patience and forgiveness. By being thankful, you'll realize that every trouble you've ever faced was a blessing in disguise.

Don't dramatize

When you have a victim mentality, you distort things for the worst. A small problem seems like a catastrophe. Even a blessing may look like a terrible adversity. Then you think that problems will engulf and destroy you. To dramatize is to make a big deal out of something insignificant. When you dramatize, you exaggerate the size of your problems. You look at them as if they were monsters and you consider them to be insurmountable barriers.

Every time you exaggerate a hardship, you're limiting yourself. You see yourself as weak and incapable, while you make your ordeals seem formidable. You don't recognize how great and competent you are, so you overlook your abilities and advantages.

To be a positive person, change the way you see your problems and the way you see yourself. Realize that your problems aren't so big and you aren't so small. The problems aren't formidable and you aren't incapable. You aren't below your difficulties, but above them. You aren't lost or drifting. You have complete control over the situation.

You're bigger than your problems. You're competent and able to handle them. You won't be submerged and destroyed by your adversities. You'll endure them and you'll win. You'll be a victor because there's nothing impossible for you to face.

As you look at your past, you can see how many times you were wrong when you thought it was all over. You thought something was too big for you to handle and because of that, you became desperate. However, you were mistaken. You survived what seemed to be impossible and you climbed what looked to be an insurmountable mountain. You faced all those troubles and difficulties that you imagined you couldn't handle.

You exaggerated the problems you faced, while you took your ability to face them for granted. Stop exaggerating and look at your problems in a more positive and rational way. Instead of seeing the problems you face as tragedies, look at them as they are. In other words, reduce the size you give to your problems so you don't feel overwhelmed.

Recognize your abilities and strengths. You need not diminish or limit yourself. See yourself as a strong and competent individual. Believe that you're able to handle anything that comes your way. There's nothing too great or too hard for you to overcome. Nothing will be impossible if you believe in yourself.

Accept your problems

When you act like a victim, you have difficulty accepting your problems. When they occur, you become disappointed and frustrated.

You act as if you have to be perfect all the time and that problems are out of the question.

To face problems in a positive way, give yourself the right to have problems. Don't act as if everything has to be perfect all the time. It's impossible to live without facing adversity every now and then. You need to learn how to cope with difficulties so you don't become upset when you have them.

I'm not saying that you must conform to mediocrity. There's a difference between accepting problems and accepting yourself. You may accept yourself while you don't accept your problems. The fact that you love yourself when you're facing problems doesn't cause you to be comfortable with them. Although you love and accept yourself unconditionally, you do everything to get over your troubles.

Accepting problems isn't the same as surrendering to them. It doesn't mean that you don't deserve better, but that you accept yourself in any situation. You can value and love yourself even though you don't surrender to your problems.

It's interesting to observe that most of the time, people who don't accept themselves are the ones who conform to their adversities. Although they become upset and hate themselves for what happened to them, they stay in their present situation. Being angry doesn't help solve their problems.

People who are more capable of getting over difficult situations are the ones who are positive in the way they face their problems. They don't complain or mourn their fate, they don't accuse other people, and they don't grieve for a long time. As soon as something happens, they start thinking of ways to deal with the problem. As a result, they recover faster than those who pity themselves and don't accept their situation.

One reason you don't accept your problems is because you don't love yourself when you have them. Another reason is because of pride. When you're addicted to praise and approval, you may regret having problems because you think they prevent you from being praised. You think that hardships will cause people to have a negative impression of you and that they won't think you're important and special, as they once did.

Being humble helps you accept problems. You don't worry that a problem will cause people to reject you. You aren't dependent of their approval. You don't crave applause and prestige, because you aren't afraid of being belittled when you face difficulties.

3.
Take Responsibility

To see yourself as a victim is a way of not taking responsibility for what happens to you. You feel uncomfortable with your past mistakes, so you try to blame something or someone else. You don't want to face the fact that you made poor choices, because you feel guilty, and avoid the pain of confronting yourself by blaming other people or circumstances.

Brenda was one of my piano students. She always had an excuse for not practicing. She was sick, she had too much homework, she'd gone to Disneyland, or her grandmother had come to visit her. On summer vacation, she stopped all of her activities, including piano, so she could rest and have some fun. In other words, it wasn't her fault that she didn't study. She was a victim of circumstances. As she said, she liked playing piano, but she didn't study because she had too many things going on in her life. Consequently, she stayed on the same level for more than a year.

On the other hand, Margaret was always on top of her circumstances. She started studying with me at the same time as Brenda and at the same level. She never had an excuse not to practice. Like Brenda, she had school assignments, she traveled, she had relatives visit, but she always practiced. Every week, she had one or two songs ready. Even on vacation, she'd take lessons. She developed so fast that in only one year, she had advanced three levels.

The problem with Brenda is that she considered herself a victim. She didn't feel as if she had control of her life. She was at the mercy of every situation, while Margaret believed that she could do everything she wanted. She was above her circumstances and she owned her life.

When you have a victim mentality, you think you don't have control over your life. You feel powerless and impotent. You assume that everything or everyone else has power over you, so you don't own yourself. You feel incapable of realizing your dreams. You're at the mercy of the people and circumstances that surround you.

Although avoiding responsibility seems to get you out of pain, it actually brings more pain than happiness. On one hand, you feel incapable and incompetent. On the other hand, you don't make the decisions or take the actions to change your life. Instead of making your life the way you want it, you stay put and complain about your situation.

Recognize past mistakes

Recognize what you've done wrong that caused you to be where you are today, and then take responsibility for your past mistakes. Stop blaming other people or things for the present condition you created by the choices you made and the actions you took. Here are a few examples:

You ate fatty food.
You ate too much.
You didn't exercise.
You smoked.
You drank too much alcohol.
You used drugs.
You watched too much television.
You didn't use your time wisely.
You didn't study for a test.
You dropped out of school.
You didn't read.
You didn't meditate.
You didn't engage in long-lasting self-improvement.
You quit studying the piano.
You didn't have a list of goals.
You were in the company of bad people.
You allowed people to influence you.
You didn't say no.
You engaged in gossip.
You criticized people instead of praising them.
You were sarcastic.
You didn't give attention to your family.
You didn't have a monthly budget.
You borrowed money and didn't pay it back.

You were dishonest.

You didn't pay your bills on time.

Although you may think awareness will cause you suffering, it's quite the opposite. By recognizing your mistakes, you feel powerful. You realize that you aren't a robot, controlled by people or circumstances. You're always in charge. Even when you think you're in the hands of people and circumstances, you're still in absolute control. You choose to do what people want you to do. You let people and circumstance take control of your life. You aren't a victim, since you're the one who allows circumstances to influence you.

You're the creator of your destiny

It's an illusion to think that the results you get in your life are due to things outside of yourself. More than ninety percent of what happens to you is a result of your own decisions and actions. You're the creator of your destiny. What you are today is a direct consequence of previous choices you made.

When you're aware that you're the cause of your present situation, you realize that you're also the only one who can change it. You can make your life different by the choices you make and the actions you take today. You can create wonderful results when you decide to take control of your life.

To make your life the way you want it to be, start making good choices. Decide what you want to do and then go for it. Make a list of things you wish to accomplish and start doing them. Stop blaming someone or something else and take action. Your list of decisions could look something like this:

Read every day.

Meditate every day.

Make a list of goals.

Start counseling therapy.

Read self-help books.

Attend seminars.

Thank your family for the positive difference they make in your life.

Dedicate more time to your family.

Exercise every day.

Don't eat fast food.

Avoid eating too much sugar.

Eat healthy food.

Go back to school.

Develop your skills.

Get more knowledge about your profession.

Learn to play a musical instrument.

Do your best in every area of your life.

Be more respectful to your boss and your co-workers.

Treat your employees with dignity.

Be more organized.

Clean your garage.

Pay your bills on time.

Your list may be long, but it'll be worth the effort. It's a fundamental step in changing your life for the best. It'll create the results you want and make your future better than your present.

Cause and effect

According to the law of cause and effect, every action, good or bad, brings good or bad results. It's that simple. If you don't like the results you're reaping today, realize that the decisions you made and the actions you took in the past weren't good. You're the one who brought bad consequences into your life through bad decisions and actions. Here are some examples of cause and effect:

You drink and drive, and crash your car. You're prosecuted, and lose your driver's license.

You don't give quality time to your children, so they become obnoxious and misbehave.

You betray your spouse, end up divorced, and lose the company of your children.

You eat fatty food and have a heart attack or a stroke.

You don't update your knowledge in your profession, so either you aren't promoted or you get fired.

You don't study for the test, so you get an F.

You spend more money than you have and have to declare bankruptcy.

You mistreat people and end up alone.

You don't exercise, so you tire easily and don't have much energy.

You don't read self-help books and meditate, so you develop a negative attitude, you don't relate well with people, and you're stressed.

Look at the signs

You'll know if you've made bad choices by looking at what's happening in your life. Here's a list of signs that indicate whether you've made good or bad choices:

You're either fat or in good shape.

People either like to be with you or they avoid your presence.

You're either having a wonderful relationship with your spouse or you're not.

You're either loved or hated by your children.

You're either happy or sad.

You're either having fun or you're stressed.

You either have money or debt.

You're either satisfied with your job or you'd like to pursue another career.

Make your own list. Make a self-analysis. Look at the results you're experiencing and decide if there are things you need to change. If you find that you're taking the wrong path, make the necessary corrections. Don't keep doing the wrong thing over and over just so you can complain.

Stop blaming

One thing to do in order to take control of your life is to stop blaming circumstances. The problem with blaming is that you end up believing it's true. You convince yourself that you really can't do anything to change the situation and that you're a victim.

Here are some examples of avoiding responsibility by blaming something else:

1. You're late to your job and say that you were in a traffic jam when you could have left home half hour earlier to avoid traffic.

2. You say you didn't study for a test because you had to take your mother to the hospital, but you could have started studying a week earlier so that you only would have had to look at your notes the day before the test.

3. You say you did something wrong because everybody else was doing it, even though your mother told you not to be in the company of those people—but you didn't listen.

A list of alibis and excuses could be infinite. Realize that you're allowing things to shape your destiny by your own choice. You're being controlled by the circumstances instead of controlling them.

Ner was my mathematics teacher when I was in middle school. One day, when the class was taking a test, a girl asked him to postpone it because she hadn't had time to study. Ner told her that her lack of time wasn't an excuse for not studying. He told her that he'd been able to graduate from college while working full time. He'd had to study late at night to have good grades and to realize his dream of becoming a mathematics teacher. He'd never used his fulltime job as an excuse for not studying. That experience taught me never to use time as an excuse for not fulfilling my responsibilities.

When you have a victim mentality, you have a tendency of looking for a scapegoat for your problems and failures. You think that everything that goes wrong in your life is caused by someone else. Here are some examples of people or entities you might have been blaming for your present situation:

God: You make a bad choice and then say that the bad result was God's will. You think God wants you to suffer, when your suffering is caused by your own actions.

Parents: Blaming parents is a very common excuse for our lack of self-esteem and for all our past failures. We say that if our parents had loved us during our childhood, we'd be in a much better situation. We think that all our relationship problems are derived from our past relationship with our parents. We don't realize that our lives are in our own hands. True, our parents exert a tremendous influence on us, but we can change the course of our lives by the choices we make and the actions we take today. We can neutralize our parent's influence by reading books, meditating, and taking control of our lives. We aren't mere spectators of our fate. We're the creators of our own destinies. Our parents will be the creators of our future only if we decide to sit back and not do anything to change the path of our existence.

Spouses: Many people blame their spouses for their hardships. They blame their spouse for financial problems, for their children's misbehavior, or for their unhappiness.

Joseph was seventeen when he learned an important lesson about how to rise above relational problems and not to allow other people to shape his circumstances. He was in the second year of his theology course when he went to visit Sheila, his girlfriend, on the weekend. Although their relationship hadn't been good and they'd broken up once before, Joseph didn't know that something bad would happen that weekend. On Sunday morning, both his girlfriend and her mother started accusing him of many negative things. Apparently a young lady from his university who liked Joseph had invented some stories and told his girlfriend's mother, expecting her lies to make Joseph's girlfriend dump him. She was successful in her plot and Sheila broke up with Joseph that Sunday.

Joseph was devastated, and to worsen the situation, he had a test the next day. Although he tried to study, he couldn't pay attention. All he could think about were the horrible things he'd heard his girlfriend's mother say about him. He decided not to take the test and to explain to his teacher what had happened, hoping the teacher would give him another chance. However, Joseph's teacher didn't give him another chance, and told him that he had to learn not to allow people influence him to that point.

"When you graduate," said the teacher, "and you have a job, you'll have to go to work even if you had fight with you wife the night before. You'll have to do your best, even though you might be broken inside."

When you are used to blaming people for your mistakes, you do it so often that you aren't aware of it anymore. You may even deceive yourself into thinking that all your failures are caused by other people. If you want to be a winner, throw away all your excuses. Look in the mirror and face reality. You aren't a victim. You're the one giving other people permission to control you.

Don't give other people the power to make you unhappy. Don't allow them control of your life. People will influence you only to the extent that you agree to their influence.

You're never right when you feel victimized by others. You have a choice: make your own decisions or let others decide for you. You have to assume responsibility for your choices. If you give other people permission to influence you, you can't accuse them of having wronged you. They only did what you allowed them to do.

You're capable of changing your life. You're strong enough to take control of your own destiny. You're the captain of your ship, the one who gives the orders, so don't give anyone else power over your future.

The more you think of yourself as a victim, the more you resent other people. The more you blame them, the more you're upset with them. Don't accuse them for what's happened to you. Even if they hurt you, don't hold on to it. Remembering injustices and misdeeds only creates a wall between you and others. You can't be kind to people when you feel like their victim.

Don't blame yourself

What causes you to avoid taking responsibility for your actions is your tendency to blame yourself. You can't accept your mistakes, so you deny them. You make excuses so that you don't have to suffer the pain of confronting them.

To take responsibility for your mistakes, look at them—and still love yourself. Recognize your flaws, but accept yourself.

There's a difference between taking responsibility for your mistakes and condemning yourself. When you condemn yourself, you aren't valuing yourself the way you are. You think your mistakes cause you to be inferior. When you take responsibility for your mistakes, however, you value yourself, even though you recognize your mistakes. You don't have to despise yourself for having failed.

When you feel guilty, you don't believe in your ability to change the situation. You don't believe that you're capable of doing differently. When you take responsibility, however, you believe you can do a better job. You're capable of making the changes you need to. You can take the steps to make your life the way you want it to be.

Blaming yourself prevents you from thinking about what you could have done better. You don't want to recognize your mistakes because it causes you pain. As a result, you stay put in your mistakes and don't grow. You can't overcome your mistakes unless you recognize them. Living in denial doesn't help you to become a better person. If you want to change your life for the best, you need to confront yourself. Instead of blaming yourself, analyze your decisions and actions to see what you could have done differently. Think through the whole situation to find out what you could have done better.

People don't trust you when you don't take charge. They don't want to give you responsibilities because they think that you'll find an excuse for not fulfilling your tasks. To be trusted, you need to be on top of the circumstances. Instead of being led by circumstances, you need to lead and to take charge of your life.

When I was a chaplain, the hospital board had to find someone to fill an important position, and there were two candidates. One of them had a good education, but wasn't reliable. He gave excuses for not completing his tasks. The other one, despite not having the proper education, was a very accountable person. He was on top of his circumstances, and never made excuses for not completing his tasks. He did everything possible to get the job done and he was always willing to help out. As a result, the hospital promoted the one who didn't have the education but was reliable. They knew they could count on him. Although his credentials weren't the best, his accountability spoke volumes. He knew how to make things happen.

Instead of blaming circumstances or people, take the steps necessary to change your life. Don't complain about the situation—do something to change it. If your marriage is causing you trouble, read books about marriage and go to counseling. If your children are obnoxious and you don't know how to handle them, read books about parenting and look for a therapist. If you leave home at 7:00 and are sometimes late to work because of morning traffic, leave at 6:45. If your car isn't reliable, fix it or buy another car. If your employee isn't doing his work appropriately, either train him or replace him.

Do whatever you need to have the life you want. Make your life better by taking action. Blaming people or circumstances won't change anything, because you aren't taking action. Make decisions that will bring you the results you desire.

Don't be approval-addicted

You act like a victim when you're afraid of being rejected. You think that people won't accept you for a mistake you've made, so you blame something else so you don't lose their approval.

To overcome a victim mentality, get rid of your fear of rejection. The only person you need approval from is yourself. If you approve of yourself, you won't fear other people's disapproval. You won't need to make excuses, because you won't be concerned if others don't accept you. You accept yourself, so you believe that they accept you, as well.

4.
Expect the Best from People

When you victimize yourself, you think that people are against you. The victim mentality is like a fog when it comes to seeing people as they truly are. You can't see them because the fog is too thick. Every action they take and every word they say is distorted in the fog. You see them as your enemies and think they want to harm you.

When you feel like a victim, you think other people are strong and that you can't resist their strength. You exaggerate their capacity to hurt you and think that you're incapable of facing their wrath.

The problem with exaggerating people's power is that you also exaggerate what they do to you. A simple word may seem like an insult. A joke seems like a racial slur. An argument seems like abuse. You amplify everything people do, creating a whole drama in your mind.

To overcome a victim mentality, see people as they are and don't exaggerate their power. They're human beings who can be hurt. They're made from the same material as you, and they don't regard themselves as superior to you. They may even think that you're stronger than they are. They may be afraid of you and imagine that you want to hurt them.

When you exaggerate other people's power, you diminish your own strength. You see yourself as wimpy and weak. You think you can't resist their wrath, and that you're going to succumb to their force, but you need to have a realistic vision of yourself and others. Instead of seeing a huge gap in strength and power between you and others, see that you're as strong and powerful as they are. Don't overestimate their force or underestimate your power.

You can hurt people

When you believe that people are too powerful, you think they can't be hurt. You think they're so strong, that no matter what you do to defend yourself, you won't be able to hurt them. You assume that in order to defend yourself you have to use a great amount of force. You feel that if you're calm and polite, people won't respect you. As a result, you become rude and abuse others through your words and actions. You may even resort to violence. However, even though you may use extreme ways to get their respect, you still feel powerless.

You don't need to take extreme measures to impress people, nor do you need to be violent or throw things to gain their respect. You can be calm and serene and still impact others. The important is how you feel when you talk to them. If you think you're weak and they're strong, you'll be unable to get their respect. However, if you don't exaggerate their power and don't underestimate your strength, you can impact others.

Harshness doesn't impress people. Although you may hurt them and cause them pain, you won't impact them. They'll still sense your weakness. They'll look past your apparent strength and see your insecurity. They'll realize that you're being rude because you're afraid. Being rude and aggressive just shows how impotent you feel. It isn't a proof of your strength, but of your weakness. You may scream, be harsh, and violent, but inside, you're afraid. You act like a child who fears their parents' wrath. As a result, instead of getting people's respect, you'll only hurt them.

To impact people, you don't need to change your actions, but your feelings. It isn't how you talk or what you do, but what you feel when you talk and when you do. If you doubt your strength, you can scream or curse, but you'll still feel powerless. When you look at others and yourself in the same way, you throw away all your defenses, you believe in their respect, and you're calm and kind. Your authority doesn't come from an impulse of rage, but from a serene feeling of self-confidence.

The connection between power and love

When you feel like a victim, you associate power with evil. You think other people are strong and evil while you're weak and good. You think that because other people are stronger than you are, they want to use their strength to harm you. You become paranoid, always fretting over how they're going to hurt you.

Evil can't be associated with power. One who is rude and hurts others isn't strong and powerful. People act violently because they're afraid. They think that the others want to harm them, and because they're too weak to stand up to them, they act violently in order to make up for their sense of weakness. They imagine that by being harsh, they'll be able to impress others.

You don't need to be afraid of those who are impolite and rude. They're impolite because they fear you. They aren't tough because they're powerful, but because they feel weak. Inside of them is a person with low self-esteem, incapable of trusting others.

All the violence and cruelty in the world come from a sense of weakness. From the least impoliteness to the strongest evil, every bad act that's committed comes from a feeling of insecurity and fragility. People scorn, scold, criticize, abuse, and even kill because they're afraid.

When you realize that abusive people are weak, you don't fear them anymore. You understand that the more aggressive and abusive they are, the weaker they feel. Actually, they think that you're powerful and they're weak. They want to prove to you that they're stronger than you are. Therefore, there's no reason to fear them. You don't need to fear people who fear you.

When you look at history and analyze people such as Hitler, Erodes, and Nero, who committed atrocities, you'll understand that they all felt weak. They were evil because they wanted to defend themselves. They felt that others were evil, so they attacked those people before they attacked them.

Every abuse, verbal or physical, comes from a sense of fragility. The spouse who criticizes their partner, the parent who spanks their children, and the boss who mistreats their employees, all of them are afraid. Even the criminal who shoots their victim or the rapist who violates a little child sees themselves as weak and brittle.

Really powerful people are the most kind and polite. They aren't afraid of you, so they're capable of treating you with respect and love. They believe they deserve your love, so they love you, as well.

Feeling like a victim makes you the persecutor

When you feel like a victim, you end up becoming the persecutor. You think that people want to harm you, so you become defensive. When you're defending yourself, you're actually attacking others. Although you're only trying to protect yourself, in other people's eyes, you're attacking them.

Dennis had a tendency to think that other people didn't like him and that they were always plotting against him. He was certain that his co-workers were persecuting him. When they talked among themselves, he thought they were gossiping about him or planning against him. If they joked, he thought they wanted to belittle him. He started mistreating his co-workers and avoided their presence, and they became defensive. He mistreated them, so they mistreated him back. A vicious cycle ensued. Since Dennis couldn't believe in his colleague's friendship, he quit his job. However, the problem didn't end there. He thought that his wife disliked him and that she was his archenemy. One day, he tried to strangle her to defend himself, and they ended up divorcing.

The real victim isn't the one who's attacked, but the one who doesn't defend. When you defend yourself from imaginary persecutors, you become the real persecutor. You think you're defending yourself from a villain who's hurting you and end up being the real villain. If you attack people to defend yourself, they'll end up persecuting you to defend themselves—you'll attract to you what you think of them.

Imagine the changes that will come about when you stop acting like a victim. When you change the negative thoughts you have about yourself and others, you'll see how your relationships will change for the better. People will notice that you trust them and will react positively to your confidence. They'll become friendlier, because they'll sense your friendship.

You can believe that other people are your friends and want the best for you. You can open your eyes and see that you aren't a victim and that you deserve to be loved. When you see people as they truly are, you'll be able to admire their loveliness and grace. You'll look children and appreciate their innocence and enchantment. You'll look at adults and notice their beauty and uniqueness. You'll be in a state of bliss, because you'll feel all the love and grace coming from others.

However, when you feel like a victim, you distort what other people are. An innocent child becomes a ruffian. You look at your children and are blinded to their grace. You're incapable of recognizing how special and precious they are. You look at their innocent mischievousness and think they want to irritate you. You take what they do personally, when in the reality, they're only being children.

I was watching the news one day when I saw a story about a woman who'd thrown her son into traffic to be run over. As the cameras rolled, an officer was comforting the boy by bouncing him in his arms. The officer thought of the boy in a completely different way than his mother. The mother looked at her son and saw the bane of her existence. The officer saw only beauty and innocence.

Can you imagine what it would be like to look at every person as that officer looked at that child, to look at your child and be enchanted, to look at your spouse and sense their beauty and uniqueness, to stop looking at other people as if they were your persecutors and to believe in their love and good intentions?

Feeling like a victim causes you to idolize others

When you victimize yourself, you think that being evil is equal to being superior. You assume that other people are superior to you because they're evil and have the power to harm you. You, on the other hand, are inferior because you're good. You assume that when they hurt you, they're above you. You're the victim of their wickedness and abuse, so you are inferior to them. They're winning and you're losing.

The result is that you despise goodness because you associate it with being inferior. You believe that being evil equals superiority, while being good equals inferiority. You think you're good because you don't have the valor and courage to defend yourself. If you were strong, you wouldn't allow others to step all over you. You wouldn't be afraid of them, and you'd hurt them as bad as or worse than they hurt you.

Therefore, you assume that in order to be valuable, you need to retaliate and hurt other people. Otherwise you'd be at a disadvantage. However, when you act that way, you aren't making yourself superior. You aren't superior when you lose the battle against hatred. If feelings of revenge overcome you, you lose.

Being evil doesn't make someone superior. Just because someone wrongs you doesn't mean they're superior to you. You aren't at a disadvantage when people mistreat you. The winner isn't the one who's bad, but the one who's good. If someone has wronged you, you're the winner, because you aren't the one who did the wronging. The other person has lost, because they're the one who hurt you.

The reason people lose when they hurt you is because they're overcome by evil. The worst battle isn't waged outside, but inside. The worst combat is against evil, hatred, and selfishness. When people are overcome by their own hatred, they lose. Even if it appears as if they have the advantage, inside, they're at a disadvantage, because they can't do what's right. Evil rules them. Although it seems as if they're the persecutors, they're really victims of their own evil.

Thinking that you're at a disadvantage causes you to resent others. While you think they have the advantage, you can't forgive them. You're unable to pardon them because of personal importance. You think that in order to restore your dignity, you need to get payback.

Some time ago, I did a series of lectures to a group of people in a home. One night, I spoke about the victim mentality. I explained that you are never in disadvantage when you are the one who was wronged. The next night, Jesse, one of the attendants, talked about how my lecture the day before had changed her life. A decade ago, her husband had started dating his secretary and then left her. She could never forget that incident. She felt as if she'd been humiliated and was at a disadvantage. She harbored hatred and resentment and wanted revenge.

Jesse said that she had a paradigm shift when she understood that she hadn't been the victim. She understood that her ex-husband and his secretary were really the victims, since they were the ones who cheated. She wasn't at a disadvantage because she had integrity.

Can you imagine how liberating it is to realize you aren't the victim of people's dishonesty and hatred? Can you imagine how good it will be for your self-esteem when you understand that every time people betray, mistreat or wrong you, you aren't the one at a disadvantage?

When you realize that you aren't inferior every time people hurt you, you can let go of your resentment. You can forgive them, because they were never superior to you. You don't need to see them suffer for their wrongdoings in order to recover your dignity. You don't need to reestablish your value by getting even, since you never lost your value in the first place.

When you feel victimized by what people do to you, you give them power over your emotions. You make them responsible for your state of mind. If they're nice, you feel good, but if they're bad, you feel miserable. You become like clay in a potter's hands. Your attitude fluctuates according to the way people treat you.

Stop placing your mood in people's hands and realize that your happiness depends on you. You have power over your emotions. People may wrong and abuse you, but they can't force you to hate or resent them. You don't have to feel inferior and think that you're at a disadvantage. You can rise above your hatred and self-pity and forgive others. You can choose to feel valuable, even in face of humiliation and injustice.

5.
Learn To Lighten Up

When you act like a victim, you feel as if you're too weak to handle your ordeals. You think that your problems will engulf you and eventually destroy you. It's as if the pain caused by your problem is beyond your capacity of resistance.

When you think you're too sensitive to face hardships, your emotional pain intensifies. You suffer more because you *expect* that you'll suffer more, but excess suffering is an illusion. You suffer an excruciating amount of pain because you feel that's the amount of pain you *should* suffer.

You're only as weak as you think you are. If you think the suffering caused by a problem is more than you can endure, you increase the pain you feel. Much of the pain you've gone through in your life was unnecessary. You thought you'd suffer, so that's what happened.

Albert and Alice's son, Joseph, had been struggling with cancer for a year and despite the bleak prognosis, they couldn't bear the thought of Joseph dying. They ignored the facts, because it was easier for them. When Joseph died, they were overwhelmed and couldn't get over the tragedy. Fifteen years later, they were still coming to terms with Joseph's death.

The stronger you think you are, the less you suffer. You can get through anything that comes your way. Nothing can happen that you can't handle.

Saving people

When you feel weak, you have an obsession to save people. If you see someone suffering, you want to ride valiantly to their rescue. You exaggerate their problems as you exaggerate your own. When they stub their toe, you want to drag them to the hospital. You assume they can't get through the pain, so they need your help.

Being overwhelmed by other people's ordeals may cause you to lose balance. You go to extreme lengths to help others and ignore your own limitations. You become so obsessed that you even forget about your family and loved ones.

Instead of saving people who don't need to be saved, help them see that their problems aren't that big. When you feel overwhelmed by their problems, you end up overwhelming them. Instead of helping them be stronger, you reinforce their defeated image.

Carlos knew a woman who was going through a tough time. Not only did he want to help her, but he wanted to marry her. Although he'd just met her, he wanted to do everything for her.

When I started meditating and understanding my own problems, I wanted to help everyone, even if they didn't ask for or need it. I wanted to use my new insights about human emotions to counsel everyone in trouble. When they refused my help, I took it personally and felt rejected.

When you learn to lighten up, you don't make a big deal out of other people's problems. If they make a fuss, it doesn't affect you. You can analyze their problems in a realistic manner. You can help them without losing balance and being overly worried.

Don't worry

When you act like a victim, you worry too much and dwell on all your problems. You worry about your marriage, your children, your work, your future, and your health. You have difficulty relaxing and enjoying life.

Dwelling on your problems won't solve them. On the contrary, the more you think about your problems, the more they'll confuse you. By thinking too much about your problems, you obscure your mind. Although the solution may be right in front of you, you're blind to it. You spend so much energy thinking and worrying that you don't have anything left for working toward a solution.

To solve your problems, you need a positive state of mind. The more relaxed and happy you are, the more you can overcome. If you focus only ten percent on your problems than you usually do, you'll solve them much more efficiently. Your brain works best when it's relaxed and peaceful. By engulfing your brain with concerns and negative expectations, you drain the power it needs to deliver the insights and ideas that will help you to overcome the problems you're facing.

Instead of focusing on problems, focus on solutions. The difference between negative and positive people is that negative people think about their problems and positive people think about solutions to their problems.

When you focus on your problems, you have trouble breaking away from them. You're so intent on your hardships that you can't stop thinking about them. Even when you sleep, you can't put your problems aside. You dream about your boss hounding you about unfinished work. Your mind is constantly overwhelmed with negative thoughts. It's no surprise that you end feeling hopeless. You become tired and moody. If you want to be successful, learn to lighten up.

You're not slave of your thoughts. You think what you choose to think. If you choose to think about problems and negative expectations, it's your decision. However, if you want to focus on the positive, you can break away of the negativity. No matter how long you've been filling your mind with trash, you can break through of that behavior.

From now on, every time a negative thought comes to your mind, replace it with a positive one. The best way to overcome negativity is by stopping it in the very beginning. Think about solutions, visualize yourself achieving your goals, or just imagine an exotic getaway. Believe you're the owner of your mind and that you can do with it whatever you choose. You can choose to be depressed or you can choose to think positively.

Being happy or unhappy is a question of habit. You're stressed because you've always been stressed and you don't know any other way to be, but you can change. You just need to think positively to the point that you become a positive person.

Worrying causes distraction

When you worry too much about your problems, you become distracted. It's as if you lose touch with reality and retreat within yourself. By focusing too much on your problems, you forget about other important aspects of life. As a result, you make silly mistakes. You forget to turn off the oven, you shut the door and forget the keys inside, or you forget an important appointment.

The day before my children's choir had its first concert, I was stressed. We rehearsed from 7:00 to 9:00 p.m., but I didn't think we were ready. At 11:00, I finally left the church. I was so distracted that I stopped at a red light and thought it was a stop sign. I finally accelerated—right in front of another car. To avoid an accident, the driver swerved to the left and narrowly missed me. I learned that when you worry too much about something, you become irresponsible.

We tend to think that the more concerned we are, the more responsible we'll be. We confuse stress with responsibility and we think that relaxation and happiness are an antonym to accountability. The facts, however, show the opposite. Focusing too much on a particular aspect of your life causes you to ignore other important aspects that need your attention. As a result, you become irresponsible, despite being stressed.

Life is like parents with a large number of kids. Every child is important and deserves attention. If you focus on just one child, the other ones feel abandoned and develop psychological problems. In order to be a successful parent, you have to give equal attention to each child.

It's helpful to see your life as a grid with many boxes. You have a career, bills, a family, and time to relax. To be a responsible adult, give each of these things the attention they need. You can't focus solely on your career to the extent that your family fades into the background or you don't have any fun. You can't focus too much on your family, either, or you won't have time for work. You need to learn to distribute your attention to everything you do. When you're at work, be there, body and spirit. You can't be planning your next vacation while you're working on an important report. On the other hand, while you're in a motel in Malibu, let go of your work responsibilities.

Excessive worry causes materialism

When you worry excessively, you become materialistic. You're so overwhelmed by your work that there isn't space in your mind for your family. You come home from work and go to your room without acknowledging your children's existence. Corporeally, you're in your house, but mentally, you're still at work. Your family senses a wall between you and them and feel excluded.

When you learn to lighten up, you'll be able to notice your loved ones. When you leave your job, you'll let go completely of all the problems and worries involved with it. From that time on, you're the property of your family. You won't take your body home while you leave your mind at work.

Focusing too much on other people is also a form of materialism. If you worry excessively about your children, you become distant. You become so engulfed with their behavior, their grades at school, and their extra courses that you can't relax and enjoy their presence. Your worry about them prevents you from having fun with them.

Being worried makes you selfish

When you learn to focus on other people, you become less worried and stressed. By shifting the center of your attention from yourself to other people, you're able to lighten up and be more relaxed. The best way to attain perfect happiness is to be involved with others. Serving others helps you realize that your problems aren't as big as you thought they were. You can shift your attention from yourself to your spouse, children, or parents. You can be more involved with your church or your community.

Volunteering is another way to dedicate yourself to others so you can be less absorbed on your own problems. When you volunteer, you meet people whose problems eclipse yours. You realize that you've being making a big deal out of your problems. By becoming involved with the world's problems, your problems become smaller and you realize that there's no reason for you to be so worried about yourself.

When you become more involved with other people's lives and interests, they become more involved with yours. You give more support, so you receive more support, which helps you solve your problems. The fact that you help other people causes them to want to help you.

Step Eight
Overcoming Fear

1.
Overcoming Fear

When I talk about fear, I remember a woman I'll call Vera who I helped when I was a chaplain. When she was six, her parents sent her to private school. She couldn't sleep because she was afraid, so she'd cry and ask for company in the night. When she became an adult, the fear didn't go away. She was afraid of riding in elevators, so she avoided them at all costs, which caused problems, because in Brazil there are many skyscrapers, so she got lots of exercise when going up and down stairs in twenty-story buildings.

She was also scared of thunderstorms, which are frequent in Rio de Janeiro and are usually accompanied by a lot of lightning. Vera had a unique way of coping. When her husband wasn't home, she'd take the kids and go to a neighbor's. If Vera wasn't at home, she'd go into *anyone's* house, even the home of a complete stranger. Her fear of storms and elevators were only two of many, so you can imagine how limited she was and how much pain she endured.

Fear isn't a positive feeling. It brings stress and unhappiness. It's a chain that prevents you from realizing your dreams.

Fear and childhood

Fear is developed in childhood. When children don't feel loved, they become insecure. They don't see their parents as their protectors, but as enemies. They don't trust their parents to help if something bad happens. Their parents are a part of the problem, not the solution.

There are parents who actually feed their children's fear. They say that if little Johnny goes to his room, there will be a cockroach there or if he disobeys, they'll take him to the doctor to get a shot.

Gina and I wanted Carolina to grow up strong and confident. Carolina used to go to her grandmother's home, which was close to the jungle. She was attracted to all kinds of animals and insects and would watch them closely. One time, she was playing with a frog. She'd put the frog in her arms and the frog would walk through them. She brought it to the house and showed it to Gina and me. I was afraid that the frog would jump on me, but I hid my fear. I didn't want her to be influenced by my fears, so I acted as if holding the frog was a natural thing.

Some parents want their children to fear them. They don't trust their children's love for them, and so they think that to get respect and obedience, they have to threaten their kids. When the children disobey, they retaliate in an abusive fashion. A child raised that way won't trust other people. They'll assume that everyone is rude and abusive, they'll be afraid of other people's reactions, and they'll expect people to hurt them, just as their parents did.

The fearful child has difficulty showing affection. Fear and love can't exist together. If fear enters the heart, love goes away.

Love has the power to bring goodness. When children love, they're motivated to obey. When they don't love, they harbor feelings of hatred and retaliation. They do things out of their fear. Their obedience is artificial and mechanical.

There are two things that will help your children not to be afraid. The first is to show unconditional love. Show them that you're their friend and protector. By being patient, kind, and understanding, they'll trust you and see you as their shelter. The second thing is to not overprotect them. When you spoil your children, you're telling them they're weak. Your exaggerated worry makes them feel brittle and vulnerable, which doesn't help them develop self-confidence.

Sheila was twenty-six, unemployed, and living with her parents. She dreaded looking for a job because she didn't think she could do it. When I visited her, I was appalled by the way her parents treated her. They acted as if she was a baby. They had a maid who took care of the home and cooked. There wasn't anything left for Sheila to do, so she felt worthless. She'd graduated with a degree in literature and had even written a book of poems. She was brilliant, but she didn't know it.

Sheila's parents had sabotaged her future by the way they treated her. In the name of love, they had made her feel weak. They worried over her and protected her too much. By surrounding her with too much care, they had prevented her from developing self-confidence.

Fear is caused by an inferiority complex

The cause of fear is the thought that your worth depends on what happens to you. What you fear isn't the problem, but the fact that your problems might make you inferior. For example, you may be afraid of losing your job, divorcing, or becoming sick because you attach value to those things. When you don't know that your real fear is the loss of importance, you fight the problem artificially. You may work long hours so you won't lose your job, you may try to control your spouse so you won't lose them, or you may take a lot of medicine to avoid being sick. However, you aren't combating your inferiority complex, and you won't overcome your fear. The problem is spiritual and not material. What you need to do in order to overcome fear is combat your low self-esteem. No matter what comes your way, you can never lose your worth. You're important, no matter what.

To place value on exterior things is like building a house on sand. You can be sure that when the wind blows or a storm hits, it'll collapse. The same thing happens if you place value on your job, your spouse, or your health. You'll always be afraid of losing your worth and you'll always feel inferior. The solution to fear is placing your value on your own existence. In other words, you don't need to be employed, to have a spouse, or to be healthy to be valuable. You just need to be alive.

Don't worry about other people's opinions

Another thing that causes fear is worrying about other people's opinions. You're afraid of something bad happening to you because you think that people will belittle you. The dread of being criticized or losing your reputation makes you afraid. You're afraid of disease because you think people will reject you. You fear speaking in public because you assume that if you make a mistake, they'll dislike you.

Behind fear is the question: What will other people think if something happened? For example: What will people think of me if I flunk school? What will they think of me if I get sick? What will people think of me if my spouse abandons me?

To overcome fear, don't worry about what other people think of you. The less you care about other people's opinions, the less you'll be afraid when something bad happens.

You worry about people's opinion because you don't believe that they love you unconditionally. The fear of not being loved is the result of not loving yourself. You assume that people won't love you if something bad happens because you wouldn't love yourself, either. For example, you fear speaking in public and being rejected because you wouldn't accept yourself if you made a mistake.

When you accept yourself, you aren't afraid of not being accepted by others. When you love yourself, you're bold. You don't fear people's rejection because you don't reject yourself. You don't fear that they'll abandon you if something bad happens because you trust their love. You expect them to support you and nurture you in times of adversity. No matter what happens, you know you can count on them.

Fear doesn't prevent you from having problems

Problems hunt those who fear. The more you fear something bad will happen, the more likely it is that that *will* happen. Fearing sickness may make you sick, and fearing failure may bring failure. Fear is like a magnet that attracts negative things.

John worked in the hospital and dreaded losing his job. His fear had a paralyzing effect, preventing him from having the attention necessary to perform his work. As a result, he committed several mistakes and was very slow. His supervisor warned John that if he didn't perform better, he'd lose his job, but that only made him more afraid, crippling his ability to do his job even further. What he feared most happened. He was fired.

In my experience as a piano teacher, I've noticed the negative influence of fear on my students when they have a recital. Sometimes they're prepared to give an outstanding performance, but their fear makes them make mistakes they wouldn't have made if they were calm and confident about themselves.

The best way to avoid the problems that come your way is not to fear them. The secret to being good is not to fear being bad. The less you fear, the less you have to fear.

Fear is the opposite of faith

When you fear, you're pessimistic. You live constantly in fear of imminent danger. If you have something good, you think you're going to lose it. You assume that problems are the rule and blessings are the exception.

Tom was an employee at the school where I was getting my bachelor's degree in Theology. He was intelligent and could memorize entire books, yet he was a failure, due to his pessimism. When someone asked how he was, he'd say he was lonely, underpaid, and poor. Every time we talked, he'd compare himself to me. He'd compliment me and degrade himself. His negative attitude was a magnet that attracted problems.

If you expect the worst, you'll bring the worst upon you, but if you expect the best, you'll attract the best. It's unlikely that you'll get more than you expect. The secret of success is expecting it. If you want to be a winner, don't count on failure—count on victory. Counting on failure makes you turn stagnant. You don't have the energy to pursue your dreams because you don't believe in yourself. If you want to be successful, believe in yourself. Having a positive attitude makes your brain work at its peak level and you'll have optimum performance. Thinking positively helps you have clarity of mind so you know what to do and how to do it. Fear attracts problems, because it gives you a negative attitude that makes you go in the direction of the very problems you fear. To be successful, see failure as the *exception* to the rule.

Fear is the result of pride

When you crave applause, you fear the opposite. You become afraid of performing poorly and of being rejected. You want everything to be perfect in your life because you think you can't handle disapproval. The more you expect to be honored, the less you accept being humiliated. To overcome fear, don't crave compliments. Don't be addicted to other people's approval. Don't waste your life trying to please everyone. Be bold enough to handle contempt without feeling sorry for yourself. Learn to accept yourself in the middle of rejection. Your desire for applause won't get you applause. The more you fear contempt, the more you'll attract it.

Suffering by anticipation

When you fear, you suffer in anticipation. The mere possibility that something bad may happen makes you suffer. One example is a young person who's afraid of dying. Death is something that won't happen for at least sixty years, so a twenty-year-old should be enjoying life instead of worrying about death.

Katie feared that her husband, Oswald, would betray her. Whenever Oswald got home late, she thought he'd been with another woman. Yet the years passed and Oswald never betrayed her. She realized that she'd been suffering in vain and finally understood that there wasn't any reason to suffer for something that never happened.

Being afraid is to bring something from the future to the present and then suffer in anticipation. Although it's likely that the expected problem will never happen, you live your life suffering unnecessarily. The problem is that while you're suffering, you aren't enjoying the good things happening in your life.

To overcome fear, live in the present. Don't focus on what may happen. Live the present and enjoy all your blessings. If you're going to divorce someday, enjoy your marriage now. Instead of thinking about the possibility of divorce and suffering, take advantage of the fact that you're married. If you're a pianist and have a concert next week, don't spend the whole week worrying about your performance. Just relax and practice.

Most of the things you fear won't happen. More than ninety percent of your fears don't come from reality, but from your negative expectations. You believe in things that aren't real and won't happen unless you imagine them. By fearing, you waste time you could spend being happy.

The more you expect, the more you fear

When you demand that something happens, you become afraid that it won't happen. For example, if you have a test and you demand that you pass it, you'll be afraid of not passing. If you demand that someone say yes, you fear getting a no. If you demand perfection, you'll fear mistakes.

You fear because you're a perfectionist. You have a series of expectations and don't accept yourself if things don't happen exactly as you planned. You establish too many requirements for happiness and assume that you can't be happy unless those requirements are met. If you have unrealistic expectations, you'll always be afraid that you won't realize them.

The best way to overcome fear is to lower your expectations. Diminish your list of expectations. If you don't expect too much from life, you won't fear that things won't happen like you want them to. Accept yourself as you are and don't establish a standard so high that you'll fear not reaching it.

To accept things as they are doesn't mean you'll conform to mediocrity. You can still have dreams and goals. The only difference is that you won't put your self-acceptance at stake because of your dreams. You may dream of being rich, but you don't need wealth as a requirement for accepting yourself. You might have a test, but you won't dread flunking it, because you love yourself unconditionally.

Can you imagine the burden you'll be rid of when you learn to love yourself unconditionally? You'll be bold and won't fear anything because you'll accept yourself, no matter what happens. As a result, you'll always be relaxed and you'll have a lot of fun. When you overcome your fears, studying for a test, seeking your dreams, working, and being married will be pleasurable. You won't be thinking about what might happen in case you fail, because you'll accept yourself anyway. You'll enjoy the present without worrying about the possibilities of the future.

There's nothing wrong with wanting to be wealthy, married, employed, or healthy. The problem is when you attach your self-acceptance or happiness to those things. When you do that, you become afraid and you aren't happy anymore. In other words, being rich, married, employed, or healthy aren't requirements for happiness and acceptance. If you want to be happy, take all the *ifs* out of your vocabulary. Don't say, "I will be happy *if* (I am rich, I am married, I am employed or I pass the test)." Say, "I'm happy because I'm alive. Even if I lose my wealth, get separated or fired, or I flunk the test, I'll be happy because I exist."

Fear is caused by a feeling of fragility

You fear because you think that you're too sensitive and you can't handle problems when they come. You think that things are going to overwhelm you and as a result, you'll be completely submerged in your problems.

Fragility is a farce. If you think you'll suffer too much as a result of a problem, you'll suffer not because of the problem, but because you think you'll suffer. You expect to suffer and therefore, you do. Your pain is the result of the idea that you're weak. You create the pain when you think you're too sensitive.

To overcome fear, change the concept you have of yourself. Picture yourself as a strong person. Believe that you're able to face adversities. You can bear any problem and any disappointment that comes your way. You're able to face ordeals. See yourself as a fortress, not a fence.

Behind any fear is a feeling of incompetence. For example, you may fear having a child because you doubt your ability to be a good parent. You may fear marrying because you think you're unable to fulfill someone's emotional needs. You may fear starting an enterprise because you think you're incapable of being successful. You may fear speaking in public because you don't believe you can articulate what you're trying to say.

The secret to overcoming fear resides in believing in yourself. By believing in yourself, you feel confident about your endeavors and don't expect to fail.

Stretch your comfort zone

One of the best ways to overcome fear is to stretch your comfort zone. When you avoid doing things because you fear the result, you prevent yourself from overcoming fear. If you wait for fear to go away before doing something, you'll never overcome fear and you'll never do what you want to do. Some people think they need to overcome the fear inside themselves before they try anything. Actually, it's the other way around.

By doing the things you fear, you send a positive message to your brain. You tell it that you can do what you fear and that you're capable of handling the fear. As result, you get a little bolder every time. It's like learning to drive a car. In the beginning, you can't even turn the wheel because you think you'll go to the wrong place. You grab the wheel tightly and want to keep it straight. However, every time you drive, you feel a little less stressed and a little more relaxed. Little by little, you clutch the wheel less tightly until you're comfortable.

If there's something you fear doing, that's the very thing you need to do. Every time you face a fear and you do it anyway, you become less afraid.

Panic

Behind panic is a deep lack of self-esteem and an extreme sense of vulnerability. Although you don't have an actual reason to be afraid, you're *afraid*. You fear your own fear. You're afraid because you think you can't handle your fear and that you might go insane.

I can talk about that feeling because I lived like that for more than ten years. When I went to private school, I felt a terrible depression. I was fourteen at that time, and my depression stemmed from a fear of not being able to handle my depression. Since I couldn't sleep, I tried to get help from my friends. I talked to them until late at night so I didn't have to be alone.

Unfortunately, the method I used to combat my fear was ineffectual. I try to avoid thinking about it, but it always resurfaced. Although I ran from my fear, it ran after me. I did everything I could to be in the company of someone at all times. I latched onto people as if they were lifeguards. That kind of fear was cyclic. I'd be depressed for two months and then it disappeared for two months.

Even after counseling, I had the worst part of my depression for a year. The solution came when I decided to read and meditate every day. Until that point, I had tried to escape my fear by not thinking about it. That approach wasn't working, so I decided to face my fear. Instead of fleeing from it, I looked it right in the eye. It began to disappear gradually until a year later, it went away forever.

Don't fear the fear. Since your fear isn't based on reality, there's nothing to fear. The thought that fear will destroy you is a lie. You're stronger than your fear, and you'll overcome it.

Fear of people

When you're fearful, you have a tendency to fear people. You think they're powerful and that you can't resist them. You think that if you don't please them, they'll hurt you. Consequently, you have difficulty saying no. That will be discussed in a deeper way in the next section.

Step Nine
Self-Control

1.
Don't Demand from Yourself

One feeling we need to overcome in order to master our emotions is our tendency to demand from ourselves. We demand that we be thin, that we study, that we become rich, or that we become more loving. We feel frustrated that we don't have the power to change. The problem is that demanding is disempowering. The more we demand, the less strength we have to do the things we want to do.

When we demand from ourselves, we place our value on the future. We think that when we're rich, thin, or have our diploma, we'll be valuable. However, when we get there, we establish other goals in order to be valuable, and die before valuing ourselves.

There are many books that speak about success. We want to get to a point where we feel great about ourselves, but we'll never feel successful if we don't value ourselves in the present. We may conquer the world, but we'll still feel worthless. We'll think that there's still something missing and we'll try to achieve it.

You'll never feel successful if you don't value yourself. You can obtain everything, but if you don't love yourself, you won't be fulfilled. You can feel successful right now if you accept yourself the way you are. I've seen many people who are successful in terms of the popular vision of success who still feel empty and unfulfilled.

Success can't be measured by material accomplishments. Success is a feeling. If you want to be successful, you need to feel successful right now. Just accept yourself the way you are and you're successful.

You might think that if you value yourself the way you are, you'll be complacent and won't have the drive to achieve more. However, it's the opposite. The more you value yourself, the more you want to succeed.

Love is powerful. If you love yourself, you have the energy to push forward. Hatred is all about weakness. If you don't love yourself now, you won't have motivation.

Demanding comes from childhood

We learn to hate ourselves in our childhood. Parents convey the message that we aren't okay the way we are. They communicate subliminally that we need to be obedient, to study, and to do a good job in order to be loved and accepted. We believe them and assume that people don't like us the way we are. We start a frantic search for being a person worth being loved. We try to find the reason why they don't love us. We think that it might be because we don't have the perfect body shape, a diploma, or assets. We assume that if we were famous, rich, or had a doctor's degree, they'd love us. We become stressed about becoming someone worthy of respect. We become workaholics in our search for people's approval. We immerse ourselves in a search for meaning, to the point that we don't have time for others. Although they're close to us, we're busy looking to deserve their love. We study, work, and make plans, all with the intention of gaining their respect, when they just want to be connected.

Roger divides his time between working and studying for his doctorate degree. He wants to feel important and be respected. He comes home and closes the door of his office to focus on his goals. His children, Sara (two) and Junior (four), knock on the door, but Roger's wife, Meire, explains that Dad is busy. They listen and seem to understand, but when she leaves, they knock on the door again. Roger gets upset. He feels that his children are an obstacle in his path to success. He opens the door, yells at them, and looks at his wife as if she's responsible for the kids' disturbance. Meire, who's already feeling alone, is sad because he doesn't value what she does. She puts the kids to bed and then goes to bed herself while Roger is still studying. Although Roger is trying to get other people's respect, he doesn't realize that if he'd open up to his family, he'd get all the love he's looking for.

When you try to acquire things in order to be loved, you're searching for something that's right in front of you. It's like wanting to go from Los Angeles to San Francisco, a one-hour trip by plane, but you make a stop in New York. You get distracted by something in New York and never get to San Francisco, but you keep remembering that's where you want to be. Instead of making such a long trip to people's love, you could go straight to them.

We want to get the diploma, the money, or the status so we'll be loved. We want to tell people, "I have a doctor's degree, I'm rich and famous, so I want you to love me and recognize how important I am."

We don't realize that we don't need to get anything to be loved. We just need to believe in other people's love. Their love is already there for us to enjoy. If we aren't enjoying other people's love, being famous or rich won't change anything. If we don't change our hearts, we'll travel the world without ever reaching our destination.

Roger is looking for people's respect because he has an empty love tank. If he'd just open the door of his office, let Sara and Junior enter, and have a good time with them, he'd feel much happier than getting his doctor's degree all alone. If he'd go to bed earlier and celebrate his relationship with his wife, he'd feel richer than the richest man in the world.

I'm not saying we shouldn't have dreams or try to accomplish things. The problem lies with the motive. If we try to get people's love through our accomplishments, those people become secondary. We put other things ahead of them.

Although what I'm going to say might seem odd, if you want to feel loved, you need to decide to feel loved. Love is abstract. You can't touch it and you can't prove it. When you look at other people, it's hard to say that they love you. Everyone is different, so every person has their own way of conveying their love. If you want to feel loved, stop making assumptions. Just believe.

Although it's easy, we make it complicated. We work day and night to be someone worthy of being loved when we already have everything we need to be loved. It's like wanting to make a cake for a party. You go to the grocery store to buy the ingredients, then go home and make a cake, but it burns and you have to start all over again—when the party's already going on and they already *have* a cake. You could go to the party and eat cake, but since you ignore the fact that it's already made, you're busy trying to make one of your own.

The cake is the love you're looking for. I invite you to stop trying to make a new cake and enjoy the cake that's already there. Stop trying to get people's love and just feel loved. Stop looking to deserve love and celebrate the love that's already yours.

Conditional love

When we demand from ourselves, we want to do things by force. We say that we *have* to do this or that and don't give ourselves the right not to do the things we want. We become slaves of ourselves.

We don't *have* to do anything. We don't have to be rich, have knowledge, or be famous. We have the right to choose. Love and freedom complement each other. When we love ourselves, we do things because we *want* to and not because we *have* to. We don't force ourselves to do things and we don't accuse ourselves for not doing what we think we should.

When you demand from yourself, you don't have any motivation. You can't be motivated when you don't have self-respect. If you're always pushing yourself to do something and punishing yourself for not having done what you think you should, your progress becomes a burden. There's a war going on inside you, and it's anything but motivating.

The more freedom you have, the more motivated you are. When you don't coerce yourself, you do things for pleasure. As a consequence, you have fun in everything you do. You feel excited to study, work, or make plans. You love your activities because you love yourself.

Obligation and condemnation are connected to each other. When you demand that you do things, you generally condemn yourself for not having done them already. You accuse yourself of being too slow and demand that you go faster. That mix of obligation and condemnation creates an inner conflict. You're constantly abusing yourself to achieve more. That's why demanding is the most ineffective method you can use to reach your goals.

When I was younger, I was very demanding of myself. Practicing the piano was a war. I couldn't accept my failures and every time I made a mistake, I punished myself. As a result, I couldn't even look at my hands, for fear of seeing them play the wrong note. That approach to everything I did made me very unhappy.

Many people give up on their dreams because of such inner conflict. They find it so boring and tedious pursuing a goal that they quit. They think the problem is the activity, but the problem is their attitude toward the activity. When they change their attitude, they find it exciting and enjoyable.

I developed much faster as a pianist when I stopped demanding from myself. My practice became more fun and I got more out of it. Instead of being worried about my performance, I paid more attention to the beauty of the music. That attitude caused me to want to play more and to get a better outcome.

If you want better results, stop demanding from yourself. The more you demand from yourself, the more you distance yourself from the very things you want to accomplish. Wanting too much is the same as not wanting at all. If your desire is an obsession, you may end up not desiring anymore.

You can test that concept in your approach to people. When you demand that people do things for you, you take away their motivation. By forcing them to do something, you make them not want to do what you ask. I realized that with my students. The students who perform better are those whose parents know how to motivate them. When kids are demanded from their parents, they lose interest. There was a mother who was always putting her children down and criticizing them for not practicing. She accused them in front of me, which made them embarrassed. She didn't compliment them when they practiced. She acted as if practicing was an obligation, so they were only doing what they were supposed to do. There was a lot of pressure and accusation, but no encouragement or recognition. The result was that they quit.

On the other hand, two other siblings developed faster because their mother knew how to motivate them. She didn't force them to practice. She just told them how she believed in them and was proud of them. Her daughters saw piano as a game. They enjoyed it as much as if they were playing outside.

If you want to be successful, stop demanding from yourself. You don't need to quit your dreams or change them. You just need to change your method. If you stop forcing and condemning yourself, you'll enjoy what you do. Instead of being stressed, you'll be happy and excited. You'll enjoy everything you do. As a result, you'll develop much faster and perform better. The process can be as exciting as the end. By not demanding from yourself, you can feel the joy of growing.

What makes you enjoy the growing process is love. When you love yourself, you have self-respect. You're not a slave to your dreams. You put yourself above your dreams. You have integrity. You're at your side, no matter what happens. If you fail or if you do a bad job, you continue to love yourself. You love yourself when you achieve your goal and you love yourself while you're getting there—and if you don't get there, you love yourself, anyway. You're not emotionally attached to your dream. You aren't your dream. It's not the dream that defines you, but a deep sense of worth no failure can shake or remove.

The more you demand to achieve a goal, the more you fear not achieving it. The fear may be so intense that it paralyzes you or cause you to make silly mistakes. If you have to speak in public, play an instrument, or sing and you demand that you don't make a mistake, you become so stressed that you end up making mistakes. Your performance is inversely proportional to your demanding. The more you demand perfection from yourself, the more mistakes you make. By demanding less from yourself, you decrease your fear and feel more relaxed. That relaxation causes your brain to work better and you give a superior performance.

In order to get a good result, you need to know your nature. Your brain doesn't like to be pushed or mistreated. When you abuse yourself, you make your brain suffer. You create a cloud around your brain that prevents it from thinking clearly. You become so stressed that your brain tries to escape the situation to alleviate the pain. As a result, you become distracted.

That's precisely what happened to me when I practiced the piano. My stress was so intense that I couldn't focus on the song. My fingers were touching the piano, but my mind was elsewhere. By not focusing on the song, I could prevent myself from listening to my mistakes and not abuse myself. Then I got mad at myself for not focusing, I punished myself for not focusing, and I demanded that I focus. The result was that I focused even less. I entered an endless loop of pain. I demanded to play well, lost my focus, demanded more focus, and focused even less.

If you have difficulty focusing on what you're doing, you need to relax. The secret to relaxing is in loosening your grip. Renounce your demanding attitude and love yourself unconditionally. If you abuse yourself for not focusing and demand more focus, you'll only make matters worse. Accept your lack of concentration and don't assume that you have some terrible mental problem.

Demanding is tiresome. When you demand and criticize yourself, you spend more energy than normal. You get exhausted after a short time. You become more tired from your abuse than from what you're doing. As a result, your mind can't work at peak level because you deprive it of the energy it needs to perform. Energy is proportional to love. The more you love yourself, the more energy you have, and the less you love, the less energy you have. The best way to energize your brain is through loving yourself. Stop the abuse, the demanding, and the criticizing, and you'll have strength and power. Your brain will deliver the maximum result.

When you demand from yourself, you have a tendency to rush. You don't want to accept the normal process of development. You want to get to the end fast because you think you can love yourself only when you get there. Therefore, you press, hasten, and push yourself to get there as fast as you can. However, your rush causes you even more pain. Your stress increases and your performance decreases. The result is that instead of speeding up the process of growth, you make it slower.

I observed it with students and parents. I was in a home when a mother was doing homework with her daughter. She got upset because the girl didn't understand quickly. The girl was made anxious by her mother's pressure and couldn't think. The mother got even more upset and the girl started crying. The mother had blocked her daughter's thinking by trying to rush the learning process.

I was giving a piano lesson when I got upset because the student couldn't play the song at the right tempo. I made him repeat it several times and the more upset I got, the more frustrated he became. To worsen the situation, his mother came to help, putting even more pressure on him. I understood that it was time to back off. I told her about the laws of the mind and that my impatience was the cause of his difficulty. I had blocked his thinking by demanding that he learn quickly.

I came to their home a week later, and he played the song again. To my amazement, he played it perfectly the first time. I concluded that he'd already learned the song the week before, but he couldn't play it right because he was afraid of my reaction. He wanted to please me and his mother so much that he kept his brain from giving him the result.

Before you begin any endeavor, be aware of the growth process. A journey of a thousand miles starts with one step. The mind has its own timing that wasn't created by you. You can't make your brain work faster than its natural pace. There are also unexpected things that can happen that will make results to be even slower. For instance, I started writing this chapter yesterday morning and intended to finish it the same day. However, I had to do a lot of things and when night came, I was so tired that I couldn't finish. Today, at midnight, I finished it. It didn't happen as planned, but I'm happy anyway.

When you demand from yourself, you lose balance. You focus so much on one aspect of your life that you forget other things. You might even become irresponsible. For example, if you want to be rich, you might work so hard that you don't have time for yourself or your family. If you want to get a doctorate degree, you might immerse yourself in your studies to the point that you live at other people's expense.

The example of the grid with different boxes is also applicable here. When you think your worth depends on your dreams, you become neurotically attached to them. That attachment may result in disappointment. If you fail, you don't have anything to fill your sense of purpose.

Demanding and believing

Your demanding is inversely proportional to how much you believe in yourself. You demand from yourself because you don't believe in yourself. When you feel incapable, you look at your dreams as if they were almost impossible to reach. You assume that you have to work as hard as you can or you won't not achieve your goals. However, because you don't believe in yourself, you don't have power and lack the motivation to reach your dreams.

Strength comes from believing in yourself. When you believe in yourself, you have power and motivation. You press forward because you believe you'll get what you want. Demanding is an attempt to compensate for lack of energy. You want to substitute faith with force.

Faith is strength, while demanding is weakness. If you want to have the motivation to reach a dream, you need to believe in yourself. The more you demand from yourself, the less strength you have to achieve your goals, because you don't believe in yourself. On the other hand, the less you demand from yourself, the more you believe and the more strength you'll have.

Demanding is an artificial motivation. It doesn't come from the heart. Real strength is spontaneous, so you don't realize when you're strong. When you feel capable, you have a natural strength. You don't need to push yourself to do something. You're already motivated, so you press forward.

If you want to have strength, stop demanding from yourself. Believe that you already have all the strength you need. Demanding and believing won't coexist in your heart simultaneously. If you want to believe in yourself, let it go of demanding. When you stop forcing yourself, faith will come and you'll have power.

Demanding isn't an alternative to being incapable. If you're incapable, no matter how much you demand from yourself, you won't reach your dreams. Therefore, there's no purpose in demanding. Besides not helping you to achieve your goals, it makes the process painful. You don't reach your dreams because you demand from yourself, but in spite of it.

Demanding and responsibility

You demand from yourself because you don't believe you're accountable. You assume that you aren't a good person and that you don't want to do what you should do. For example, you demand that you do a good job because you think you don't want to do a good job. You demand that you study because you think you don't want to study. You demand that you're a good person because you think you're evil. You have a negative self-image, so you think that if you don't force yourself to do the things you should do, you'll never do them.

Such demanding also happens in relationships. You nag your spouse because you have a negative image of them. You don't believe in their goodness, so you think you have to force them to do the right thing. However, when you don't believe in them, you send a negative message that disempowers them. When they realize you don't believe in them, they lose the motivation to do the very thing that you ask.

It's like the mother who demanded her children study the piano. The more she demanded, the less they wanted to study. The problem was that her demanding revealed her lack of faith in their willing to practice. She saw them as negligent and irresponsible. The subliminal message behind her demanding was "I don't trust you. You're irresponsible and don't want to do what you should do." She wasn't only draining her children's motivation to play, but she was also making them think they weren't good people.

There's a difference between demanding and encouraging. Encouragement comes from faith, while demanding comes from distrust. When you demand that someone do something for you, you show your disbelief, which ultimately disempowers them. However, when you encourage them, you believe in their good intention, you trust that they can do it, and they *want* to do it. You send a positive message that empowers them to do what you want.

2.
Self-Control

"You will know the truth and the truth will set you free" (Romans 8:32)

Behind all emotional problems is a difficulty in controlling oneself. Every negative emotion comes from an obsession. You don't choose to hate, to retaliate, to put people down, or to feel inferior. You just feel an urge that you can't control. You become a hostage of your emotions. You don't do what *you* want to do, but what your *impulses* want you to do. You don't own yourself—your impulses own you.

If you're dominated by your emotions, you're a slave to yourself. It's as if you were dead. Instead of living, you're being lived. Your emotions control you instead of you controlling them. You have a biological life. You walk, talk, and eat, but you're emotionally dead. You can't love, because hatred dominates you. You can't be humble, because pride controls you. You aren't generous, because egotism subjects you. You don't live in the spirit, but in the flesh. You aren't governed by principles, but by feelings. You do whatever comes to mind. You don't do what you want, you do what you don't want. You're a spectator. You see yourself making mistakes, but you can't do anything about it. You have self-destructive behavior, but you don't have the power to change.

Goodness comes from self-control. If you want to have integrity, you need to have freedom. The secret of love lies in freeing yourself from hatred. That's why loving is a choice. Hate, however, is the opposite. You don't choose to hate. Hate chooses you.

Imagine that you're in the living room and you want to watch a show on television, but someone else has the remote control and switches from channel to channel while you feel powerless. The same thing happens in the emotional realm. When you hate, you aren't doing what you want to do, but what evil wants you to do. Evil possesses the remote control that changes the channels of your actions and feelings. As a result, you aren't living, you're being lived. Evil makes you do whatever it wants and you can't do anything about it.

You were created good. Inside you is love, humility, generosity, faith, courage, freedom, and kindness. Therefore, evil isn't you, because you're good. Evil is an intruder. It comes from the outside and infests you like a virus, preventing you from being all you can be. It controls you and makes you do what you don't want to do. When evil enters you, it imprisons goodness and subjects you with obsessions, impulses, and addictions.

When hatred enters your heart, it captures love and locks it away. Then you take things personally, you resent, you hate, you retaliate, and you abuse. You know you're wrong, but you don't have self-control. You condemn and disapprove of yourself, but you don't have the power to change.

The same happens with selfishness. When selfishness invades your heart, it takes generosity and imprisons it. Then you use people, take advantage of them, don't give, and you're dishonest.

When you hate, fear, abuse, degrade, or are selfish, you aren't being yourself. You aren't doing what you want to do, but what evil wants you to do. You're being controlled and manipulated. You aren't a bad person. Bad is the evil that resides in you. You're good. Inside you are all kinds of virtues. You're loving, kind, humble, generous, and courageous. Hatred, unkindness, selfishness, and cowardice don't come from you, but from the evil that resides in you. Therefore, no matter what you do, you're still good. When you act badly, it's not you, but the evil that's inside you.

To be yourself, you need to expel evil from your heart. You need to free yourself from all the negative emotions that control you. You must reclaim yourself. You aren't your emotions. You're above them. The path to freeing yourself from evil is through self-control. You need to believe that you have a choice. You don't need to dawdle on the couch watching evil handle the remote control of your emotions and actions. You've given the remote control of your life to evil, so it's you who needs to take it back. You just need to believe that you're capable of taking back the remote control.

There are many people who feel powerless to say no. They feel like hostages to other people. They're easily influenced by people's agendas and weaknesses. However, you'll never be able to say no to others if you can't say no to yourself. The way to be free from others is to be free from yourself. When you have self-control, no one can control you. The same way you say no to yourself, you say no to them.

Everything we do and feel is the result of habit. We create the habit of eating too much, cracking our fingers, bad-mouthing, complaining, and cursing. We create the habit of hating, resenting, having a victim mentality, fearing, and feeling guilty. We assume we are that way and we can't change, but the secret to change lies in believing in ourselves.

We're conditioned to think that we can't change and that we have to be the way we are. We even tell people that if they want to be with us, they have to accept us as we are because we can't be different then we are. That's a myth. We aren't our impulses, we aren't our obsessions, and we aren't our addictions. We can control our appetite, our desire for sex, our urge to smoke, our obsession with bad-mouthing, and our willingness to retaliate. We can be whatever we want to be. We don't have to be what we've been. We can change at any moment if we believe we can.

For example, let's say that you eat too much and think it's impossible to change your habit. Imagine that you were suddenly kidnapped and taken to a country where starvation was commonplace. You'd be worried about how you could survive without eating lots of food like you've done all your life. In the beginning, your stomach would make all sort of noises and you'd feel weak, but over time, you'd get used to eating less food until it would be normal to you. You'd feel some hunger and discomfort, but it wouldn't be as big of a deal anymore. However, you don't need to be kidnapped to change your habit of eating too much. You just need to believe that you can change.

My wife, Gina, was overweight for nine years until she decided to change. She told me that in the beginning she felt weak. She'd programmed her mind to think that she needed lots of food. She decided how many times per day she'd eat and how much. When she felt the urge to eat at other times, she drank water instead. For eight years now, she's maintained her normal weight.

Everything you are is the result of conditioning. You've conditioned yourself to eat too much, to overspend, and to think negative thoughts. You've conditioned yourself through the habits you created, especially those you developed in childhood.

The secret to change is through reconditioning. Research shows that if you change a habit for thirteen weeks, you'll be able to stick with it. After that, you lose the urge you had. For example, when I was in Brazil, I was used to eating certain kinds of foods. I liked those foods so much that I couldn't imagine not eating them. When I came to America, I couldn't find those foods anymore, and I missed them. I thought about traveling to Brazil, going to the same restaurants I'd gone to before, and eating as much as I could. However, for seven years I couldn't go back, and over time I lost the desire to eat that food. Now I even don't want them anymore. I simply don't feel attracted to them. I changed my notion of what tastes good.

Not only can you change, but you can experiment with what works better for you. You can switch from one behavior to another and then go back and forth. You can use the method of trial and error. If something doesn't work, change it, and if that doesn't work, change again. If you feel that having dinner is causing you problems, eat only salad at night. However, if you feel that eating salad is also not good for you, eat fruit. If you feel that eating fruit isn't good, drink only water. Then, if you feel that water isn't good, go to bed without eating or drinking anything. Although it might seem comical, my point is that you can change as many times as you want.

The good thing is that every time you change, you become more confident in your capacity to change. You realize that you *can* control yourself. You don't always have to be the same. You're not your habits, obsessions, and feelings. You're above them. They don't own you, you own them. You become stronger every time you change until you reach a point where you don't have problems changing. You take complete ownership of yourself.

However, you can't change through demanding or forcing. You can't overcome obsession with obsession. Don't ever say, "I *have* to do it." For example, don't say you have to eat less, to study, to change, to be more loving, and to stop cursing. By saying you *have to*, you disempower yourself. Your demanding reveals a lack of faith in your ability to change.

The way to freedom is through self-control. Believe that you can be whatever you want to be. You can choose. Instead of saying, "I *have* to do it," say "I *will* do it." For example, say "I will be more diligent, I will be more kind, I will say thank you, and I will be generous." When you say *I will*, you show confidence in your ability to change. You don't have any doubt that you can be whatever you want to be.

Still more powerful is when you say "I *am*," as in "I am diligent, I am kind, I am appreciative, and I am generous." You might think that affirming in the present would be a lie, because you haven't still overcome your limitations, but as I said before, you're good. You're not your faults. If you err, it's because you have a negative image of yourself. You are what you think you are. When you say you're diligent, you're sending a positive message to your subconscious mind, which will believe what you're saying and act upon that belief.

Another reason you don't have self-control is because you pity yourself. You think that if you don't have what you want, you'll be inferior. You connect your worth to the thing you want, so you become emotionally attached to it.

You say to yourself, "I'm cursed. I've lived with this my entire life and now I can't have it!"

Many of us were spoiled in our childhood by our parents or other people. They unconsciously conveyed the message that if we didn't have everything we wanted, we wouldn't be happy. We believed that we had to satisfy all our impulses, so we want to be pleased all the time. Happiness isn't the result of having everything our way, but of accepting things as they are. Our addictions are the result of connecting our happiness to things other than ourselves. We think that happiness comes from having sex every day or from smoking, drinking, buying things, or having people do everything we want.

Imagine that you're driving your car, as happy as you can be, until you see a bar. From that moment on, you aren't happy anymore, because you think that you can't be happy unless you enter that bar and have a beer. However, that sensation is a fantasy. You were happy before you watched the bar, so how can you suddenly be unhappy because you saw a bar? You're lying to yourself. Your unhappiness is an illusion. You don't need to drink beer to be free of the illusion. You just need to realize that you have everything to be happy inside of you.

That way of thinking has helped me change my eating habits. When I feel the urge to eat food that's harmful to me, I ask myself if I'm fantasizing that I need that food to be happy. For example, I was eating too much dessert until I realized that I was placing my happiness in eating dessert. I understood that eating dessert didn't change my state of mind. Dessert won't make me happier than I am. It might even make me unhappier, because the sugar and fat can cause heart disease or diabetes.

You might also think that if you don't have what you want, you'll suffer too much. You assume that the pain will be beyond your limit to endure. That's what happens to overweight people. They have an unconscious belief that if they eat less, they won't be able to bear their hunger.

In order to change your eating habits, believe that you can endure eating less. It won't be as hard as you think, and you *can* bear the change. If you expect too much pain, that's what happens. You feel a lot of pain, not because it's painful, but because of your expectation. You create the pain in your mind, which made you suffer. As a result, you can't change.

Happiness is a choice. You have many reasons to be unhappy. Life isn't fair and things won't always happen as you expect. Therefore, if you wait for circumstances to be perfect in order to be happy, you'll never be happy. That's why you need to choose to be happy.

Happiness comes from self-control. Depression, sadness, and bitterness are obsessive. You develop the habit of being unhappy and then find reasons to support your negative attitude.

When you wake up in the morning, make a decision to be happy.

Tell yourself, "Today, I'll be unconditionally happy."

If the traffic is bad, if you don't get everything done, or someone disapproves of you, remember that you have a choice to be happy or unhappy. Nothing can make you unhappy, unless you allow it to.

Anger is also an addiction. When you're angry, you lose self-control. You say and do things you regret. The way to overcome anger is to realize that you have a choice to stay calm. If you get angry, you're giving people or circumstances the remote control to your emotions.

Anger is a habit we create in childhood. After we condition ourselves to be angry, we think we can't change. However, like any other habit, we can overcome anger. We can recondition ourselves to be patient and calm.

Resentment is also a habit. When you develop a habit of resenting, you mull over every little thing people do to you. You become obsessed about remembering what people did to you. To overcome resentment, create a new habit of not taking things personally. You can make a choice of not thinking about what people do to you. Refuse to focus on the negative things they do to you, and as soon as they hurt you, delete it from your mind. You might think it's impossible to do, but I promise that it's absolutely possible. It's just a question of self-control. You can do it if you believe you can. I want to invite you to test it right now. If you hold a grudge in your heart, make a decision that you won't resent the person who hurt you anymore. Don't give importance to what they did to you and don't think about it anymore. You'll feel happy when you test and prove that you don't have to keep bad memories. You can feel whatever you want to feel.

Love is a choice. You may not feel as attracted to your spouse as you once were, but you can rekindle the flame by choosing to love. Somewhere along the way, you decided not to love. You lost the admiration and respect you had before because of things you didn't like, but you can make the decision to love again. Make a list of the positive things you see in your spouse and choose to feel attracted. It's that simple. You're the one who complicates what is simple.

One of the most difficult things to control is your tongue. There are many ways you show your inability to control your tongue, such as bragging about yourself, bad-mouthing, scorning, or saying hurtful things. Silence may be also an obsession. There are occasions when you should say things and you don't, and others you shouldn't say things and you do say. In other words, you talk when you should be quiet and you're quiet when you should talk.

We have a tendency to defend ourselves when people accuse us. Even if we're wrong, we want to justify ourselves. If we feel insulted by people, we insult them back. We can't take abuse for granted. As a result, we want to make sure that we counteract every offense with an equal or greater one.

Jesus was an example of self-control. People were stunned by his nonchalance. Although he was accused for things he hadn't done, he remained silent. He knew that defending himself wouldn't help. However, his silence was his best argument and his loudest defense. It showed his self-control and his ability to respond to hatred with love.

You can control your tongue. You don't need to complain, bad-mouth, scorn, or scream. No matter what people say to you, you can choose to be respectful. You need to know when to say something and how to say it. What you say may be right, but if you say it at the wrong time and in the wrong way, your message might not get through. Speaking the truth, just because it's the truth, is sometimes unwise.

Some couples say a lot of hurtful things to each other, just for the sake of retaliating. They feel an urge to hurt because they feel disrespected. They aren't looking for a solution. They just want to retaliate and make the other person feel as bad as they do.

If you don't have a positive purpose for saying something, don't say it. Don't say things when you're angry. Only use your tongue to build up, to compliment, and to love.

Anger is usually associated with verbal abuse. If you don't have the power to control your emotions, you also don't have power to control your tongue. In order to control your tongue, start controlling your emotions. When you discover that you don't need to be angry, you also discover that you don't need to accuse, scorn, or scream. Even if someone is cursing or criticizing you in a disrespectful way, you can still be quiet.

Step Ten
The Art of Saying No

1.
Self-Confidence and Communication

If you want to be independent, you need self-confidence. Believe in your wisdom and ability to make choices. You're able to make a distinction between right and wrong. The more you believe in your wisdom, the more you're able to make good choices. If you lack self-confidence, you end up making poor decisions. The problem isn't that you can't make good choices, but that you don't *believe* you can.

Your self-confidence is conveyed through the way you communicate. When you don't have self-confidence, you exhibit insecurity. Your message may be excellent, but the tone of your voice and your body language reveals your lack of confidence. The subliminal message behind what you say is "I don't trust myself. I'm not sure if what I say is right." That uncertainty keeps your message from getting through and you end up not getting other people's respect.

When people realize you lack confidence, they aren't sure if they can accept your message. They think they can't trust your wisdom. They unconsciously assume that if you don't believe in yourself, they can't believe in you, either.

Your lack of confidence may affect your communication in many different ways.

1. **Being silent**. You assume that you don't have anything interesting to say, so it's better if you stay quiet. You leave the responsibility of speaking to those you think are more mature and wise.

2. **You assume that people don't want to hear from you.** You think that people see you as you see yourself. You assume they

aren't interested in what you say and don't respect your ideas. Why to bother saying something if they'll reject you?

3. **Disengagement**. When you don't believe in your wisdom, you disengage from communication. You retreat inside yourself and become distant. You live in your own little world. It happened to me. I didn't believe that people respected my ideas, so I disconnected. My body was with them, but my mind was elsewhere.

4. **You speak cautiously**. When you don't trust what you say, you speak reluctantly. You're afraid of saying something foolish. You fear that people might make fun of you or become irritated with you.

5. **You're rude**. This is another extreme. You're harsh in the way you speak because you anticipate rejection. You think that by being rude, you're going to impose your thoughts. You assume that if you're calm and respectful, they won't respect you.

6. **You want to prove you're right**. When you don't believe in what you say, you want people to believe in you. You want to replace your confidence with their confidence. You want to prove to them because you want to prove it to yourself. When you believe in yourself, you aren't worried about what they think of you. What's important is that you believe in yourself.

7. **You don't want to hear people's opinions**. When you want to prove you're right, you have difficulty listening. You're so obsessed with being respected and appreciated that you can't hear what other people say. You're worried about what you say. While they're speaking, you're already thinking about what you're going to say. You interrupt them so you can convey your opinion as soon as possible.

8. **You feel rejected when people disagree with you**. You take other people's opinions personally. You think that by rejecting your ideas, they're rejecting you. You think that if they love you, they'll accept everything you say and will applaud your ideas. You feel frustrated and sad when they don't agree with you.

9. **You want to impose your opinion**. You assume that if people don't accept your opinions, they don't love you. You want them to show their love by agreeing with everything you say. You become selfish. You forget that people might want to be heard and accepted. You ignore their need to be approved of.

The secret to getting your message through lies in your self-confidence. When you believe in what you have to say, you speak confidently. That assurance is revealed through your tone of voice and your body language. You have an appearance of honor and dignity. You're neither afraid nor defensive. You speak in a friendly way. You believe that people respect your ideas and want to hear from you. You don't see them as enemies, but as friends. You feel loved and accepted.

When you believe that people respect your ideas, you can focus on what they say. You aren't preoccupied with proving you're right, so you hear them better. You don't feel threatened by their ideas and opinions. You respect their opinions because you believe you deserve to be respected.

In order to get your ideas through and communicate with people, follow the steps below:

1. **Believe in what you say.** You can't make people believe in you if you don't believe in yourself. Believe in your wisdom and your ability to make a distinction between right and wrong.

2. **Speak with poise and confidence.** According to research, only seven percent of communication depends on the words we say. How you say something is more important than what you say. Sometimes you disagree with yourself. You say something, but the tone of your voice and your body language say something else, and your message is splintered. Your tone of voice and body language need to backup what you're saying. They all need to say the same thing. By believing in yourself, you send a clear message.

3. **Believe the other person wants to hear what you say.** Believe that the other person respects your opinion. Believe that they support you. Don't think they're against you. Believe in their friendship.

4. **Be friendly.** When you trust the other person, you speak in a friendly way. You're calm and kind. As a result, you're able to develop a rapport. They sense your confidence in them and respond positively to it.

5. **Accept people's influence.** When you believe in yourself, you can listen to people's opinions without feeling disrespected or rejected. You don't feel the urge to defend yourself. As a result, you have a greater chance of getting your ideas through. When people feel that you respect their opinions, they listen. The secret to influencing people lies in accepting their influence. If you want them to hear you, hear them first. Seek to understand so you can be understood.

Follow your gut

When you're insecure, you feel childlike. You assume you don't have the maturity to distinguish between right and wrong. As a result, you want people to decide for you and to guide you. You ask their opinion and open up your life to them. You tell them things they really didn't need to know. You get different opinions, but you don't know which one to follow.

Other people are no better than you. They have the same chance of making a wrong decision. In addiction, no one understands you more than yourself. You know yourself better than anyone else.

Instead of hiding in other people's opinions, believe in your own wisdom. Trust that you can make a good decision. Believe you're mature and capable of making a good choice. Nothing can substitute for your self-confidence. The truth is inside you, so trust your gut.

Opening your life to other people can be devastating. Most of them can't handle it. They might see you as weak and insecure and lose respect for you. They might even tell other people. If you need to seek advice, look for a counselor, a cleric, or an expert. Read books pertaining to the subject. Above all, trust yourself. Most of the time, the problem lies in a lack of confidence instead of a lack of knowledge. Knowledge without self-confidence is like a car without fuel.

When people realize you lack confidence, they want to dominate you. They think you need their input and direction. They assume that if they don't control you, you might perish.

Although Isabella was separated from her husband, George, he still controlled her. She complained that he wanted to make all decisions about their divorce and her future. She asked people to help her influence George. She talked about her problem with a counselor and asked him to convince her ex-husband to do what she thought was right. She didn't believe that she was able to make decisions herself. She wasn't bold enough to follow her gut without having her ex-husband's approval.

2.
Freedom and Childhood

Some parents have a negative image of their children. They see them as rebellious and mischievous and assume they don't want to obey. Those parents think the only way to get their children to obey is by force. They feel that if they don't threaten and instill fear, their kids won't respect them.

Dictatorial parents don't believe they deserve respect. They think that if they don't intimidate, they won't get obedience. When parents believe in themselves, they believe in their children's goodness. They trust their own authority and don't think they need to force things.

When parents don't respect their children's individuality, they hurt their self-esteem. Children who are controlled don't have self-respect. They don't believe they deserve to have opinions. They think they don't have the right to choose, and they have to do whatever other people want.

I've seen parents who pride themselves in controlling their children, even after they're married. Claire lived with her daughter, Kris, and Kris' husband, Thomas. She thought that Kris and Thomas had to give her complete and total obedience. She controlled Kris through blackmail and guilt. Thomas felt disrespected by his mother-in-law's manipulation, but Kris wasn't bold enough to break her dependence.

Another mother, Shirley, prided herself in controlling her daughter, Nadir, even after she was married. She spanked her right before her marriage to prove that she was still in control. After Nadir was married, Shirley gave unsolicited advice about how she should treat her husband. She made Nadir open up about her problems and talk about intimate things in her marital life.

Parents such as those don't realize the problems they're causing. By controlling their children, they take away their ability to think for themselves and to make choices. Such children grow up immature and dependent. They won't have self-confidence, so they look for other people's guidance. They're easily influenced by anyone and have difficulty establishing boundaries.

If your adult children still follow your guidance and accept your manipulation, it's not a sign of victory, but of failure. If it makes you proud, you don't understand the concept of creating an independent and self-supporting adult.

As parents, we won't be around our children forever. They'll have to follow their own destiny. Therefore, we need to teach them to trust themselves and help them believe they can make good choices. Sometimes we think we need to save our children. We want to rescue them every time they fail. Maybe we need to save them from our fear and insecurity.

Our inability to believe in our children reveals our own inability to believe in ourselves. We think we need to save them because we think *we* need to be saved. We don't believe we're mature enough to take care of our lives, so we think they are, too.

To help their children fly, a mother eagle throws them into the air. Although it might seem mean, in her perspective, it's an act of love. What would happen if the mother eagle left her children in the nest for fear they'd get hurt? They wouldn't be able to survive. Some parents give their children everything but wings. They overprotect to the point of draining their offspring of the self-confidence necessary to live.

A woman was talking to me about how easily she was influenced by other people because of how she was raised by her mother. She couldn't establish boundaries. Her mother had made her think that she didn't have the right to have an opinion.

As parents, we need to teach our children values. We want them to be people of character. However, we also need to give them the right to question our values and beliefs. To become mature and independent, they'll have to think about the values we've taught them and decide what's good and what's bad. They will accept some values and reject others. If our child is a replica of us, our rearing was a failure.

Some parents are very sensitive to their children's different beliefs, especially when it comes to religion. They have a hard time accepting that their offspring have different views. They want to force their beliefs through guilt, fear, persuasion, and blackmail.

Parents need to learn to let it go. Giving children wings to fly is a question of self-control. Giving unsolicited counseling and advice to adult children is disrespectful. Even if children ask for their parents' opinion, they need to be cautious in their approach. When that happens, parents need to tell their kids that they're capable of finding the answer by themselves and that they believe in them. Make it clear that you're only giving your opinion and that you'll support their final decision.

When children grow up, parents need to treat them as friends. It's a sign of respect and love when parents treat their children as equals. Many children avoid their parents because they're not respected as adults. Every time they meet their parents, they're criticized and given advice.

Trying to be too intimate might make you lose your connection to your children. The more you respect your children's freedom, the closer you'll become. They'll understand your space as a sign of love and won't be afraid of being intimate with you. They'll feel comfortable opening up because they know you won't take advantage of their closeness. As a result, you'll influence them more.

Dealing with controlling parents

If you were over-controlled by your parents during childhood, you might feel that it's hard to break the umbilical cord. You might assume that resisting your parents' manipulation is a sign of disrespect. You feel that if you love them, you have to accept their control.

The more you subject yourself to your parents' dominance, the more they disrespect you. Parents unconsciously know their children need independence. Although they try to manipulate them, they're proud when they have the guts to break away. Don't worry if your parents resist your attempts to be free. You can be sure that in the end, they'll be proud of you and your relationship will improve.

Sometimes it might be necessary to keep a safe distance. If your parents are unable to respect your individuality, you might have to retreat for a while until they give you the space you deserve. Explain the reason why you are avoiding too much proximity. Say that you feel as if they're taking away your freedom and that you need to find your own individuality.

Becoming independent of your inner parent

In every section of this book, I've stressed the importance of breaking through the negative records registered in our mind from our childhood. Mastering ourselves is ultimately about becoming independent and gaining self-control. It's necessary to go deep inside of ourselves, opening all the drawers of our subconscious mind and making a reevaluation of every belief we've recorded. We need to know which beliefs are empowering and which are disempowering.

It's not easy to break through disempowering beliefs. Some of them contain a lot of guilt and fear that prevent us from rejecting them. We're so afraid to question them that we can't even think about their validity. Although we unconsciously feel there's something wrong about them, we irrationally defend them, for fear of punishment. We prefer to stay in our comfort zone and in the bubble of protection created by our parents. We fear exploring new terrain and discovering more empowering beliefs.

The hardest beliefs to question are those related to our parents' religion. We think that if we reject their beliefs, we'll be rejected by God. Although on a subconscious level we know that isn't true, we don't bring it out of our subconscious for fear of chastisement.

Jesus said, "You will know the truth and the truth will set you free." (John 8:32)

God created us with a brain to think and to question. He created us with the ability to test him. Where there's no freedom, there's no love. God doesn't want us to be like robots without free will.

It was hard for me to test my father's beliefs. My father is a man of character and did everything he could to plant good principles in my mind. I owe this book and all my victories to him. However, I've given myself the right to test his teachings and to reject some of them. Although we have the same religion, we diverge in the way we practice it. He'd like me to be like him, but I hold on to the right to be different and to keep my individuality sacred.

3.
The Art of Saying No

If you were controlled by your parents, you might have a problem saying no. You transfer your parents' image to other people and think they want to control you like your parents did. You assume that because you didn't have the right to say no to your parents, you can't say no to other people, either.

When you think that people want to control you, you transfer the same anger you had for your parents to them. You see them as selfish and dictatorial, and you may do what they want, but you resent it.

You misjudge people when you think they want to manipulate and control you. It's a figment of your imagination. You're the one who's controlling and making you do what they want. When you allow people to control you, you aren't obeying them, you're obeying the mental image you've formulated of them.

If it isn't people who enslave you, that means you're always in control of yourself. Even when you think they're manipulating you, you're the one who's allowing them to manipulate you. The thought that other people are enslaving you is a fantasy. You enslave yourself through them. You accept their control and then you accuse them for controlling you, although you gave them the right to do so.

People can't force you to do anything. Even if they torture you, you can say no. If you're independent, you'll die before they can control you. No matter how authoritarian or persuasive they are, you'll maintain your freedom. Blackmail, threatening, or torture will mean nothing to you.

As I've already said, one thing that makes you surrender is the thought that other people are strong. You think they're evil and will hurt you. You exaggerate their power and diminish your strength. You think you can't face their might. When you have difficulty saying no, you distort other people's power. You see them as formidable enemies. When you believe you *can* say no, you realize that people aren't that strong.

Carlos was controlled by his wife, Sonja. Although Sonja was small compared to Carlos, he thought she was strong and powerful. He feared her as if she was the devil made flesh. The result is that he allowed her to dominate him. He was unable to keep his individuality, for fear of her reaction.

You don't have to change people in order to be free. You don't need to convince them they must respect your individuality. If you change, they'll change, too. If you believe you can say no, they'll sense your courage and back down. They'll respect your limits and give you the space you claim.

Don't waste your time trying to convince them you can do whatever you want. You don't need to argue with them about your right to freedom. Your problem isn't with them, but with you. If you're convinced of your right to say no, you won't feel the need to convince them.

Freedom and self-esteem

Your ability to say no is directly proportional to your level of self-esteem. The more you value yourself, the more freedom you have. When you don't value yourself, you think you can't say no. You assume that everyone else has rights, but you don't. They can say no to you, but you can't say no to them. Therefore, if you ask them for something, you expect them to say no. However, if they're the ones who ask you something, you assume you have to say yes. You think you're inferior. You're the slave and they're the masters.

The solution to such a state of dependence is to value yourself. When you love yourself, you have an elevated concept of yourself. You don't assume you deserve to be coerced and subjugated. You believe you have the right to say no. To accept domination is a lack of self-respect.

When you see yourself as a slave, you create a barrier between yourself and others. You're the servant and they're the masters. You're inferior and they're superior. It isn't possible to have intimacy because there's a distance between you and them. Believing in your freedom brings you closer to them. You aren't inferior. You aren't a servant. You're their equal. You feel comfortable in their presence. There's no shame and no fear.

Wanting to be loved

Your problem with saying no stems from an empty love tank. When you don't love yourself, you desperately seek other people's love. You're willing to do anything to guarantee that you'll have their company. You think that by subjugating yourself and doing whatever they want, you'll have them. However, that's the opposite of what happens. The more you degrade yourself, the more you distance them from you. When you put yourself down, you exhibit a negative self-image. Instead of conveying respect and dignity, you show insecurity and low self-esteem. You cause people to lose their respect for you.

The more you love yourself, the more attractive you are. When you value yourself, you radiate beauty and dignity. You influence people with the image you have of yourself and make a good impression.

There's a difference between doing things because you love people and doing things because you want them to love you. When you do things because you love people, you're thinking of them. You focus on the outside and not the inside. You want to give and not receive. When you do things to be loved, you're focusing on yourself. You're being selfish.

When you do things to be loved, you send a subliminal message of selfishness. People notice subconsciously that you're focusing on yourself. They know that your actions aren't genuine and they aren't impressed by what you do. People react positively when they realize that your actions are a fruit of your love. When their subconscious mind captures your sincere desire to give, they open their hearts to you. They become thankful of your giving because they sense that you're focusing on them and not on yourself.

When you see other people as authoritarian and selfish, you have a negative image of them and it's impossible to love them. Your difficulty saying no reveals your lack of love. You do things for people out of fear. You please them so they don't hurt you.

Fear doesn't motivate you to be a good person. The more you fear, the less you do. When you feel coerced, you don't have the power to serve others. Fear causes hatred. Your difficulty saying no doesn't come from love, but from hatred. When you love, you believe you can say no, but when you hate, you think you always have to say yes.

Love is power and fear is weakness. When you love people, you have the power to please them. You do things for them, not because you fear, but because you love them. You feel pleasure in serving them.

Fear, however, is a turn-off. When you fear, you don't want to please people. You do things for them out of sacrifice. Your very existence feels like a burden. You might even express your sorrow and pain for doing what they ask of you. The problem is that you impact people negatively. They feel your reluctance and pain and don't value what you do.

It seems a contradiction. You think that if you feel comfortable enough to say no to people, you'll end up not pleasing them, but it's exactly the opposite. When you believe you can say no, you end up pleasing people more. Your courage to say no reflects the trust you place in them. You believe in their goodness and love. You trust their friendship. As a result, you want to please them. Love and freedom go together. To be free is to trust in other people's love.

Your actions will only produce a good impact if they're accompanied by love. You need to match your actions to your feelings. Real goodness comes from the heart. When you do things because you really want to do them and because you love people, you have a powerful impact. However, no matter what you do, if it comes from fear, you lose the force. It might be a grandiose act, but it doesn't produce a positive effect.

That means you may have a more positive impact saying no than saying yes. If you say yes because you fear people's rejection, you'll say yes with your mouth and no with your heart. When you love people, you believe you have the right to say no. You say no to them because you trust them. You don't see them as selfish or evil. You don't think they'll abandon or hurt you in case you don't want to please them. As a result, you say no with confidence and love. You know that they love you and will understand you. You trust that they want the best for you. You say no graciously and kindly. Your no sounds like a yes. They recognize that you feel safe enough in your friendship to say no to them.

The fear of being abandoned

Your difficulty saying no is a result of thinking that people might abandon you if you don't do what they ask. You see their love as fickle. You think that they're with you because they're interested in what you can do for them, not because they love you. Therefore, if you don't do what they want, they'll leave you.

You think that people might abandon you because you don't have anything special. You assume they're better off without you than with you. You don't believe you have anything good to offer them. They don't have anything to lose. On the other hand, you think that you have too much at stake. You think that you can't survive without them. You assume that you depend on them to live.

That fear of abandonment originates in your dependence. You think you're weak and incapable of taking care of your life. You surrender your freedom and dignity to other people in exchange for their help and support.

To overcome that fear, believe that you can take care of yourself without other people's help. You don't need them to survive. You don't need to sell your dignity and freedom in exchange for their presence. You won't perish if they leave you. You're completely able to live and thrive without them. You aren't with them because you don't have anywhere to go, but because you love them.

You're afraid of saying no because you think people aren't worried about losing you. You think they don't care whether they have you or not, so it's better if you do what they ask. You need to value what you are and what you do. If they leave you, they'll lose you. You're unique and special. You don't need to crawl on the ground to have them. You can stand up with dignity, because you're wonderful.

In order to say no, you need to believe that you can weather other people's negative responses. No matter how gracious and loving you are when you say no, some people will react in a negative fashion. No matter what you do to explain that it isn't personal, they'll feel hurt and won't accept your excuse.

Some people use unkindness and meanness to control you. They act like children. They throw a tantrum to see if you'll surrender to their manipulation. They threaten, blackmail, and intimidate. If you don't value yourself, you might think they have a right to control you. You assume you have to give in to their pressure and do whatever they ask of you.

Don't take people's negative reactions personally. Don't think they're being negative because you don't have the right to say no or because you're bad if you say no. Don't assume you have to please them. People won't love you more because you surrender to their control. Quite the opposite—they won't respect you. They'll notice your fear and they'll degrade you. The more they can control you, the less they'll respect you.

To say no, you need to be able to ignore negative reactions. You need to remain serene and peaceful, even when someone is accusing or screaming at you. Your nonchalant response is the best way to calm them down. When they realize you aren't sold, they'll stop their attempts to manipulate you.

You don't need to fear losing the company of those who don't love you. If someone doesn't respect your individuality, you're better off without them. They don't love you, so it's not like you're losing anything. You never had their love, so you aren't losing what you didn't have.

Don't seek people's approval

Sometimes you don't want to say no because you think you'll humiliate someone. You assume that in order to value them, you always have to say yes. It's important to remember the law of unconditional value. People's value isn't in your hands. You don't have the power to put them down. Saying no or yes to them won't change their value. They're valuable, no matter what you say.

If you think that saying no would humiliate them, you don't really value them. If you really value them, you'll never think you can put them down. Pitying them reveals your lack of respect.

If you think that by saying no you're humiliating them, you send a negative message that's captured by their subconscious mind. They unconsciously feel that you pity them. They realize that you don't believe in their unconditional value. Therefore, they become upset, not because you said no, but for not believing that their value surpasses your no.

We accept people's manipulation because we assume we're evil. We think that saying no is something bad and that if we were good, we'd always say yes. We want people to have a positive impression of us.

We need to say no with a pure heart. We need to believe in our good intentions and be sure that we respect and value others. When we're sure of our good intentions, we send a positive subliminal message. People feel our confidence and trust us. People are influenced by what we think of ourselves. If we believe in ourselves, they believe in us, too. However, if we think that we aren't good, they think the same. The reason is that we are what we think we are. If we think we don't value people and want to hurt them, it becomes the truth. We end up fulfilling our self-imposed prophecy.

Some people may prey upon our lack of confidence. When they realize that we don't trust ourselves, they see it as an opportunity to control us. That doesn't mean they have bad intentions. The problem is that they buy into the idea that we're evil. They think that if we're good, we'll do whatever they ask. That's why it's important that we're sure of our good intentions. When we know we don't want to hurt people and we value them, we make them believe in us, too.

To control us, some people act like victims. They pity themselves and try to make us feel bad about ourselves. It's a negative habit they've created in order to get what they want. Although they aren't conscious of what they're doing, they lack integrity. We don't need to resent them. We need to remember that they don't know what they're doing and that they're unconscious of their actions.

To say no, we need to be sure of who we are. We need an unshakable certainty about our character. Our opinion of ourselves must stand higher than the opinions other people have about us. That means we need to believe in our goodness, even when they want to convince us that we're evil. If they play the role of the victim and act as if we're degrading them by saying no, we need to maintain our sense of dignity. We mustn't change our self-image because of their criticism.

People can survive a no

Your difficulty saying no is a consequence of thinking that people are too sensitive. You exaggerate their vulnerability. That's caused by a negative self-image. You transfer your sensitivity to them. When you believe you're capable of facing no, you believe in them, too.

The secret to saying no lies in your ability to hear no. When you pity yourself, you pity them, too. If you feel too much pain when people say no to you, you think they can't face your no, either.

If you can't say no to yourself, you can't say no to others. For example, if you think you need to eat even when you aren't hungry, you have difficulty saying no to your child's requests for food. You pity them because you pity yourself. If you buy a computer when you know you don't have the money to pay for it, you can't say no to your wife when she wants you to buy a new car. You think that you need to have everything you want, so you think other people need to have everything they want.

The stronger you are, the stronger you think other people are. When you fear saying no, you feed other people's weaknesses. You sink them in their self-pity. When you gratify all your children's needs, you make them extremely sensitive. They won't take no for an answer and, as such, will have no self-control.

Opposite forces

When you think that people want to control you, you demand that you please them. You exert an enormous pressure on yourself to do what they want you to do. However, you think that the pressure comes from them. You don't realize that it's you forcing you to please them. You become frustrated for not doing what you want to do. You regret not having the courage to follow through with your desires. You try to oppose their strength. You make an enormous effort to counter their manipulation and do what you want to do.

The problem is that the two pressures cancel each other out. For example, if you try to push another person who meets your force exactly, it's as if you were standing still. By the same token, if you don't believe you can do what you want to do, no matter how much pressure you exert to make your will prevail, you won't be able to overcome it. No matter how much force you exert, you'll feel powerless.

On the other hand, the amount of force you apply to impose your will is inversely proportional to how much you believe in your freedom. The less you believe you can say no, the more force you exert. The more force you apply, the less force you have. When you really believe you're free, you don't make an effort to oppose your will. You believe in your freedom, so you have natural power.

When you exert a great amount of force to oppose other people's control, you're actually trying to neutralize your own force. It's *you* making you do what you think people want you to do, so you're opposing your own demands. You force yourself to obey people and then force yourself to disobey them. In other words, you're at war with yourself. You don't know if you should do what they want or if you should do what you want. If you do what they want, you regret not following your gut. If you do what you want, however, you fear losing their approval and love.

The more you want to please people, the more frustrated you feel for not doing what you want to do. You become more and more upset for not following your heart. You want very much to be free and follow your gut, but you don't have the courage to do so. That means that the more you want to follow your desires, the less power you have to follow them.

One of the first steps for learning how to say no is to bury your obsession to do what you want to do. The more you want to say no, the less you can say it. You can't overcome obsession with obsession. If you're obsessed with doing what you want, you'll also be obsessed with doing what people want and one obsession will cancel out the other. You'll neither have the power to please people nor to please yourself. The secret to winning lies in accepting defeat. You need to be able to renounce your desires. When you overcome your impulses, you have the strength to say no to others. You aren't obsessed with obeying them because you aren't obsessed with obeying yourself.

Pleasing people vs. following principles

When you think you have to do whatever people want you to do, you have a dilemma. What if people want you to do something immoral or against the law? Will you forsake your principles to do what they ask you so you won't lose their approval?

Some people have what I call *situational ethics*. They're like chameleons. They change according to the circumstances. There was a secretary of an organization I worked for who was desperate for approval. He was secretary during the term of a very dictatorial president. Although he knew the president's attitude was wrong, he compromised to guarantee his position. When he was talking to employees during meetings, he looked constantly at the president to see if he approved. The president was finally deposed in an assembly election and another one was elected in his place who was completely different. He was friendly and respected people's individuality. The secretary, who continued in his position, changed completely and came to disapprove of the very things he'd approved of before.

You can't be a person of character while you're seeking other people's approval. If you want to have integrity, you'll have to learn to say no. To be a person of character, you need to be courageous. You need to be willing to face disapproval and to be rejected. You need to be governed by principles instead of people's agendas and weaknesses.

You may have heard that everyone has their price, but a person of integrity will never be sold. Even in face of death, they maintain their integrity. They'll do the right thing, even if they're rejected, persecuted, or killed.

4.
Assertive Freedom

True freedom comes from the heart. To be free outside, you need to be free inside. It's not what you do that shows you're free, but what you feel. It's not simply saying no or doing whatever pleases you, but feeling free to say no, even when you say yes.

Some people think that in order to be free, they always need to do the opposite of what people would like them to do. They feel outraged when people ask them something and become very sensitive. They act like teenagers starting to affirm themselves and looking for their freedom.

Rebellious people think that doing what people want makes them inferior. When they give in to other people's pressure, they feel humiliated. They think that those who force them to do something are above them, and they want to be free to show their dignity. They compete with others to prove they aren't inferior.

Trying to be free to find your value isn't the right motive. Being a people pleaser doesn't make you inferior. Whoever controls you isn't superior to you. Being free won't make you valuable. You're always valuable, whether you're free or not. Learning to say no won't change your worth.

If you try to be free to be superior, you will never be free. If you want to be free so that people praise you for your courage, you're still worried about people's approval. You still want to make a good impression. What if, instead of applauding you, they reject you? Will you please them again so they'll approve of you? In order to be free, you need to be completely independent of people's opinion. When you look for freedom with a pure heart, you don't compete and you don't want to prove your value.

You don't look for freedom in order to be valuable, but because you *are* valuable. You can't be free if you don't value yourself. If you want to be free, value yourself first. When you recognize your value, you won't want to subjugate yourself to others anymore.

When you say no to show your value, you put other people down. By trying to show your importance, you end up humiliating them. It's like a competition. You feel inferior when they ask you something, so you say no just to show that you're superior to them. It becomes a game in which your primary interest is to prove your worth. You make the issue personal when it doesn't need to be personal. You feel inferior because of their attempt to control you, so you oppose their will to prove that you're superior to them.

Your no is real when you reject a person's request for a reason besides just rejecting. For example, if your wife asks you to go to the supermarket and you say no because you really can't go to the supermarket, you're only rejecting the request. It's not personal. You didn't feel humiliated by her request, so you don't need to humiliate her. On the other hand, if you feel humiliated because you think she's trying to manipulate you and you say no, you're taking it personally. You're competing with her and humiliating her.

When you're free, you don't take people's requests personally. You don't feel offended when they ask you things. Even if you realize they're trying to control you, you don't care. They may be trying to control you, but you don't feel controlled, because you know you can do whatever you want. Therefore, you ignore their attempts to control and focus on what they're asking you to do. If you think you can do what they ask, you do it, but if you think you can't, you don't. If you say yes, you aren't saying yes to their controlling attitude, you're saying yes to their request. You say yes because you feel that they've made a reasonable request. If they ask you something unreasonable, you say no.

Real freedom isn't a competition. When you look for freedom in the right way, you have a profound respect for other people's worth. You value yourself, so you value them, too. You don't say no to prove your superiority.

When you're rebellious, you don't think about other people's wishes. You're so preoccupied with your wishes that you don't consider theirs. You live in a selfish way. You only think about what you want and don't care about their feelings. You see them as evil people who want to manipulate you and yourself as the victim of their manipulation.

When you become free, you're able to listen to other people's opinions without feeling disrespected or outraged. Even if they're trying to control you, you listen to them with respect. You don't say yes or no to prove that you're free or to show that you aren't inferior. Your main concern is whether what they say is good or not. If you feel that they have a good opinion or a reasonable request, you follow them. If you feel that what they think or ask isn't good, you reject it. It's not personal. You aren't rejecting them, you're rejecting their idea. You don't feel inferior, so you can reject their idea and love them at the same time.

When you're rebellious, you tend to isolate yourself. You don't want other people to influence you in any way. You want to make your own decisions and do whatever pleases you without taking their opinions into consideration. However, that independence is artificial and causes alienation. You retreat to an inner world and drive other people out. They feel your disinclination to be close and feel rejected and abandoned.

When you're rebellious, you become sensitive to other people's influence. If they offer an opinion, you feel as if they're trying to control you. When they disagree with you, you feel insulted. You don't want to tell them what you think because you aren't open to their influence. You don't want them to say what they think. You don't want to tell them about your plans because you think they won't accept them and might try to persuade you to change.

When you overcome your sensitivity, you can open up to other people without fearing that they're going to control you. You're able to share ideas without feeling disrespected or trying to compete. You can listen to others without feeling stressed. You don't speak your ideas with rage. You don't need to be distant to be free. You can be close and maintain your freedom.

Isolation isn't a sign of freedom. You look for isolation when you can't say no. When you believe you can say no, you don't fear contact. You don't feel outraged when people disagree with you. You don't take it personally.

For example, you might want to move to a different place because you think you'll have more job opportunities. You don't want to ask for your wife's opinion because you think she's too manipulative and she will oppose your idea. You make your decision and then go to her with the sole intention of announcing your verdict.

When you don't fear being controlled, you can open up about your plans. You don't feel disrespected if people disagree with you. You're open to their influence and make them feel as if they're a part of your life. You break the isolation and feel the bond between you and them.

When you're rebellious, you don't want to compromise. By compromising, you think that you're surrendering to other people's control and are becoming inferior. When you believe in your value, you can look for a compromise without feeling inferior. You accept people's influence and you're willing to change your plans to reach a point that's better for you and for them.

When you're really independent, you can think about *us* instead of *me*. You don't live to please yourself. You want to please everyone around you, too. You care about other people's desires. That's helpful when you have to make decisions. When you fear other people's dominance, you don't want to hear their opinions, so you don't ask for them. When you're really free, you ask their opinions and make decisions in groups. You put your plans on the table and ask what everyone involved thinks about them. You let everyone offer their ideas and don't reject them when they're different from yours. The advantage of that approach is that you make everyone feel respected. They feel as if you value what they think and they feel as if they're a part of your life.

When you accept other people's influence, you get more help. By opening your plans to them, you make your plans their plans. They buy into your ideas much easier and want to support you.

Rebellion against laws

When you're rebellious, you think that laws were created to enslave you. You think that in order to be free you can't follow rules or principles. If you're a child who lives with your parents, you don't want them to impose rules. You don't want them to tell you when you should get home, if you have to clean your room, or if you need to go out with them.

If you're married, you don't want your spouse to ask what you're doing and you don't want them complaining if you get home late. You don't want to follow a religion because you think you'll have to obey farcical rules that will take away your freedom. You assume that in order to be free, you can't have any rules or principles.

It isn't rules and principles that take your freedom away, but your attitude toward them. It's your own demanding that makes you feel enslaved by rules. Disobeying the law won't change your inclination to demand from yourself. Instead of breaking the law so you feel free, break through with your self-demanding. If you stop demanding from yourself, you won't feel enslaved by rules and principles. You'll follow principles and still feel free.

You may have a lot of rules and still be free inside, while you may have no rules and be in bondage. Rejecting rules doesn't make you free. It just shows that you aren't free. When you're really free, you're able to obey rules and laws without feeling inferior.

Real freedom makes you a person of principles. Only free people have the power to live according to principles. They're not obsessed with doing what they want, so they can follow the guidelines. They can say no to themselves.

You can only follow principles when you don't feel enslaved by them. When you think that obeying laws takes your freedom away, you disobey them so that you'll be free. However, when you realize that it's you who takes your freedom away, you can obey the law and have freedom, too. The solution is to stop demanding. Obey the law without demanding that you have to obey it. You can abide by laws, follow principles, obey your boss, and do what your spouse asks without feeling enslaved. If you believe you're free, you can do whatever the law tells you or whatever people ask without feeling incarcerated. You can even be a slave, but if you have freedom inside, you won't feel oppressed. Freedom is an attitude. It's not what you do, but how you feel.

Free people can follow principles because they don't feel enslaved by others. They're free to do what's right. They don't give in to other people's pressure. They put principles above other people's agendas. On the other hand, putting principles above everything make us put people first. Being a person of character is ultimately about loving people. When you have integrity, you don't do what people want. You do what's good for them. You prefer to love them than to please them. There's a difference between giving people what they want and giving them what's good for them. When you love your children, you're more worried about their well being than about pleasing them. If they want something that will be destructive, you say no. You're more concerned with their education than in satisfying their desires. Children respond positively when they feel that you place their well being above their desires. They feel your sincerity and are secure in your love.

Respecting authority

When you don't have freedom, you're sensitive to authority. A mere opinion may sound like an order. You feel outraged when people disagree with you. Every different idea is seen as an insult. You think that people have to agree with you about everything.

When you have such a sensitivity, you tend to reject authority. You don't like being told what to do and you don't want your superiors to give you orders. You think that they should ask and coax you as if they were begging instead of commanding.

You don't like to be commanded because you feel humiliated. You think that if someone holds a superior position, they become superior to you. You confuse hierarchical superiority with superiority in worth. You think you need to treat people as equals so you won't feel inferior to them. You try to play with them so you don't feel inferior, but such intimacy sounds disrespectful to them.

I remember a carpenter from when I worked as a chaplain who felt disrespected by the hospital director's attempts to manage him. When the manager asked him to do something, she also told him how she wanted him to do it. He told her that no one could tell him how to do his job. He was the expert and she had to listen to him. She fired him and hired another employee who accepted her directions.

When you have inner freedom, you can hear commands and not feel insulted. You're able to follow orders without losing your self-respect. You know that a difference in hierarchy doesn't imply a difference in value.

When you fear being controlled by others, you also have difficulty having authority. If you think that you're humiliated when you're directed, you'll think the same about people when you're placed in a position of authority. You'll assume that by leading them, you're degrading them. As a result, you'll be careful how you treat them. You'll treat them as if they're your equals. In some cases, you might beg them to do something.

The result is that people won't respect you. They'll take your obsession with not humiliating them as a sign of weakness. They'll think they can do whatever they want. You're worried about not wounding their dignity, but meanwhile, they'll ignore your authority.

That's why you can only be a leader when you accept leadership. When you don't feel humiliated by other people's authority, you're able to have authority. You don't think that you're cheapening others by leading them.

If you think that you degrade people by having authority, you send them a negative message. They buy into your thinking. They feel that you're putting them down. The more careful you are not to humiliate them, the more humiliated they feel.

When you believe in other people's value, they buy into your influence. The more authority you have, the more you respect them. They see your authority as a sign that you value them unconditionally.

5.
Assertive Authority

Something that has always intrigued me is why some people control others. What motivates them to manipulate others? One thing I've noticed is that dictatorial people don't realize they're controlling. They think they're being controlled. Their effort to control others is an attempt to escape being controlled. They think they're defending themselves from others who want to control them and don't realize that they're doing the controlling.

Reasons why people tend to control others:

1. **You control others so that they don't control you.** The problem with controlling people so that they won't control you is that you always think they're controlling you. Even if they renounce their individuality and you gain total control over them, you still feel they're trying to manipulate you. While you think that they're controlling you, you don't realize that you're the one who's controlling. You can't overcome demanding with demanding. Only freedom can overcome tyranny.

2. **You control others because you control yourself.** If you're self-demanding, you don't have self-respect. When you respect your freedom, you don't accept anyone taking it away from you. You don't allow anyone to do with you what you don't do to yourself. As a result, you also respect other people's freedom. You transfer the same respect you have for yourself to them. You don't want them to be controlled because you don't want to be controlled.

3. **You control others because you don't value yourself.** Respecting other people's freedom has everything to do with your self-image. If you love yourself, you love them, too, and if

you love them, you won't want to control them. You think you don't deserve to be controlled, so you think the same about them. They're too important for you to control them. You'll respect their individuality—like you respect yours.

4. **Tyranny comes from pride.** Tyranny is an attempt to make up for someone's inferiority complex. When someone doesn't have self-esteem, they think that by controlling others, they'll be more important. They confuse status with inner value. They think that climbing the hierarchical ladder will make them superior to others. The higher they are, the more important they'll be. The problem is if there's someone above you, you'll feel inferior. The only way for you to feel important is if you're above everyone, which is improbable. On the other hand, trying to gain power in order to be valuable is a fallacy. You think your value is in your position and not in yourself.

5. **Tyranny is selfish.** When you try to get a position of authority in order to be praised by others, you're being selfish. You're thinking about you and not them. You want to take advantage of your power. You might think that by having authority, you'll be famous, praised, or rich, but true authority comes from love. It isn't motivated by receiving, but by giving. When you love people, you want to serve them. You see your position of authority as an opportunity to give. Jesus talked about real authority during the Last Supper, when the disciples were discussing who would be honored most when he established his kingdom.

   He said, "The kings of the Gentiles lord it over them; and those who exercise authority over them call themselves Benefactors. But you are not to be like that. Instead, the greatest among you should be like the youngest, and the one who rules like the one who serves. For who is greater, the one who is at the table or the one who serves? Is it not the one who is at the table? But I am among you as one who serves." (Luke 22:25-27)

6. **Trying to get other people's praise.** One thing that makes people attracted to power is thinking they'll be admired and praised. It comes from an empty love tank. They want to make up for their lack of self-esteem by being esteemed by the others. Other people's praise won't heal your inferiority complex. You can't replace your lack of self-esteem with theirs.

7. **Tyranny is addictive.** We've all heard the saying "power corrupts." Authoritarian people become dependent of power. They don't want to lose their grip over others. I realized it

when I worked for an organization where there were two leaders who were very totalitarian. They were so dependent on power that they did everything possible to defend their positions. When elections came, they tried to protect each other, because they knew that the majority of the staff wanted to get rid of them. They managed to last three terms before they were finally deposed. When it happened, they took it personally and became resentful. They acted like victims and complained that the workers had taken them for granted. They tried to justify themselves, saying they were deposed because they wanted things to be right. They didn't take responsibility for their mistakes.

8. **Thinking that other people don't love you.** When you have an empty love tank, you think that people don't care about your wishes. You assume they're selfish and want to impose their ideas. You take it personally when they don't agree with you or don't do what you want. You think that if they love you, they'll renounce their desires, opinions, and individuality and subjugate themselves completely to you. The solution is to believe in other people's love. When you believe in their love, you don't take it personally when they disagree with you or don't do what you want. The more you believe in people's love, the less you demand. Demanding is a turn-off. When you demand that people do things for you, they lose their desire to do them. They may do it out of fear or for guilt, but not out of love, and if they don't do it for love, they do it mechanically, against their will. They don't have pleasure in doing, because there's no pleasure in tyranny. Believing in people's love is an investment. When you believe they love you, you motivate them to please you. Love and freedom are inseparable. Love is the power to get what you want from people. By loving them, you respect their individuality, and by respecting their individuality, you make them interested in doing what you want.

I've seen it in many marriages. When a partner demands attention from the other, they usually don't get it. The more they want it, the less they get. Demanding, complaining, and criticizing aren't inspiring. They drive people away instead of bringing them closer.

9. **Not believing in one's authority.** The less you believe in your authority, the more despotic you are. You think you have to make an enormous effort to influence people because you don't have faith in yourself. You think you don't deserve respect. As a result, you try to get respect by force. You

blackmail, threaten, lose your temper, and scream to make up for the authority you think you don't have. The solution is to believe in your authority. You need to have a good self-image. When you respect yourself, you believe in other people's respect, too. You don't think you need to force them to respect you. You think that it's natural that they're going to respect you, because you deserve it. Even if you have a good self-image, there will be people who won't respect you. They won't disrespect you because of you, but because of them. They don't think they deserve respect, so they think you don't deserve it, either. You don't need to be frustrated and take it personally. You don't get respect through threatening or hurting people. Your tyranny reveals your weakness. People unconsciously feel your insecurity. They know you're trying to make up for your lack of self-respect. They might be afraid of you, but they won't respect you.

10. **Being authoritarian creates a rift between you and other people.** If you're superior, you're remote. You aren't on the same level. You may want people's praise, but the more you elevate yourself to get their approval, the more distanced you feel from them. To feel other people's love, you need to get close to them, which happens when you're humble.

Conclusion

I commend you for your self-discipline and dedication in reading this book. It shows that you're really interested in your growth. The good news is that you aren't the person you were when you started reading, and you'll never be the same again. You've changed forever.

I suggest that you to read it again or buy it in CD form and listen to it. I've done that with books I've read and the result was amazing. When I like a book, I buy it in CD form and listen to it at least ten times, until I really assimilate the message.

I also strongly recommend that you make reading a habit and spend at least thirty minutes per day at it. There's a list of books I've read that helped me in my growth at the end of this book. If you keep reading, you'll become wiser and will succeed in every area of your life.

I also want to invite you to check my website at <u>www.claudiovargas.</u> <u>net</u>. My plan is to have a new message in video there every week in English, Spanish, and Portuguese. You can use it as a tool for your growth process. The messages are free, so take advantage of them. If you wish, you can buy them through the website.

I want you to remember the ten steps to mastering yourself.

First, value yourself. You're important, not because of what you have, but because of who you are. Nothing can make you inferior. No matter what happens to you, you're always worthy. Other people can't make you inferior, and even you can't put you down. Thinking you're inferior is a fantasy. By thinking you're inferior, you suffer in vain, when you could be enjoying the fact that you're unique and special.

Second, overcome pride. Many people confuse pride with self-value. They think that by having an arrogant attitude or by putting other people down they can have self-esteem. Nothing could be further from the truth. The more worth you feel, the more humble you are. Pride shows a lack of self-esteem. You're proud because you don't believe you're valuable. You put other people down because you feel inferior to them. When you believe in your worth, you don't need to boast anymore.

Third, love yourself unconditionally. Accept yourself as you are. You can't love others if you don't love yourself. If there's a war going on inside you, there will be a war going on outside. When you love yourself, you believe in people's love and as a result, you love them. Love isn't an obsession, it's a principle. When you love someone, you don't do things for them because you feel a strong compulsion to do them. You act out of your will. When you love, you keep your promises and are a person of character.

Fourth, forgive yourself. We have a tendency to judge and condemn ourselves for things we've done in the past. Miguel Ruiz says in his book *The Four Agreements* that the human being is the only one who pays several times for the same mistake. We also condemn ourselves for things we do on a daily basis. When we mix all those condemnations together, we realize why we're so unhappy. Forgive yourself and you'll find happiness. Stop criticizing yourself and making a big deal out of your faults and you'll be a better person, for good comes from love. You'll never overcome your shortcomings while putting yourself down. The way to perfection is through forgiveness. You aren't perfect to forgive yourself. You forgive yourself to be perfect.

Fifth, overcome anger. You feel angry because you don't value yourself unconditionally. Every time you feel inferior, you become angry. You're angry because you allow things to shape your self-image. You might think that you need to be angry to get people to respect you. However, by being angry, you show a lack of self-control and an inability to love yourself and others unconditionally.

Sixth, believe in yourself. You are what you think you are. You'll never reach higher than you think you deserve. You attract to yourself the very things you expect. Expect good things, and you get good things. Expect bad things, and you get bad things. If you focus your mind on problems, failures, and fears, you'll attract them like a magnet. Victory is on the inside. Set your mind to be a victor, be positive about your future, and you'll see things turn out for the best.

Seventh, overcome the victim mentality. Your life isn't the result of outside forces and influences. If you've allowed circumstances and people to shape your destiny, it was your choice. You can't blame other people for poor results, when it was you who gave them the right to control your life. Don't give other people permission to manipulate you and to have power over your outcome. You be the one who makes the choices. Don't victimize yourself to get people's love. Crying over your fate won't prompt compassion. You don't need to be bad to be loved. You have many qualities that make you worth being loved without having to resort to self-pity to gain appreciation. You're unique, special, and talented. You don't need people's mercy, because you're a victor and not a victim.

Eighth, overcome your fears. You fear that something bad might happen because you wouldn't value and love yourself if that thing happened. You project your lack of self-love to other people and think that they wouldn't love you, either. When you love yourself unconditionally, you no longer fear rejection. You believe in other people's love because you love yourself.

Ninth, don't demand from yourself. You can do things because you *have* to do them or because you *want* to do them. Although it sounds the same, it's completely different. When you do things because you have to do them, you don't take pleasure in the doing. You can't have contentment while you force yourself and demand from yourself. When you do things because you want to do them, you receive pleasure, because you love yourself every step of the way toward getting what you want. Love makes life enjoyable. When you love yourself, you stop criticizing yourself every time you make a mistake and you don't push yourself beyond your limits. As a result, you have more fun throughout the process, which causes you to reach your goals faster.

Tenth, learn to say no. In order to say no, you need to believe in your own love and in other people's love. Saying no doesn't make you a bad person. Quite the opposite, saying no shows that you trust other people's love and you love them. You say no to them because you believe they're able to understand and love you unconditionally. Believing in other people's love lets you say no with grace and respect. Your no is so confident and polite that it sounds like a yes. You say no with your mouth, but you say yes with your heart. You aren't afraid of being rejected. You also don't doubt your intentions and emotions. You know that you're a good person and that you have other people's best interests in mind. You believe in your judgment and decisions, and you express that when you say no.

I want to thank you, dear reader, for giving me the opportunity to impact your life in a positive way. My dream was to use all the truths I've discovered through my meditations and readings to help other people. I'm happy for fulfilling my purpose in life and I'm grateful to you for helping me achieve this goal.

Claudio Vargas Ministries

Claudio Vargas Ministries focus on helping individuals reach their maximum potential in every area of life. Claudio speaks in churches, schools, and companies, giving seminars about family, self-help, goal—setting, and leadership.

Claudio is also an accomplished musician. He plays classical and jazz piano. He's a composer and arranger and has recorded CDs of his own and produced CDs for others.

He has opened a website at www.claudiovargas.net that has free video messages and he'll extend to radio and television in the near future. You can help Claudio Vargas Silva to attain these goals by buying his material or making donations through the website.

For speaking engagements or consulting:

E-mail: claudiovargas1@aol.com

Phone: (408) 806-7619

Bibliography

Following is a list of books I've read that helped me to be the person I am and to write *Master Yourself.* I strongly recommend them as a tool for helping you in your emotional development.

Leadership
Maxwell, John C. *Developing the Leader within You.* Nashville: Thomas Nelson Publishers, 1993.

Finances
Ramsey, Dave. *The Total Money Makeover.* Nashville: Thomas Nelson Publishers, 2003

Marriage
Chapman, Gary, *The Five Love Languages.* Chicago: Northfield Publishing, 1992, 1995.
Gottman, John M., *The Seven Principles for Making Marriage Work.* New York: Three Rivers Press, 1999.
Gray, John, *Men Are from Mars, Women Are from Venus.* New York: HarperCollins Publishers Inc., 1992.

Parenting
Pickhardt, Carl E., Ph.D. The *Everything Parent's Guide to Positive Discipline.* Avon: Adams Media, 2004.

Self-help
Canfield, Jack and Janet Switzer. *The Success Principles*. New York: HarperCollins Publishers, 2005.
Carlson, Richard. *Don't Sweat the Small Stuff*. New York: Hyperion, 1997.
Carlson, Richard. *Don't Sweat the Small Stuff About Money*. New York: Hyperion, 1997, 2001.
Carnegie, Dale. *How to Win Friends and Influence People*. New York: Pocket Books, 1982.
Covey, Stephen. *The 7 Habits of Highly Effective People*. New York: Free Press, 1989.
Covey, Stephen. *The 8th Habit*. New York: Free Press, 2005.
Dyer, Wayne W. *The Power of Intention*. Carlsbad: Hay House, 2004.
Helmstetter, Shad. *What to Say When You Talk to Yourself*. New York: Pocket Books, 1987.
Hill, Napoleon. *Think & Grow Rich*. New York: Random House Publishing Group, 1960.
Jeffers, Susan. *Feel the Fear and Do It Anyway*. New York: Ballantine Books, 1988.
May, Rollo. *Man's Search for Himself*. New York: Delta Publishing, 1953.
Osteen, Joel. *Your Best Life Now*. New York: Warner Faith, 2004.
Peale, Norman Vincent. *The Power of Positive Thinking*. New York: Ballantine Books, 1996.
Peale, Norman Vincent. *You Can if You Believe You Can*. New York: Fireside Books, 1987.
Robins, Anthony. *Awaken the Giant Within*. New York: Free Press, 1991.
Robins, Anthony. *Unlimited Power*. New York: Free Press, 1986.
Ruiz, Miguel. *The Four Agreements*. San Rafael: Amber-Allen Publishing, 1997.
Spencer, Johnson. *Who Moved My Cheese*. New York: G.P. Putnam's Sons, 1998.

Teenagers
Covey, Sean. *The 7 Habits of Highly Effective Teens*. New York: Fireside, 1998.
McGraw, Jay. *Closing the Gap*. New York: Fireside, 2001.
McGraw, Jay. *Life Strategies for Teens*. New York: Fireside, 2000.
Pelzer, Dave. *Help Yourself for Teens*. New York: Penguin Group, 2005.